For Debbie —
Positively

Michael
Mercer

ABSOLUTELY FABULOUS
ORGANIZATIONAL CHANGE™

STRATEGIES FOR SUCCESS FROM AMERICA'S BEST-RUN COMPANIES

MICHAEL W. MERCER, PH.D.

Castlegate Publishers, Inc.

This publication is designed to provide accurate and authoritative information on the subjects it covers. It is sold with the understanding that the publisher and author are not engaged in rendering legal, accounting, financial, investment, medical, mental health, or other professional services. If legal, accounting, financial, investment, medical, mental health or other professional services are required, the services of an appropriate, competent professional should be obtained.

Library of Congress Cataloging-in-Publication Data
Mercer, Michael W., 1950 -
    Absolutely fabulous organizational change / Michael W. Mercer.
        p.   cm.
    ISBN 0-938901-21-4
    1. Management.   2. Organizational Change.   3. Leadership.   I. Title.
    658.406 - dc21   2000
                                                        99-076325
                                                        CIP

The following are Trademarks of Mercer Systems, Inc.:
 ◆ Abilities & Behavior Forecaster™
 ◆ Abilities Forecaster™
 ◆ Behavior Forecaster™
 ◆ Forecaster™
 ◆ Hire the Best Tool Kit™
The following are Trademarks or Registered Trademark of The Mercer Group, Inc.:
 ◆ Hire the Best – & Avoid the Rest™
 ◆ Absolutely Fabulous Organizational Change™
 ◆ Turning Your Human Resources Department into a Profit Center™
 ◆ Intensive Coaching®
The following is a Registered Trademark of Castlegate Publishers, Inc.:
 ◆ Spontaneous Optimism®

Printing number

10 9 8 7 6 5 4 3 2 1

CONTENTS

Preface

I wrote this book for a number of reasons.

First, I have delivered many speeches, workshops and management retreats on *Absolutely Fabulous Organizational Change*™. After my presentations, participants always ask how they can obtain my book on this topic. Apparently, since I wrote quite a few other books, they assume I wrote a book on *Absolutely Fabulous Organizational Change*™. After telling people countless times I had not yet written a book on organizational change, I finally decided to write this book so my audiences and others can benefit from it.

Second, from my consulting, research and management experience, *I delineated the three ingredients that go into every highly successful organizational change*. It does not matter if the organizational change is a merger, acquisition, restructuring, supply chain enhancement, turning a cost center into a profit center, reengineering, computerizing work previously done by humans, turnaround, or hatching a brand new business inside an existing company. In all cases, the same three ingredients are present – or else the organizational change would not have met or exceeded the desired measurable results. This book explains

- ◆ my three-ingredient model
- ◆ examples of how superb companies put my three ingredient model into action

Third, I always notice that managers and executives possess a keen yearning to find out how America's best-run companies operate. Whenever I deliver a speech or workshop, audience members always intently listen every time I give an example from a big-name company. (Note: I only give such examples with the permission of the company or executive I am speaking about.) Usually, such insights are available only to people working for – or consulting to – those companies. Or, sometimes business periodicals give a brief glimpse into how a remarkable company carries out its work. Given this huge appetite to find out how superb companies operate, I decided to focus much of this book on examples from big-name companies. Specifically, *I will show you how the following fantastic companies use my three-ingredient model to produce incredibly successful organizational change:*

- Egghead.com
- Excell Global Services
- Harley-Davidson
- IBM
- Intuit
- City of Indianapolis
- Robert Mondavi Corporation
- Outback Steakhouse, Inc.
- Ritz-Carlton Hotel Company
- VF Corporation
- Washington Mutual

These companies are known by huge numbers of people. Also, millions of investors own shares of these companies, either by owning stock or mutual funds. As such, knowledge of how these fantastic companies plan and implement organizational change will satisfy a yearning to know how *America's best-run companies* got that way.

Fourth, as a business psychologist who consults to companies, I find the personalities, interpersonal skills, motivations and mental abilities of leaders proves totally crucial to their success or failure. In fact, I developed a widely used pre-employment test – the *Abilities & Behavior Forecaster*™ test – that many companies give to job applicants to help predict which applicants are most likely to succeed, if hired.

Unfortunately, very little *objective* data is written about the behaviors and mental abilities of spectacularly effective leaders. There is some *subjective* conjecturing, but very little *objective* data.

So, I did research to fill this need for *objective* data. Using my *Forecaster*™ tests, I tested many executives and managers who led immensely successful organizational change. Their *Abilities & Behavior Forecaster*™ test scores reveal fascinating insights into their

- interpersonal skills
- personalities
- motivations
- mental abilities

This book reports:

◆ Research on the *Abilities & Behavior Forecaster*™ test scores of incredibly successful executives and managers

◆ Recommendations of customized testing, interviewing and other hiring tools to choose job candidates with a high likelihood of success

Fifth, one of my three ingredients of organizational change is how the leaders manage their emotions, thoughts and actions while they lead organizational change. Such information has been barely researched and reported in other publications.

To fill this knowledge gap, in this book I report crucial aspects of successful leaders' (A) optimism, (B) attitudes, (C) expressions they use a lot, (D) life themes, (E) formative childhood events, and (F) role models. This provides fascinating insights into the real people who implement amazingly successful organizational change.

Sixth, I intensely feel the importance of a crucial human aspect of organizational change: I find organizational change – when successful – vastly benefits hundreds, thousands and sometimes even millions of people. This includes employees, customers, and investors – plus their families and friends. Given this situation, I feel confident my book can help individuals and organizations produce absolutely fabulous organizational change that benefits millions of people.

Finally, I always enjoy talking with executives and managers who make things happen. *Anyone who reads this book can feel free to contact me to discuss questions they have about using the techniques and tools I discuss in this book.*

Positively,

Michael W. Mercer, Ph.D.
The Mercer Group, Inc.
& also
Mercer Systems, Inc.
Barrington, Illinois, U.S.A.

Acknowledgments

I tremendously thank the following people for their help, advice, suggestions, and encouragement: George Arteaga, Robert Cormack, Bruno Cortis, Barbara Jennifer Dahl, Annie Danser, Guy DiSpigno, Margaret Gonzalez, Brian Hess, Sr., Brian Hess, Jr., Robert Hoffman, Dale Kerkman, David Kuhlmann, Ashley Lapp, Mary Ann Lluberes, Michele Manahan, Sandi McCarty, Vincent J. McNamara, Leah Nelson, Karen Olmstead, Ariel Oshen, Peggy Pistilli, Sheryl Shatford, Donald Shepherd, Heather Victoria Sterling, Michael Thacker, J.D. Thorne, Joseph Troiani, Jan Vermillion, Sue Williford, and Thomas G. Williford.

I always cherish the enthusiasm, cheerfulness and help given to me by Mary Ann Victoria. She is my absolutely fabulous delight.

My mother and father, Rhea and Philip, aunt Idelle, and sister and brother, Meridith and Jeff, have expressed a lot of encouragement for many of my endeavors, and I appreciate all of it.

1

How You –
& Your Organization –
Can Tremendously
Profit from this Book

I deliver a lot of speeches, workshops and management retreats at business conferences and companies. At each presentation I deliver, I always meet managers and executives who hunger to find out what *really* works. They also like to hear my first-hand knowledge and examples of how America's best-run companies produce absolutely fabulous organizational change.

And that is exactly what you will discover in this book.

You will find out about techniques and tools that really work to plan and implement *astoundingly successful* organizational change. All the methods you will read about are proven to work in the real world. I purposely left out any academic or theoretical jargon or gibberish that impresses students in a classroom, but does not help managers working in the real world of organizations. As such, you benefit from finding out what actually works.

For many years I have been a management consultant, helping companies across the United States and Canada. Prior to that, I served as a manager in two major corporations.

From my extensive consulting and management experience with many organizations, I discovered a "secret" to organizational change: All change that meets – or exceeds – its desired results contain three key ingredients. Specifically, the executives and managers who plan and implement effective change always include the three ingredients of *successfully*

1. leading the organizational change
2. handling employee problems that arise during organizational change
3. managing their actions and emotions while they lead organizational change

Importantly, I will show you exactly how some of America's best-run companies plan and implement absolutely fabulous organizational change – using my three ingredient model. You will read the success stories of these organizations:

- Egghead.com
- Excell Global Services
- Harley-Davidson
- IBM
- Intuit
- City of Indianapolis
- Robert Mondavi Corporation
- Outback Steakhouse, Inc.
- Ritz-Carlton Hotel Company
- VF Corporation
- Washington Mutual

Ingredient 1: Successfully Leading the Organizational Change

Ingredient 1 – successfully leading the organizational change – includes key elements. It includes making sure the organizational change fits in with the company's culture and also its vision for a big, exciting future. This also requires effectively setting measurable goals in certain ways, as well as harnessing the power of teamwork to accomplish the goals. When the goals are met or exceeded, successful leaders hold celebrations to reward team members and help them emotionally bond due to having succeeded together in a worthy cause.

Ingredient 2: Successfully Managing Employee Problems during Organizational Change

Ingredient 2 – managing employee problems that pop up during organizational change – proves crucial. Despite the wonderful plans of leaders and the lofty results those plans can accomplish, the fact remains that some employees inevitably will do everything possible to undermine the change endeavor.

They will resist. They will kick up a fuss. They will act nutty. They will badmouth the leaders and the organizational change behind the executives' backs.

With such enemies within the organization, a key requirement is for the leaders to realize how their employees resist or undermine the change – and do something about it. After all, the executives are not running a mental health clinic for rebellious or upset adults. The executives need to achieve desired results, without which the entire organization could suffer. But, with achieving the change's desired results, the organization, employees, customers and shareholders all will benefit.

As such, the leaders who need to effectively handle employee problems are dealing with urgent, make-it-or-break-it potential catastrophes. Fortunately, this book tells you how America's best-run companies handle employee problems during organizational change.

Ingredient 3: Successfully Managing Yourself during Organizational Change

Ingredient 3 – the fact that leaders must manage their emotions and interactions with employees – is absolutely essential for any organizational change to achieve its desired results.

My research and observations continually find that highly successful people are incredibly optimistic. This fact even is borne out in test results of successful leaders who took the pre-employment tests I developed that are used by many companies – the *Abilities & Behavior Forecaster*™ tests. You will read about these eye-opening *Abilities & Behavior Forecaster*™ test results in this book. Also, incredibly successful leaders invariably hold key attitudes and repeatedly use certain phrases that convey their upbeat, confident approach to work and, in effect, life in general.

As a business psychologist who consults to many companies, I find out a lot about the interpersonal skills, personalities, motivations and mental abilities of high-achievers. The spectacular leaders who plan and implement absolutely fabulous organizational change are not just carrying out their leadership duties in the here-and-now of daily business life. Instead, they have lived their entire lives so they develop amazing mindsets, skills, and talents – starting in childhood – that now serve them well in their leadership roles.

You will see how spectacularly successful managers and executives developed into fantastic leaders through the themes that define their lives, formative childhood (1 - 21 years old) experiences, and their relationships with people they consider their role models. The result is that highly successful *leaders* really are, in many crucial ways, highly successful *people.*

They steered their careers into leadership positions to express something deep in their psyches. And now their brainpower, optimism, attitudes and approaches to life benefit their organizations, employees, customers, and shareholders.

You Benefit from Examples of How America's Best-Run Companies Use My 3 Ingredient Model

Importantly, this book shows how my three ingredient model of organizational change has been put into action in some of America's best-run companies. You will benefit from reading exactly how incredibly successful managers and executives in these companies use the three ingredients. As such, you will discover real-life, field-tested ways to create absolutely fabulous organizational change.

Also importantly, every example from America's best-run companies includes actual results of the company's absolutely fabulous organizational change. After all, the main purpose of all organization change is to produce improved bottom line results. This book shows you magnificent measurable results organizational change produced in America's best-run companies.

Now, You Can Produce Absolutely Fabulous Organizational Change

With your knowledge of my three ingredient model of organizational change – and with many dramatic examples of companies using the three ingredients – you can confidently proceed to plan and implement absolutely fabulous organizational change.

Go for it!

2

3 Ingredients
of
Absolutely Fabulous
Organizational Change

As I consult to executives and managers at many companies, I discovered highly successful organizational change requires three key ingredients. If any of the three ingredients is missing or incomplete, then even the best plans for change invariably fall apart or do not achieve the desired results.

Fortunately, when a company uses all of my three ingredient model, I find the organization's planned changes

♦ actually get implemented
♦ produce fabulous, measurable improvements – often beyond what was planned!
♦ create qualitative results that dramatically help the organization and its employees

With this in mind, let's delve into an overview of the three-ingredient formula I devised. Later, you will read many detailed examples. These examples show you how *America's best-run companies* used my three ingredient model to produce *successful* organizational change. These organizations include well-known, highly respected companies and even one government organization:

♦ Egghead.com
♦ Excell Global Services
♦ Harley-Davidson
♦ IBM
♦ Intuit

- ◆ City of Indianapolis
- ◆ Robert Mondavi Corporation
- ◆ Outback Steakhouse, Inc.
- ◆ Ritz-Carlton Hotel Company
- ◆ VF Corporation
- ◆ Washington Mutual

My three ingredient model required for all successful organizational change is the following:

Ingredient 1:   *Successfully Leading the Organizational Change*

Ingredient 2:   *Successfully Handling Employee Problems during Organizational Change*

Ingredient 3:   *Successfully Managing Yourself as You Lead Organizational Change*

Now, let's delve into an explanation of the three ingredients.

Organizational Change Ingredient 1:
Successfully Leading the Organizational Change

Successfully leading your organizational change requires four key actions:

Action 1: Pinpointing your organizational culture – and making sure your proposed changes fit in that culture

Action 2: Creating a big, exciting vision for your organization's future

Action 3: Goal-setting to implement the changes and move your organization closer to its vision

Action 4: Teamwork to achieve the goals that, added together, produce the desired, profitable organizational change

Let's look at each action individually.

Action 1: Pinpointing Your Organizational Culture

Important: The *only* – I repeat, *only* – organizational changes that prove successful are those that more or less fit into the company's culture! Any brilliant changes you conjure up that do not fit into your organizational culture either will not get implemented or will not achieve the desired results!!

This significant matter raises the question: What is an organization's culture? An organization's culture is the sum of the *behaviors and values the organization most recognizes and rewards.*

How do you uncover exactly what your organization's culture is?

I devised a quick method to pinpoint what a company's culture is. Specifically, a corporate culture is conveyed perfectly by the *story* every employee knows and tells. Usually the story involves the company's founder. The following example will illustrate how my *story = culture* works.

My last corporate management position – before I started my own consulting firm – was at a company called American Hospital Supply Corporation, commonly called "American." The company was based near Chicago. It was a very well-managed $3-billion/year company, listed on the New York Stock Exchange, with about 30,000 employees. American was taken over by Baxter International, a large healthcare supply company.

I started working at American on a Monday. I heard the following story on Tuesday, only my second day on the job. All of the thousands of employees I spoke with during my years of working at American heard the same story within the first five days of working for the company. Here is the story:

On the Day Promised

American Hospital Supply Corporation was founded by a gentleman named Foster McGaw. He founded the company to enable hospitals to order all their supplies – bandages, bedpans, tongue depressors, surgical instruments, and lots more – from one company, namely, American. Prior to this, hospitals needed to order supplies from hundreds of different suppliers, which proved horribly inefficient. So, McGaw built a warehouse in which he stocked hospital supplies from hundreds of medical supply companies.

Foster McGaw would go into hospitals to take their order for the many supplies they needed. And – importantly – he always promised each hospital that he would deliver the supplies ordered on a specific day. For example, if he promised to deliver the supplies on the next Tuesday, he made 100% certain he delivered the supplies on Tuesday – exactly as he promised.

The Chicago weather often complicated his promise. McGaw founded the company before there were motorized vehicles, such as trucks or cars. He would deliver the supplies in his horse-drawn wagon.

Well, bad Chicago weather sometimes made his promised delivery date awfully difficult to achieve. For instance, Chicago sometimes has huge snowfalls. And the blowing and drifting snow makes it hard to drive a car or truck. So – you can imagine – how difficult it was to get a horse-drawn wagon through the deep snow and snowdrifts!

So, here is how Foster McGaw handled that. Let's say he promised to deliver supplies to a hospital on Tuesday. On Tuesday, he would load his wagon with the supplies, and then set out for the hospital. Whenever he reached a snowdrift he could not get through or around, he would get off his horse-drawn wagon, pack the hospital supplies onto his back, strap on snowshoes, and walk over the deep snow to deliver the hospital supplies – on the day he promised.

What does this repeatedly told story about the founder convey about the corporate culture? The corporate culture definitely was the following: *Succeed despite all odds.*

Isn't that exactly what the story tells? And, while working at the company, employees knew they always needed to *succeed despite all odds.* For instance, if someone had a huge project with a seemingly impossible deadline, that person nevertheless finished the project *by the promised completion date.* If an employee needed to carry out an assignment with too low a budget, it did not make any difference! The employee would do the assignment at or under budget. Why? Because the company's culture in a thousand ways valued, rewarded and recognized the company's permanent need to *succeed despite all odds.*

Throughout this book you will read many companies' oft-repeated stories, usually about the company founder, that – upon reflection – perfectly convey the organization's culture.

As for organizational change, as stated before, any organizational change that does not in some way fit into the company's culture is doomed to failure: It will not achieve the desired results. This explains why a company that flops in making organizational changes – if you examine its culture – often wasted time and money trying to put into action a change that did not fit into its culture.

A classic example is the fiasco of Quaker Oats buying the Snapple beverage company. Quaker Oats is a very established food company with very traditional marketing and ways to operate. Executives at Quaker got the idea that the company should buy the Snapple beverage company, because Snapple's beverages could be distributed through Quaker's vast distribution network.

As soon as I heard about this takeover, I *immediately* knew this was a very unwise acquisition. (In fact, I considered selling short the stock of Quaker Oats!) Why? In brief, Quaker's culture was one of *tradition* and a "normal" big-business way to do things. In hugely sharp contrast, Snapple was an extremely non-traditional, entrepreneurial company. Even its distribution was non-traditional. People heard on radio shows that they could become Snapple distributors. They signed up to distribute Snapple beverages in their local areas. This wildly differed from Quaker Oats' traditional corporate-type distribution methods, handled by wage-earning Quaker employees – not entrepreneurial people like at Snapple.

Here are devastating results of this unwise takeover of Snapple by Quaker Oats:

◆ Quaker Oats lost tons of money
◆ Quaker Oats eventually sold-off Snapple for a loss of over $1-billion
◆ CEO of Quaker Oats left the company after this disaster

Many years ago, Dr. Sigmund Freud, the founder of psycho-analysis, said that for individuals "anatomy is destiny."

Well, I – Dr. Michael Mercer, a management consultant and business psychologist – say, *"Organizational culture is destiny."*

Companies can make many organizational changes, but it proves best not to stray from the company's main focus or culture. A leader who strays too far from the organization's culture probably should update his or her resume.

Action 2: Creating A Big, Exciting Vision for Your Organization

Important: Realize that a company's *vision* is *not* the usually puffy, cliché-filled mission statement adorning the company's lobby or annual report.

Instead, a company's vision is a *big, exciting* goal the organization aims to accomplish. It proves extremely compelling. For example, GE's famous vision has been something like this: *Our key goal is to be either #1 or #2 in every industry GE is in.* Is GE's vision big, exciting, and compelling? It certainly is!

It is interesting to observe that when GE sells or spins off a division, that division often is doing quite well financially.

However, it often is #3 or #4 in its industry – and, as such, that division does not fit into GE's vision of being *either #1 or #2 in every industry GE is in.*

Also, a big, exciting vision accomplishes something else that proves crucial to an organization's strategy for success: It proves incredibly exciting for employees to show up to work in a company where they play a role in a big, exciting vision. In contrast, you may have noticed that organizations top-heavy with lackadaisical or half-hearted employees usually articulate either no clear vision or a small, unexciting vision. In fact, at many such organizations, the employees' main goals are to show up for work, breathe air, and do enough work to avoid getting fired!

In this book, you will see the *big, exciting visions* of America's best-run companies. Here are some examples:

The Ritz-Carlton Hotel Company's *Vision:*

*Our key goal is to be the
premier worldwide provider of luxury travel
and hospitality products and services.*

Intuit's *Vision:*

Our key goal is to revolutionize the way people do financial work.

Robert Mondavi Corporation's *Vision:*

Our key goal is to be the world's preeminent fine wine producer.

Importantly, every successful organizational change I have consulted on or participated in helps the company progress toward achieving its big, exciting vision. I never witnessed an exception to this rule. Indeed, the chief purpose of any organizational change must be, by its very nature, to move the organization closer and closer to its vision of a big, exciting future.

Action 3: Goal-Setting to Implement the Changes

Even the finest plans for organizational change get nowhere unless executives, managers and employees set goals. These goals form the steps that create the staircase to the grand scheme of the organizational change. The goals give employees specific, measurable targets, along with deadline dates to accomplish each goal.

> *"In the long run, people hit only what they aim at.*
> *Therefore, they had better aim at something high."*

HENRY DAVID THOREAU

I learned how to successfully use goal-setting in my first management job I held after I finished by Ph.D. I worked at a division of a huge company. My duties included starting and managing the company's goal-setting system. From doing this, I learned management-by-objectives (MBO). Most importantly, I especially learned from first-hand experience with hundreds of managers what works and also what does not work.

My first discovery: Goals must directly help move a company toward achieving its big, exciting vision. They do not exist in a vacuum separate from the company's overriding reason for being.

A second discovery I made: Goals "trickle-down" from the top executives to each rung on the ladder below them. Despite all the pseudo-egalitarian rhetoric some people spout, successful business planning and goal-setting goes from the top downward. It does not bubble up from the bottom of the organization to the executive suite. So, top executives must lead in setting goals. Then, they need to require each layer of employees below them to set goals that will combine to achieve the executives' "big-picture" goals.

My third lesson I learned is that goals must contain two key components:

◆ measures
◆ deadlines

Measures should include improvements in dollars, numbers, or percentages. The deadlines assure the goals get achieved by set dates – despite all odds.

Later in this book, you will see key goals set by executives of some of America's best-run companies.

Action 4: Teamwork to Achieve the Goals

One executive or manager – regardless of how brilliant, ambitious, or energetic – cannot work alone to produce major organizational changes. Instead, teams of employees must collaborate to achieve goals needed to implement the changes. Some teams consist of co-workers in the same department or work-group. Other teams are interdepartmental – made up of people from an array of departments or divisions. Some teams are permanent, while others exist for only a short time to accomplish specific goals. In this book, you will read many examples of how teams work to produce organizational change.

How did executives leading organizational change get employees to use teamwork plus interdepartmental collaboration? Here is an example.

At Egghead.com – the large company that sells technology products and services – president and chief operating officer (COO) Jeffrey Sheahan and CEO Jerry Kaplan cleverly package two activities every Tuesday and two activities every Friday to assure (A) teamwork, (B) interdepartmental cooperation, and (C) achievement of business goals.

Teamwork Activity 1: Tuesday, Noon - 2:00 p.m. over lunch - Executive Staff Meetings

The company's top executives participate in this weekly meeting: (1) CEO Jerry Kaplan, (2) President & COO Jeffrey Sheahan, (3) Chief Financial Officer, (4) Chief Technology Officer, (5) Vice President of Human Resources, and senior vice presidents of the various functions. The meeting focuses on strategic as well as operational issues. The overwhelming chief focus is on strategy, but on-going significant business issues are addressed as well.

Teamwork Activity 2: Tuesday - Weekly Key Data Pack

Each manager submits a "5 - 15 Report." This report takes a manager 15 minutes to write, and it takes Sheahan 5 minutes to read. Each "5 - 15 Report" shows precisely how the manager is progressing on his or her key performance "metrics" or measurable goals the manager is working to accomplish. Also, every "5 - 15 Report" is brought to the weekly Friday Senior Staff Meeting to help focus the discussion about operational issues and how the company can improve.

Teamwork Activity 3: Friday morning - Weekly Senior Staff Meeting

Participants are all the company's middle managers. These are managers who report directly to the top five executives, namely, the CEO, COO, CFO, CTO, and VP-HR.

Each middle manager communicates how he or she is progressing on achieving the measurable goals. This proves crucial. As Sheahan points out, "When you're moving at e-speed, this gives us a chance each week to get together and keep each other on track."

Teamwork Activity 4: Friday - 3:30 - 3:50 p.m. - "Social"

All employees get together for a 20-minute stand-up meeting (no sitting allowed!). Ice cream and cake are served. People sing praises about – and also reward – individual employees who accomplished wonderful things for the company.

A word about Teambuilding Sessions. In this book, you will read examples of using "Teambuilding Sessions" to promote teamwork and collaboration.

What are *Teambuilding Sessions?* I can speak from my experience. I devised a *method that helps teams or work-groups measurably improve their productive teamwork and collaboration.* Teambuilding Sessions I conduct at a company include many elements, including:

- ◆ Identify the team's work-problems which, if overcome, will improve the team's productivity
- ◆ Overcome interpersonal problems among team members that stop them from collaborating productively; I do this using a unique, non-threatening method that I devised
- ◆ Create solutions to the team's work-problems

When I do Teambuilding Sessions, I conduct three with each team: One extensive session and then two follow-up sessions. The follow-up sessions make sure the team members *actually* implement the work-problem solutions and *really* do overcome their interpersonal problems.*

Organizational Change Ingredient 2:
Handling Employees Who Resist or Undermine the Organizational Change

Surveys of executives reveal many organizational changes fail to meet their stated objectives due to "people problems." In many respects, these "people problems" fall into two main categories. Specifically, some employees

- ◆ resist
- ◆ act rebellious

---

*To obtain information about how Dr. Mercer conducts *Teambuilding Sessions,* you can refer to the Materials You Can Order section in the back of this book.

The *resistance* takes the form of employees objecting to – or flinging roadblocks in the way of – the change. *Rebellion* by employees seems akin to teenagers boldly flaunting a defiant act in front of authority figures, in this case executives and managers instituting change.

In each example of absolutely fabulous organizational change in this book, you will find a lot of specific examples of how

◆ employees resisted change
◆ executives overcame the resistance to make the change a reality

Every manager implementing organizational change needs to realize employee problems will pop up. For instance, some of the many employee problems encountered in organizations include employees

◆ slowing down their work pace
◆ mouthing public support for the change, but putting it down in private
◆ not collaborating in a productive fashion

One of my prouder moments in the media spotlight occurred when I appeared on business television shows – and also was quoted in national magazines – concerning employees' emotional reactions to organizational change. I had just delivered a speech on the topic at a national conference. At the press conference after my speech, reporters snapped to attention and later quoted me when I said the following: *"The major emotional reaction of employees during organizational change is that they feel like their spouse or lover just walked out on them!"*

Why did my statement attract so much media attention? I think it is because I summarized the ultra-uncomfortable, emotionally charged feeling of *betrayal* practically everyone has felt. Every person has felt betrayed by someone in his or her personal life. But, we seldom think about employees feeling betrayed by their employer. Well, employees who have a difficult time handling change often feel betrayed. They get used to everything being done in the company in a certain way – just like a person gets used to a spouse or lover typically acting in a certain way.

But then, all of a sudden – like horribly loud thunder that makes a person's heart race – if a company or spouse or lover suddenly changes how they act, the person feels a huge loss. This conveys the sense of betrayal employees often feel during major organizational change.

Unfortunately, it cannot be ignored, because people who feel betrayed often figure out ways to "get back at" the company or person who betrayed them. For instance, employees can obstruct organizational change in many ways. If enough employees rebel or undermine change, this slows down or derails the change the organization needs to survive, grow, and prosper. I found key *emotional reactions* of employees who harmed or slowed down organizational change were the following:

- betrayal
- anger
- gloominess
- cynicism and skepticism

So, the urgent question arises: What methods proved most effective to handle employees who resisted – or undermined – organizational change? My research on executives in the trenches uncovered that these are among the most useful methods:

- communicate why the change is a business necessity
- terminate, lay-off, or fire
- involve employees in making decisions
- incentive pay for producing key measurable results
- insist employees achieve goals within set deadlines
- insist on teamwork – which creates peer pressure to "get with the program"
- celebrate successes – so everyone wants to participate

This brings up a crucial concern: Employees who did fine *before* the organizational change may not do well in the company *after* the change is implemented. I refer to these as *"old-style"* employees and *"new-style"* employees. Note: I am not referring to an employee's age. Instead, I mean that people who do work that proved fine prior to the change often need to work in a different – or new way – after the change.

From my consulting to many organizations, I often find these vital differences between *old-style* and *new-style* employees:

Old-Style Employees	New-Style Employees
Works in 1 department	Interdepartmental
Solo work	Teamwork
Likes receiving direction	Likes independence

Prefers to be told what to do	Prefers shared leadership
Focus: Seniority & experience	Focus: Updating & expanding skills
Human robot	Thinks to do work

A successful leader *transforms* the *old-style* employees into *new-style* employees. Important: The word *transform* means more than meets the eye. "Transform" derives from two words: *trance* and *form*. Let me explain. Most people spend most of their time in a type of *trance*. I do not mean the stage hypnosis trance in which a hypnotist slowing swings a pocket watch to "hypnotize" someone into a "trance." Instead, I mean most people are in a *trance* in that they do most actions by habit – without thinking.

For example, you probably have a *habit* of doing certain actions in the same way without thinking about them – tying your shoes, turning on the light in a particular room, and even some interactions with people. If you needed to think much before doing such everyday actions, you would waste a lot of time and energy. So, you just do those actions without thinking – by habit. As such, you do many actions, in effect, in a normal, everyday *trance*. This, of course, usually works to your benefit.

However, when an organization implements changes, the effective leader helps employees *form* new habits for doing certain actions – or *form* new *trances*. That is, the successful leader *trance-forms* the *old-style* employees into *new-style* employees.

For example, at Excell Global Services, Lori Ulichnie, vice president of human resources, found four methods work particularly well to help transform *old-style* employees into the *new-style* employees the company needed after Excell's highly successful organizational changes:

◆ Incentive pay
◆ Thrill of employees receiving upper management attention when their projects produce great results
◆ Determine strategy, be clear about it, and live by it
◆ "Communicate 500 Times" – keep repeating the company's strategy to employees

Along the way, in many organizations, some of what I call *"de-employment"* is needed. Some employees simply fail to improve. Other employees prove ill-suited to make the change due to inability to develop new skills or knowledge. Still others – the ultra-rebellious ones – keep resisting, objecting, undermining, and erecting roadblocks. At some point, such problem employees may need to be "de-employed." This could be layoffs, firing, or other terminations. Some companies transfer employees to other departments where they could be productive.

One time I was conducting my workshop on *Absolutely Fabulous Organizational Change*™ at a company's "management retreat."*

At one point in my presentation, an executive in charge of a division of that company dramatically stood up. He announced to the group: *"As our organization undergoes major organizational changes, we always seek to cure the wounded. But, we will shoot the dissenters."*

Everyone in my management retreat workshop sat shocked and silent for a few moments. Then, all of a sudden, everyone burst out laughing. Reason: They suddenly recognized the wisdom of what they heard. Indeed, effective leaders find it highly useful to

- ◆ "cure the wounded"
- ◆ "shoot the dissenters"

"Cure the wounded" implies helping employees who sincerely want to help the organization improve, grow, and prosper. "Shoot the dissenters," of course, this does not mean to actually "shoot" or harm rebellious employees or "dissenters." Instead, this means it proves *ultra*-necessary to get rid of (fire, layoff or transfer) employees who refuse to help implement change. After all, a company's goal is to grow and prosper. A company's goal is not to run a counseling center to treat rebellious employees.

Importantly, a fantastic way to avoid employee problems in times of change is to *not* hire employees who could become problem employees! As I rhetorically ask in workshops and speeches I deliver based on my book *Hire the Best – & Avoid the Rest*™, "What's the fastest, cheapest, easiest way to have employees who are productive, dependable, and honest?" My answer: "Hire people who are productive, dependable, and honest!!"**

---

*You can obtain details about Dr. Mercer's workshops and speeches by using the Materials You Can Order section in the back of this book.

**Information on Dr. Mercer's pre-employment tests, workshops and materials on *Hire the Best – & Avoid the Rest*™ is available through the Materials You Can Order section in the back of this book.

Given this truism of hiring great employees, I advise companies undertaking organizational change to alter what they look for in job applicants. In general, America's best-run companies look for job candidates who already possess the behaviors (interpersonal skills, personalities, and motivations) and mental abilities of the *new-style* employees they need to produce spectacular results from their organizational change. Improved hiring methods often include evaluating job candidates using *customized*

◆ tests
◆ interviews

Organizational Change Ingredient 3:
Successfully Managing Yourself during Organizational Change

I find it astounding how managers use many management techniques for planning and implementing organizational change – but do not look at something incredibly important: How they manage their attitudes, actions, spoken words and emotions during organizational change. They act like their personality is disconnected from the success – or failure – of the wonderful organizational change they envision!

From my experience consulting to executives who *successfully* carry out organizational change, I continually find certain key characteristic among these absolutely fabulous change leaders.

First, they are very intelligent. I had executives from some of America's best-run companies take Mercer Systems' *Abilities Forecaster*™ tests to measure how intelligent these magnificent leaders really are.* They scored high on the Problem-Solving Ability test (a test of general intellectual ability) and on tests of other key mental abilities. That is, incredibly successful leaders are incredibly smart – as measured by the widely used *Abilities Forecaster*™ test. You will read more on this later in this book.

Second – and perhaps even more important – these fantastically successful executives are quite optimistic. This was

---

*You can obtain information on Mercer Systems' pre-employment tests – the *Abilities & Behavior Forecaster*™ tests – by referring to the Materials You Can Order section in the back of this book.

verified in research – which you will read about in this book – using Mercer Systems' *Behavior Forecaster*™ test. This test predicts 13 work behaviors:

♦ 5 personality traits – including optimism
♦ 3 interpersonal skills – including teamwork, friendliness, and assertiveness
♦ 5 motivations – including customer service, money, and power motivations

Of all the traits that emerge as key to a successful leader's ultimate success, I find his or her *optimism* is one of the most important. Optimism proves so significant that I developed two premises for managers and executives.

Premise 1: The leader is *the* role model for employees in the organization.

Premise 2: Highly effective role models are optimists.

This calls for a definition of what is an optimist. I co-wrote a book entitled, *Spontaneous Optimism*™: *Proven Strategies for Health, Prosperity & Happiness.** Our book and related materials report on the

♦ key role of optimism in career, physical and emotional health, and financial success
♦ techniques to boost optimism in work and personal life

In *Spontaneous Optimism*™, my co-author and I give this definition:

In brief, an optimistic person

♦ *possesses a clear vision of an exciting, meaningful life*
♦ *works on goals to help progress toward his or her exciting vision*
♦ *has a confident, "Can-Do" attitude*
♦ *takes high levels of self-responsibility*
♦ *lives a prosperous life*

Without exception, as you will see in this book, leaders at some of America's best-run companies all felt optimism played a huge role in successfully implementing major organizational changes. Their optimism helped them keep plugging away despite obstacles, negative people, and other roadblocks.

---

*Details on the *Spontaneous Optimism*™ book, audiobook and Intensive Coaching® sessions are available through the Materials You Can Order section at the back of this book.

One key trait of optimists is this: Optimists focus on solutions. In sharp contrast, pessimists focus on complaining or problems. This distinction proves vital, because when employees see their role model focuses on solutions – and not on problems – they learn they should do the same.

Or, to put it another way, *attitudes are contagious.* If the leader complains and focuses on problems – not on solutions – then that manager should expect employees to "pick-up" that behavior and act similarly. Indeed, any organization that allows complaining, blaming and a focus on problems creates an environment in which it is hard to implement successful organizational change.

After all, success in business and life-in-general requires focusing on opportunities and solutions. Failure in business and personal life consists of wallowing in the mud of problems. *Successful* executives and managers I have tested – or consulted to – are optimists. Fortunately, optimism is a skill anyone can learn. And pessimism is a skill anyone can unlearn.

Interestingly, I discovered a great way to gain insights into a person's outlook on life: Ask the person for his or her favorite story. When a person tells you his or her favorite story, the person reveals a tremendous amount about what he or she considers truly important in work and personal life.

For example, Robert Hughes, manager of IBM National Accounts Payable, and his team figured out how IBM could save a ton of money. And they succeeded on a massive scale: *IBM ended up saving $1-billion using improved vendor processing.* Along the way, they helped IBM create new technology and systems IBM now sells to other companies, plus they won numerous highly prestigious awards for their pioneering achievements. Hughes' favorite story is the following:

The Little Train That Could

In this classic story, a little train went on an incredible journey. At one point, it needed to travel up a steep hill, which proved extremely difficult. Throughout this ordeal, the Little Train kept saying, "I think I can! I think I can!!" And, eventually the Little Train did reach its destination.

What makes *The Little Train That Could* such a significant story to this highly successful leader? For him, the story illustrates the importance of persistence. Or, as he puts it, "Anybody can do anything if they put their mind to it."

Also, when Hughes told me his favorite story, he noticeably emphasized the little train used the word "think" – "I *think* I can! I *think* I can!!" This is intriguing. Reason: The placard displayed on the desk of IBM's founder, Thomas Watson, Sr., contained only one word – "*THINK.*" As such, Hughes' favorite story – *The Little Train That Could* – complements the IBM founder's "*THINK*" motto.

Interestingly, *The Little Train That Could* is an exceptionally popular story among high-achievers. How do I know this? The story came up many times in research I did to develop a pre-employment test. To decide what test questions to ask applicants, I started by asking a series of questions to groups of high-achievers and underachievers in certain occupations. From their answers, I pinpointed which test questions to use in the final pre-employment test – as well as discovering how high-achievers' answers differ from underachievers' answers.

One question in the test development centered on the person's favorite story. The most frequently cited story among the high-achievers was *The Little Train That Could*. No underachievers chose that story! This classic story conveys universal truths about (A) the value of persistence, (B) focusing on achievement, and (C) how someone can succeed despite all odds.

I also discovered from testing and interviewing many candidates for management and executives positions that a person's most formative events in childhood – ages 1 - 21 years old – give insights into how a person behaves on-the-job. For this reason, I asked executives leading major organizational change at America's best-run companies to reveal their most formative childhood events. These shed a lot of light on how they grew as people and, by extension, executives and managers. For instance, Tim Gannon – co-founder and senior vice president of Outback Steakhouse, Inc. – described his most formative childhood events, as follows:

> *At age 12 years old, I sold newspapers in the street – and from that I knew that although I came from a poor family, I could go out and make as much money as I want.*
>
> *At age 14 years old, I had 900 customers and two employees. The average newspaper seller had only 150 customers and no employees. I was riding high, earning about $75 per week – which was a lot of money for a 14 year old to earn.*
>
> *So, I had all the money I wanted – and I never knew I came from a poor family.*

From his incredibly formative childhood experiences, Gannon offers this advice: "How hungry are you and how deep is your hunger? If you don't have deep hunger, then you'll never achieve great success."

Another powerful insight into successful leaders, I discovered, is to find out who their role models are plus the most important lessons learned from each one. For example, Dyan Beito – the senior vice president who leads acquisition integration at Washington Mutual, one of the USA's largest financial institutions focusing on retail consumers – says two of her role models provided lessons that she carries into her work and personal life.

Role Model 1: Father. *Lessons Learned:* "Optimism and moral values. My father was the most optimistic person in the world. I also learned lots of moral values from him. He would say, 'If you're going to do a job, do it right the first time – or don't do it at all.'"

Role Model 2: Regional manager at Beito"s third banking job. *Lessons Learned:* "Time management and discipline in doing the activities she needed to do to succeed each day. She stuck to each task until she completed it."

It seems apparent that a major reason for Beito's career success and success as a leader stems from her applying lessons she learned from her two role models:

♦ optimism
♦ moral values
♦ "do it right the first time" approach
♦ time management discipline

Summary of My 3 Ingredient Organizational Change Model

Based on my many years of consulting to corporations – plus my previous work as a manager at two companies – I found organizational change achieves desired results when three key elements are managed effectively:

♦ *Leading* the organizational change
♦ *Handling employee problems* during the organizational change
♦ *Managing yourself* – so you are a tremendous role model for your employees

3

Test Scores Reveal Personalities & Intelligence of Managers & Executives Who Lead Absolutely Fabulous Organizational Change

When I consult to highly successful executives and managers, I *subjectively* notice they share certain traits. Fortunately, I developed a way to objectively discover the personalities and mental abilities of people who lead absolutely fabulous organizational change: Test them with a widely used test that normally is used to test job candidates. So, I did this.

I used a pre-employment test I developed – the *Abilities & Behavior Forecaster*™ test – in my research. Usually, *Forecaster*™ tests are customized to help companies predict which job applicants are likely to become productive, dependable employees.*

For this project, I had many executives and managers who led highly successful organizational change fill-out the *Abilities & Behavior Forecaster*™. With this data, I came up with *objective* "benchmark" test scores. These are the *Forecaster*™ test scores typically gotten by people who lead highly successful organization change.

---

*You can obtain information on using Mercer Systems, Inc.'s pre-employment tests – *Abilities & Behavior Forecaster*™ tests – by referring to the Materials You Can Order section at the end of the book.

3 Ways You Can Use the "Benchmark" Test Scores of Highly Effective Executives & Managers

This "benchmark" information on the *Abilities & Behavior Forecaster*™ test can be useful in three main ways: First, you can use the *Forecaster*™ test with these "benchmark" test scores to help you evaluate and pick candidates for management and executive jobs. You readily can compare your job candidate's *Forecaster*™ test scores to the scores of proven successful executives.

Second, you can compare your company's current managers' *Forecaster*™ test scores to the scores of amazingly successful leaders at some of America's best-run companies. This can help you (A) decide which employee could lead change management and (B) develop employees' talents on crucial leadership traits.

Third, you can *customize* the *Abilities & Behavior Forecaster*™ test for almost any job in your company. For instance, if you need to hire good salespeople, customer service representatives – or people for many other jobs – you can do your own "benchmarking" study on each job in your company. Then, you can use your company's "benchmark" test scores to readily compare each applicant's *Forecaster*™ test scores against the test scores of your *successful* employees in each job. You, of course, probably would prefer to hire applicants who

◆ score similar to your company's *successful* employees in each job and also

◆ do well in other prediction methods you use, such as interviews and reference checks

Test Scores of Spectacularly Effective Executives & Managers

The highly effective executives you will read about in upcoming sections of this book – *Absolutely Fabulous Organizational Change*™ – took the *Abilities & Behavior Forecaster*™ test, along with other remarkably successful leaders I tested. So, you get to see *cumulative* test scores of successful leaders in America's best-run companies. Note: You will read about combined test scores from all the leaders I tested for this project. For ethical and professional reasons, you will not see the test scores of any individual executive who participated in my unique *benchmarking study*.

The "benchmark" *Forecaster*™ test scores of highly successful leaders at some of America's best-run companies are shown by the parentheses in Diagram 1. For instance, on the *Forecaster*™'s

Teamwork scale, the "benchmark"parentheses indicate the successful leaders usually score 8 - 11 points. That shows they are extremely teamwork-oriented. Or, on the Problem-Solving Ability scale, these successful managers and executives typically score 8 - 11. This indicates they possess a very high level of general intelligence. Indeed, they are super-smart.

Diagram 1. **"Benchmark" Scores on the** *Abilities & Behavior Forecaster*™ **Tests: Test Scores of Leaders of Highly Successful Organizational Change**

BEHAVIOR FORECASTER™ Test

	1	2	3	4	5	6	7	8	9	10	11	
Inaccurate						(				)		Accurate

INTERPERSONAL STYLE

	1	2	3	4	5	6	7	8	9	10	11	
Unfriendly				(				)				Friendly
Passive					(					)		Aggressive
Prefers Solo Work							(			)		Prefers Teamwork

PERSONALITY

	1	2	3	4	5	6	7	8	9	10	11	
Lax to Follow Rules, Policies & Procedures			(				)					Rigidly Follows Rules, Policies & Procedures
Subjective				(				)				Objective
Pessimistic					(			)				Optimistic
Calm			(					)				Excitable
Feeling-Focused				(					)			Fact-Focused

MOTIVATIONS

	1	2	3	4	5	6	7	8	9	10	11	
Low Money				(				)				Strong Money
Low Helping People					(			)				Strong Helping People
Low Creativity					(			)				Strong Creativity
Low Power			(				)					Strong Power
Low Knowledge		(					)					Strong Knowledge

ABILITIES FORECASTER™ Test

	1	2	3	4	5	6	7	8	9	10	11	
Low Problem-Solving							(	)				Strong Problem-Solving
Low Vocabulary						(		)				Strong Vocabulary
Low Arithmetic						(		)				Strong Arithmetic
Low Grammar						(		)				Strong Grammar
Low Small Detail Speed & Accuracy				(				)				Strong Small Detail Speed & Accuracy

Note: Parentheses show "benchmark"/typical scores of successful leaders.

Source: Research by Dr. Michael W. Mercer, using Mercer Systems, Inc.'s *Abilities & Behavior Forecaster*™ tests, www.mercersystems.com.

The *Abilities & Behavior Forecaster*™ tests predict how a person will act on-the-job in four major arenas:

◆ 3 interpersonal skills
◆ 5 personality traits
◆ 5 work motivations
◆ 5 mental abilities

The *Behavior Forecaster*™ tests job applicants to predict three interpersonal skills, five personality traits, and five work motivations. The *Abilities Forecaster*™ is composed of five tests of mental abilities: Problem-Solving, Vocabulary, Arithmetic, Grammar, Spelling & Word Use, and Small Detail Speed & Accuracy.

Another way to understand the successful executives' *Abilities & Behavior Forecaster*™ test "benchmark" score is shown in Diagram 2.

Diagram 2. **Explanation of "Benchmark" Test Scores of Highly Successful Managers & Executives on the *Abilities & Behavior Forecaster*™ Tests**

Explanation of Leaders' "Benchmark"/Typical Test Scores	"Benchmark" Scores (scores = 1 - 11 points)
Behavior Forecaster™ Test	
Interpersonal Skills	
✓ Moderately Friendly	4 - 9
✓ Strongly Assertive	6 - 11
✓ Very strongly Teamwork-oriented	8 - 11
Personality Traits	
✓ Flexible about Following Rules	3 - 8
✓ Fairly Objective Reactions to criticism	5 - 9
✓ Strongly Optimistic	7 - 11
✓ Moderate on Calm-to-Excitable continuum	4 - 9
✓ Fact-Focused (not Feeling-Focused)	5 - 10
Motivations	
✓ Above-average motivation to make a lot of Money	5 - 10
✓ Strong motivation to Help People	6 - 11
✓ Strong motivation to do Creative work	7 - 11
✓ Average to below-average motivation to exert Power	3 - 8
✓ Low motivation to increase Knowledge/do research	2 - 7
Abilities Forecaster™ Test	
✓ Very strong Problem-Solving Ability – super-smart	8 - 11
✓ Strong Vocabulary Ability	7 - 11
✓ Strong Arithmetic Ability	6 - 11
✓ Strong Grammar, Spelling, & Word Use Ability	7 - 11
✓ Average Small Detail Speed & Accuracy Ability	4 - 9

Source: Research by Dr. Michael W. Mercer, using Mercer Systems, Inc.'s *Abilities & Behavior Forecaster*™ tests, www.mercersystems.com.

How You Can Hire Highly Productive Employees

Importantly, you may be involved with hiring managers, executives, or other employees. In fact, some people you hire will lead organizational change. As such, you now need to answer two vital questions: How can you determine which

1. job candidate might turn out to be fantastic, if you hire the person?
2. seemingly "good" candidate – e.g., seems good in interview or has good resume – might flop or do poorly on-the-job?

Fortunately, I can help you answer such crucial hiring questions due to my expertise in evaluating and choosing job candidates. I

◆ developed the *Abilities & Behavior Forecaster*™ tests

◆ authored the book *Hire the Best – & Avoid the Rest*™

◆ trained thousands of managers in how to conduct customized interviews of applicants

◆ created customized interview guide forms for hundreds of jobs

◆ conducted in-depth evaluations of job candidates

As such, I prepared recommendations you readily can use. You will read these hiring tips by turning to the next chapter.

4

How You Can Hire Successful Employees

Imagine . . . you need to hire someone. Perhaps you need to hire a salesperson, manager, customer service representative, executive, production worker, or any other employee. The person you hire will impact your company's bottom line. Also, some people you hire will play key roles in organizational change or other crucial business endeavors.

Your goal: *Predict* how well each job candidate may perform on-the-job, *if* you hire the person.

Question: How can you make a good hiring decision?

Answer: You have four options to help you evaluate job candidates.

You are offered this advice here for two reasons. First, this book focuses on how to plan and implement highly successful organizational change. People you hire ultimately can make-or-break your organization. If you hire high-achievers, they help you vastly improve your company. Or, if you hire underachievers, they drag down your organization and your career.

Second, if I offered you only *ideas* about how to hire productive employees without also offering you specific *tools* to help you do this, then you would not be able to put these ideas into action. As such, I am offering you tips and tools on how to hire productive employees, because I

+ authored the book *Hire the Best – & Avoid the Rest™*
+ developed widely used pre-employment tests – the *Abilities & Behavior Forecaster™* tests
+ trained thousands of managers in how to conduct customized interviews of applicants

This chapter explains four methods that can be customized to help you choose job applicants for specific jobs in your organization.* They are

Method 1. Tests customized for specific jobs in your company.
Method 2. Interviewing skills training for managers who make hiring decisions
Method 3. *Hire the Best Tool Kit*™
Method 4. Customized evaluations of candidates for certain key positions

Method 1: Customized Pre-Employment Tests

Large-scale research shows the most accurate way to predict job performance is pre-employment tests, especially *customized* (A) behavior tests and (B) mental abilities tests.

For this reason, I spent years developing the *Abilities & Behavior Forecaster*™ tests. These tests predict

◆ 3 interpersonal skills
◆ 5 personality traits
◆ 5 motivations
◆ 5 mental abilities

My firm, Mercer Systems, Inc. has *customized* the *Abilities & Behavior Forecaster*™ tests for many jobs in many companies. These jobs include

◆ Salesperson
◆ Customer Service Representative
◆ Production Worker
◆ Supervisor and Manager
◆ Teller
◆ Many other jobs

Customizing the *Forecaster*™ tests is done via a "benchmarking" study (concurrent validity study). "Benchmarking" pinpoints the typical test scores of *successful* (productive and dependable) employees in a specific job. Then, you readily can

---

*You can

◆ find out about using Dr. Mercer's pre-employment tests, tool kits, books and workshops by referring to the Materials You Can Order section at the back of this book
◆ visit Mercer Systems, Inc.'s Web site at www.mercersystems.com.

compare an applicant's *Forecaster*™ test scores against the "benchmark" test scores of *successful* people in the job. For instance, if you want to hire successful salespeople, you could (1) do a "benchmarking" study focusing on your company's successful salespeople and then (2) test job applicants and see which applicants score similar to your company's proven successful salespeople.

Example: Since this is a book on leading organizational change, let's say you need to hire a person for a manager or executive job who will lead organizational change. Of course, you benefit by comparing each candidate's test scores against the "benchmark" test scores of *successful* leaders of organizational change. Diagrams 1 and 2 show how two applicants' *Forecaster*™ test scores compare with the scores of executives and managers who led highly successful organizational change, based on my research (reported in another chapter).

In the diagrams, the "*X*" shows the candidate's score on a test scale. "*Benchmark parentheses*" show typical *Forecaster*™ test scores of executives and managers who planned and implemented absolutely fabulous, successful organizational change. For instance, Candidate A (Diagram 1) scored 11 points on the "Teamwork" scale which is similar to successful leaders for whom the "benchmark" is 8 - 11 points. In this example, a company would prefer candidates who both

♦ score similar to the successful executives (score mostly in *benchmark parentheses*)
♦ do well in interviews, reference checks, and other evaluation methods

As such, in the following two diagrams, you probably would

♦ seriously consider Candidate A (see Diagram 1)
♦ not seriously consider Candidate B (see Diagram 2)

Reason: Candidate A scored *similar to* highly successful managers and executives; that gives a good indication of Candidate A's possible success on-the-job. In contrast, Candidate B scored *very different than* the successful leaders; this indicates Candidate B may prove lacking in crucial ways. *Forecaster*™ test scores should be looked at along with other prediction methods, such as interviews, reference check, and work history.

Diagram 1. *Abilities & Behavior Forecaster*™ Test Scores of A Candidate Who Scored <u>Very Similar</u> to Highly Successful Managers & Executives at Some of America's Best-Run Companies

Candidate A

BEHAVIOR FORECASTER™ Test

	1	2	3	4	5	6	7	8	9	10	11	
Inaccurate						(			X		)	Accurate

INTERPERSONAL STYLE

	1	2	3	4	5	6	7	8	9	10	11	
Unfriendly				(				X	)			Friendly
Passive					(			X	)			Aggressive
Prefers Solo Work							(			X)		Prefers Teamwork

PERSONALITY

	1	2	3	4	5	6	7	8	9	10	11	
Lax to Follow Rules, Policies & Procedures		(	X					)				Rigidly Follows Rules, Policies & Procedures
Subjective				(					X)			Objective
Pessimistic						(			X)			Optimistic
Calm			(		X			)				Excitable
Feeling-Focused				(		X			)			Fact-Focused

MOTIVATIONS

	1	2	3	4	5	6	7	8	9	10	11	
Low Money					(				X	)		Strong Money
Low Helping People					(				X	)		Strong Helping People
Low Creativity							(	X			)	Strong Creativity
Low Power		(				X	)					Strong Power
Low Knowledge	(			X			)					Strong Knowledge

ABILITIES FORECASTER™ Test

	1	2	3	4	5	6	7	8	9	10	11	
Low Problem-Solving							(			X	)	Strong Problem-Solving
Low Vocabulary						(		X		)		Strong Vocabulary
Low Arithmetic					(				X)			Strong Arithmetic
Low Grammar						(	X			)		Strong Grammar
Low Small Detail Speed & Accuracy			(	X						)		Strong Small Detail Speed & Accuracy

Notes: "X"= candidate's score

Parentheses show the "benchmark parentheses" where successful executives and managers typically scored.

Source: Research by Dr. Michael W. Mercer, using Mercer Systems, Inc.'s *Abilities & Behavior Forecaster*™ Tests, www.mercersystems.com.

Diagram 2. *Abilities & Behavior Forecaster™* Test Scores of A
Candidate Who Scored <u>*Very Different*</u> Than Highly
Successful Executives & Managers at Some of
America's Best-Run Companies

Candidate B

BEHAVIOR FORECASTER™ Test

	1	2	3	4	5	6	7	8	9	10	11	
Inaccurate					(		X				)	Accurate

INTERPERSONAL STYLE

	1	2	3	4	5	6	7	8	9	10	11	
Unfriendly				(X					)			Friendly
Passive				Ⓧ	(					)		Aggressive
Prefers Solo Work			Ⓧ			(				)		Prefers Teamwork

PERSONALITY

	1	2	3	4	5	6	7	8	9	10	11	
Lax to Follow Rules, Policies & Procedures		(						)		Ⓧ		Rigidly Follows Rules, Policies & Procedures
Subjective			Ⓧ		(				)			Objective
Pessimistic		Ⓧ					(			)		Optimistic
Calm				(		X			)			Excitable
Feeling-Focused					(			X	)			Fact-Focused

MOTIVATIONS

	1	2	3	4	5	6	7	8	9	10	11	
Low Money				(			X		)			Strong Money
Low Helping People		Ⓧ			(				)			Strong Helping People
Low Creativity				Ⓧ		(			)			Strong Creativity
Low Power		(						)		Ⓧ		Strong Power
Low Knowledge	(							)		Ⓧ		Strong Knowledge

ABILITIES FORECASTER™ Test

	1	2	3	4	5	6	7	8	9	10	11	
Low Problem-Solving						Ⓧ	(			)		Strong Problem-Solving
Low Vocabulary							(X			)		Strong Vocabulary
Low Arithmetic				Ⓧ	(					)		Strong Arithmetic
Low Grammar					Ⓧ	(				)		Strong Grammar
Low Small Detail Speed & Accuracy			(				X	)				Strong Small Detail Speed & Accuracy

Notes: "X" = candidate's score

Parentheses show the "benchmark parentheses" where successful executives and managers typically scored.

Circled Ⓧ shows where candidate scored different than "benchmark" scores of successful executives and managers.

Source: Research by Dr. Michael W. Mercer, using Mercer Systems, Inc.'s *Abilities & Behavior Forecaster™* Tests, www.mercersystems.com.

Two important factors go into customizing and using the *Abilities & Behavior Forecaster*™ tests. First, you conduct a "benchmarking study" to *customize the test scoring for each job in your company for which you want to test applicants.* I created a 5-step method to conduct a customizing "benchmarking study" in a very time-efficient manner. As soon as you finish your company's "benchmarking," you can start testing applicants. Then, you readily compare each applicant's test scores to the "benchmark" or typical scores of successful employees in each job for which you test applicants.

Second, you can have job candidates fill-out the *Abilities & Behavior Forecaster*™ tests using either of these two ways:
◆ *Forecaster*™ test questionnaire booklet
◆ Internet-based *Forecaster*™ testing

If you have applicants complete the *Forecaster*™ tests in the test questionnaire booklet at your company's office, then your company quickly scores the tests using Mercer Systems, Inc.'s test scoring software.

Or, if you have applicants take the *Forecaster*™ tests using Mercer Systems' Internet-based testing, then your company immediately obtains test scores and reports from our Internet-based testing site. The Internet-based testing allows you to easily test applicants either (A) in your office or (B) at any other location.

Method 2: Customized Interviewing of Job Candidates

Managers need to interview job applicants.

Problem: Research shows most managers do *not* know how to make accurate predictions of applicants' possible on-the-job success based on the interview.

Solution: I conduct customized interviewing skills workshops entitled, *Hire the Best – & Avoid the Rest*™. Prior to the workshop, we customize the interviewing method and questions for each specific job in your company. Then, we deliver a workshop to teach your company's managers and other interviewers how to
◆ conduct the interviews we customized for each job
◆ ask useful, customized questions
◆ interpret answers given by applicants
◆ assess how likely a candidate could do well on-the-job

Such customized interviewing methods help a manager predict which applicants could succeed, if hired – and which ones might flop. Also, they help managers feel more confident of (A) how to interview applicants and (B) make wise hiring decisions.

Method 3: *Hire the Best Tool Kit*™

The third method to assess the job candidates combines key ingredients of customized testing and interviewing – plus more. Mercer Systems, Inc. developed a *Hire the Best Tool Kit*™. The *Hire the Best Tool Kit*™ can be used to evaluate candidates for most jobs. It includes four items or "tools":

Tool 1: Tests – Mercer Systems' *Abilities & Behavior Forecaster*™ Tests
Tool 2: Interviewing System Customized for Specific Jobs in Your Company
Tool 3: Method to Rate Job Candidates
Tool 4: Over-the-Phone Consultation

Tool 1: Pre-Employment Tests

The *Hire the Best Tool Kit*™ includes *Abilities & Behavior Forecaster*™ tests. The *Forecaster*™ tests can be customized for specific jobs in your company. These tests are used by many companies to assess job candidates for a wide array of jobs, including (A) salesperson, (B) customer service rep, (C) production worker, (D) supervisor, (E) manager, and (F) many other jobs. Note: Also, I used the *Forecaster*™ tests in my research to uncover the personalities and intelligence of highly effective managers and executives who led organizational change, as reported elsewhere in this book.

Your company has job candidates fill-out the *Forecaster*™ tests. They take tests using either of these two ways:

♦ *Forecaster*™ test questionnaire booklet
♦ Internet-based *Forecaster*™ testing

Then, you could compare each candidate's test scores to the "benchmark" test scores of *successful* employees in the specific job for which you are hiring someone. You may want to seriously consider applicants who score similar to your successful employees.

Tool 2: Interviewing System Customized for Specific Jobs In Your Company

The second item or tool in the *Hire the Best Tool Kit*™ is a coupon to contact my consulting firm. We help you use our unique method to identify the talents and skills your company needs in the person you will hire for each specific job. Using this information, we then design for you a ready-to-use, customized interviewing system. Your *customized interviewing system* includes

◆ insightful questions that you ask each candidate
◆ procedure to quickly know what follow-up questions to ask a candidate
◆ checklists of actions by the candidate that you must observe in the interview
◆ techniques to discover if a candidate has the talents and skills needed to succeed
◆ methods to stop a candidate from lying to you – or "embellishing" the truth – about his or her talents, skills, or work experience

Tool 3: Clear-Cut Method to Rate Candidates

The rating method gives you an organized way to assess how candidates stack up on crucial talents your company needs in the job for which you are hiring someone. Armed with these vital ratings, you can make your important decision about whom to hire for the position.

Tool 4: Over-the-Phone Consultation

Many questions arise when a manager needs to make a hiring decision. Often, a lot of money, time and effort are at stake. So, the *Hire the Best Tool Kit*™ includes over-the-phone consultation with me or another business psychologist at Mercer Systems, Inc. to provide expertise in

◆ evaluating job candidates
◆ making crucial hiring decision

Method 4: Ultra-Customized Evaluation of Candidates for Executive & Manager Positions

I recommend using this ultra-customized evaluation mainly with candidates for key jobs or high-level positions, especially executive and management jobs. This method involves using the services of a business psychologist (sometimes called an industrial psychologist). A business psychologist earned a Ph.D. or doctoral degree in psychology with special training in helping companies boost productivity and profits.

Often, when I tell people I am a business psychologist, they incorrectly think I do psychotherapy! Reason: They do not know the huge difference between *business or industrial* psychologists and *clinical* psychologists. Business psychologists focus on helping organizations improving productivity and profits, sometimes including evaluating job candidates. In contrast, clinical psychologists do psychotherapy to treat mental illness – and they are *not* experts in evaluating job candidates.

You can look at the difference this way: Some physicians are neurology (brain) experts and other physicians are dermatology (skin) experts. No one would go to a neurologist for skin problems! Likewise, a company would not go to a *clinical* psychologist for problems entailing *business or organizational* problems. Instead, the company would use the services of a business or industrial psychologist.

When companies come to me – a business psychologist – to evaluate candidates for key manager or executive jobs, I conduct an ultra-customized, in-depth evaluation of the candidate. This intense evaluation of a candidate includes the following steps:

Step 1: Pre-Evaluation – Determining What the Company Needs

First, I help the hiring-executive (person the candidate would report to, if hired) list the most important talents and skills the company must have in the person it hires. Second, I uncover crucial requirements of the job and how it fits into the company's vision, business plans, and corporate culture. Finally, from this information, I create testing and interviewing custom-tailored to evaluate candidates for the specific job.

Step 2: Testing and Interviewing Candidate

First, I test the candidate, using my firm's *Abilities & Behavior Forecaster*™ tests. Second, I conduct a 2 - 4 hour extremely in-depth interview of the candidate. This intense interview delves into how well the candidate possesses talents and skills the person must have to succeed in the specific job in the company.

Step 3: Customized Report on Candidate

I write a *customized* report on the candidate, and send it to the executive who will make the hiring decision. This report focuses on how the candidate has or does not have the important talents and skills the company must have in the person it hires. Also, I include detailed recommendations.

Step 4: Post-Evaluation – Consultation to Company's Executive(s)
　　　Making the Hiring Decision

After evaluating all finalists, I discuss the candidates for the job with (A) the hiring executive to whom candidate would report, if hired and (B) other executives who must know about the candidates. We delve into the pros and cons of each candidate, as well as recommendations on how to manage the person who is hired.

Step 5: Optional – Candid Discussion with the Candidate Who Is Hired
    Some companies like me to give feedback and advice to the chosen candidate. In this incredibly candid discussion, I

◆ tell the candidate about his or her strengths and weaknesses

◆ give recommendations to overcome the weaknesses

◆ address how the person can achieve career goals

◆ talk about concerns the person has in taking the job

Summary of How You Can Hire the Best

Overall, the *goal of evaluating job applicants is to predict which candidates will turn out to be productive, reliable employees who enhance your company's bottom line.** These could be managers or executives. Or, they could be salespeople, customer service representatives, production workers, or many other types of employees.

You can assess job applicants using these techniques:

Method 1. Tests customized for specific jobs in your company

Method 2. Interviewing skills workshop to train managers how to make hiring decisions

Method 3. *Hire the Best Tool Kit*™

Method 4. Ultra-customized evaluation of manager and executive candidates

Tests, training and tool kits can be customized to help you hire productive employees. Then, you can use customized methods to help you *hire the best – and avoid the rest*™.

---

*You can

◆ find out about using Dr. Mercer's *Hire the Best* tool kits, tests, book and workshops by referring to the Materials You Can Order section at the back of this book

◆ visit Mercer Systems, Inc.'s Web site at www.mercersystems.com.

5

Examples of How America's Best-Run Companies Plan & Implement Absolutely Fabulous Organizational Change

After delivering many speeches, workshops and management retreats on organizational change – plus consulting to companies on other issues – I decided to write this book. At that point, I needed to choose the best way to convey to readers what really works. I decided readers would greatly benefit from detailed case examples of how executives succeeded at instituting major organizational change at America's best-run companies. Reason: This provides "real-world" examples of what actually works.

So, I listed companies I consult to plus others to include in this book. Then, I wrote questions to elicit details about how each company's absolutely fabulous organizational change used my three-ingredient model for organizational change. After that, I interviewed the executive responsible for each company's successful organizational change for 2½ - 4 hours each.

Also, I had the executives fill-out a pre-employment test I developed – the *Abilities & Behavior Forecaster*™ test. This test is widely used by companies across North America to evaluate job candidates so they can choose productive employees for many jobs*.

---

*You can find out more about the *Abilities & Behavior Forecaster*™ test by (1) reading about the *Forecaster*™ test scores of highly successful leaders in other parts of this book and (2) looking at the Materials You Can Order section at the end of this book.

The *Forecaster*™ test provided *objective* measurement of these fantastic executives'
- 13 key behaviors on-the-job
- 5 major mental abilities

The benefit of all this work for you is this: You can read exactly how executives at some of America's best-run companies planned and implemented incredibly successful organizational changes. These organizations include
- Egghead.com
- Excell Global Services
- Harley-Davidson
- IBM
- Intuit
- City of Indianapolis
- Robert Mondavi Corporation
- Outback Steakhouse, Inc.
- Ritz-Carlton Hotel Company
- VF Corporation
- Washington Mutual

For each company, first you will find out details of its major organizational change, along with the magnificent results. Then, you will see how each executive used my three-ingredient model of organizational change:

Ingredient 1: Successfully Leading the Organizational Change
Ingredient 2: Successfully Managing Employee Problems during the Organizational Change
Ingredient 3: Successfully Managing Himself or Herself while Leading Organizational Change

Ingredient 1 – *Successfully Leading the Organizational Change* – includes insights into the company's
- organizational culture
- big, exciting vision for its future
- goal-setting system to implement the change
- teamwork to assure goals got accomplished

Ingredient 2 – *Successfully Managing Employee Problems during the Organizational Change* – proves important, because even the best plans for organizational change fail if employees resist the change or lack needed skills. So, this part shows you
- types of employee resistance – or undermining – the executives encountered

- effective methods to handle resistant employees
- comparison of "old-style" employees who did fine before the change versus "new-style" employees needed after implementing the change
- actions to transform "old-style" employees into "new-style" employees
- "de-employment" used to make the change succeed
- hiring improvements to bring "new-style" employees on-board

Ingredient 3 – *Successfully Managing Yourself while Leading Organizational Change* – is unique. You seldom, if ever, read how a leader actually handles his or her emotions and actions on-the-job while managing change. This section starts with the premise I discovered that successful managers and executives usually are optimists.* In fact, *Forecaster*™ test scores of executives and managers who led absolutely fabulous organizational change prove they are strongly optimistic people. This is described elsewhere in this book. In upcoming chapters on America's best-run companies, you will discover how each executive uses

- optimism in making organizational change
- key attitudes to keep in an upbeat mood
- specific words, quotes and phrases to boost confidence
- a focus on solutions – not on problems

Also, in Ingredient 3 of each company example, you will discover fascinating personal experiences of the executives. These experiences helped them evolve into amazingly accomplished individuals. Specifically, you will read about each executive's

- favorite story – and how its theme enhances their success
- formative childhood events (age 1 - 21 years old) that continue to help in their careers
- role models they greatly admire – plus lessons learned from each one

---

*You can find out about Dr. Mercer's research and advice on optimism and leadership in his books and audio-books on (1) *How Winners Do It: High Impact People Skills for Your Career Success* and also (2) *Spontaneous Optimism*™: *Proven Strategies for Health, Prosperity & Happiness*. For information, you can look in the Materials You Can Order section at the end of this book.

This gives you unique insights into the personal lives of people who lead incredibly successful organizational change at America's best-run companies. You will not read such insights elsewhere. Why? Because business publications only focus on management techniques or results – and usually omit leaders' key life experiences. But, without the human dimension each executive brings to his or her organization, nothing would be accomplished.

Now, let the adventure begin!

Let's see how magnificently successful leaders at some of America's best-run companies used my three-ingredient model to create *absolutely fabulous organizational change*™.

6

OUTBACK STEAKHOUSE

Help Every Manager Make $1 Million – & They Will Make You Rich

Outback Steakhouse, Inc.'s *Vision:*
Our key goal is to create a
world-class casual dining company that endures.

Yum!!

What do you get when you combine a buoyant, upbeat atmosphere with mouth-watering steaks, glorious "blooming onions," bend-over-backwards-to-help-you customer service, a fun Australian-type atmosphere, plus restaurant proprietors who are on a fast-track to become millionaires?

This is the recipe for the monstrous success of Outback Steakhouse, Inc. According to Timothy Gannon, one of the founders and now a Senior Vice President, if Outback goes down in corporate history it will be for creating more millionaires than any other food business – perhaps even any type of business. This is done with a unique recipe that has grown Outback to a huge company. It boasts over 600 restaurants, sales in the billions, and over 40,000 employees. Such statistics make this a powerhouse business.

Interestingly, when I started telling two executives from non-restaurant companies about Outback Steakhouse, Inc., they immediately gasped in acknowledgement about how popular and successful Outback is. One of the executives told me, "There's an Outback restaurant near my house. And the parking lot is always so full of cars that it's impossible to get in there. It's that popular!" This sums up the result of years of blood, sweat and tears on the part of Gannon, the other two co-founders, and the magnificent management model they dreamed up and turned into a hugely successful business reality.

Outback Steakhouse, Inc.'s Major Organizational Change

"We will go down in history for having changed the status of the person who runs a restaurant from that of general manager of the restaurant to a corporate partner," exuded Gannon. "In doing this, we will create hundreds of millionaires."

"We changed the concept of ownership in the restaurant business from corporate ownership of restaurants with a general manager (GM) – who is just an employee of the restaurant corporation – to 'shared ownership.' In doing this, Outback went from a traditional corporate environment to a Partnership Program – and no other restaurant company is doing it."

Here is how it works. Each proprietor of an individual Outback restaurant contributes $25,000. This sum buys the proprietor 10% ownership of that one restaurant.

"Having someone write a $25,000 check is a very powerful thing. Most powerful is the fact of human nature that when people are owners, such as the proprietors, they act differently than if they are just a hired employee who manages a restaurant. It's probably only second financially to buying a house."

This produces other benefits for the proprietor. To begin with, compensation for Outback restaurant proprietors is

◆ $45,000 base salary
◆ 10% of the restaurant's cash flow

This results in total annual compensation of about $80,000 - $120,000, including the 10% of cash flow. Such compensation far exceeds most restaurant GMs who usually earn $60,000 - $80,000/year.

Crucially, the restaurant's cash flow directly results from how aggressively the proprietor generates sales. All-in-all, Outback devised a brilliant system in which each restaurant proprietor possesses a monstrous financial stake in operating a high volume, high profit operation. By doing this, says Gannon, "We truly believe the proprietors are the ones who run our business. So, that's why we put the power and authority in them to run their restaurants as they see best." After all, each proprietor has a vested financial interest in making sure his or her restaurant does exceedingly well. Plus, with a $25,000 investment and a huge financial gain down the road, each proprietor possesses a monstrous incentive to stay with Outback and make his or her restaurant successful.

And that is not all! There is even more opportunity for successful Outback proprietors. Specifically, after five years, a successful proprietor can buy 10% of another Outback restaurant. After 10 years, the proprietor can sell his or her percentages of both restaurants back to Outback Steakhouse, Inc. This could be worth about $700,000. Or, the proprietor can receive Outback stock. If the stock goes up in price, then this stock could be worth, perhaps, $1-million.

Steps Outback Used to Implement This Crucial Organizational Change

Outback put into action its *"Partnership Concept"* using three main steps. Result: "The return on the effort is incredible," emphasized Gannon.

Step 1. "Change the Vernacular"

Outback dramatically re-thought how to set-up a successful restaurant chain. The founders decided to do some things quite different than the norm. A key feature is to

- ◆ not call a restaurant manager either an "employee" or "general manager"
- ◆ call them "proprietors"

This makes a fundamental aspect of Outback markedly different from other restaurant companies. It removes the manager from the typical employee status, and immediately propels that person into a proprietor or a type of ownership status.

Also, the word "proprietor" harkens back to old-time eating establishments in which the actual owner's name was listed on the place: A sign near the restaurant's doorway would proudly display the name of the restaurant "proprietor." The sign never stated the name of the "general manager." Customers always got the immediate impression that the owner was on-site to make sure the customers had such a great dining experience that they would want to return.

*Step 2. Make Sure the Corporate Staff Does Not Manage in a Highly
        Directive or "Heavy-Handed" Way*
Again, this puts the thrill of being in-charge – and the heavy
duty of taking almost total responsibility for everything – into the
lap of the proprietor of each Outback restaurant.

Someone once told me that an early General Motors executive
said something like this: The purpose of line employees is to get
work done – and the purpose of corporate staff is to keep them
from doing it! This sounds funny. But, it also rings true in all too
many companies, especially companies that grow to a large size.
To protect against this all-too-common problem, Outback
instituted a crucial step to make sure proprietors possess the
freedom and responsibility to run their own show with minimal
meddling by corporate headquarters staff.

Step 3. "Do Share Ownership"
This step entailed drawing up many legal documents
pertaining to both partnership and ownership.

Measurable Results Produced by the Organizational Change

Outback's fantastic business model fashioned two tremendous
results that give Gannon particular pride. First, Gannon says it
"generates higher sales than we ever anticipated." Specifically,
Outback's average restaurant volume is $3.3-million/year. And
some Outback restaurants exceed $4-million/year.

Intriguing note: The company produces these phenomenal
sales volumes despite the fact that Outback restaurants only serve
dinner! They are closed for lunch!!

Outback's sales volume per restaurant is sharply higher than
the volume of Outback's average competitor, which Gannon
estimates at about $2.2 - $2.8-million/year – including all the
competitors' lunch sales.

Second, Outback has an astonishingly low turnover of
proprietors: Only seven percent. This is the lowest turnover rate of
any restaurant chain in the United States. The average nationwide
is 40 - 70% turnover of restaurant managers.

Unmeasurable or Qualitative Improvements

Outback's special way of doing business resulted in three key
qualitative enhancements.

Qualitative Improvement 1: Quality of Life for the Proprietor
Since each Outback restaurant only serves dinner – no lunch served – the proprietors can have a personal life. In sharp contrast, the typical restaurant Outback competes with is open for lunch *and* dinner. To serve lunch from 11:00 a.m.-2:00 p.m., a typical restaurant GM needs to arrive by 8:00 a.m. Then, as soon as lunch service ends about 2:00 p.m., the GM needs to get the restaurant rolling toward dinner service, which takes place about 5:00 - 10:00 p.m.

Working such long, hard days takes a tremendous toll on the typical restaurant GM. And that is not all. Waiters and waitresses often hate working the lunch shift. Reason: By working lunch, the staff actually only have opportunities to make money for about three hours, 11:00 - 2:00 p.m. By the time they arrive before lunch and leave after lunch, the staff have eaten up a hefty portion of their day – all for essentially working only three hours. In contrast, by working dinner shift only at Outback, the waiters, waitresses and other employees – as well as the proprietor – benefit from having almost all day to do personal or business activities other than work at the restaurant.

Qualitative Improvement 2: Consistent Management Philosophy for Employees
Since each Outback restaurant has one proprietor who is guaranteed to be there 5 - 10 years, employees can expect a consistent management style. Other benefits of this are
◆ very high sales volumes
◆ low turnover among employees
In contrast to Outback, many restaurant chains suffer from two critical problems due to how they are managed. First, the typical non-Outback restaurant chain has fairly high turnover of GMs. Second, the typical restaurant chain has the special problem of also having a regional manager. The regional manager oversees many restaurants – often 12 - 24. It is the regional manager who wields the real power behind how each restaurant is managed. As such, in typical restaurants, employees immediately learn that the real management philosophy, working conditions and atmosphere is based on how the regional manager operates – not the individual restaurant's GM. The GM is just a cog in the wheel – and all the employees discover this during the first week on-the-job.

However, at Outback restaurants, all employees learn on their first day on-the-job that their restaurant's proprietor actually controls how the restaurant is managed.

Qualitative Improvement 3: Quality of Food is Ultra-High

By serving only dinner, Gannon explained, Outback restaurants can serve much better food than restaurants that are open for both lunch and dinner. He pointed out food does not sit in warming wells all day. Also, food is fresher, because it is prepared only for dinner – and not lunch and dinner. On top of that, Outback's salads are crisper; in contrast, at a typical restaurant the salad that is not served at lunch sits around all day until it is served at dinner. Outback does not foist this food problem on its customers, because food is prepared for only one meal – dinner – and for no other meals.

Organizational Change Ingredient 1: Successfully Leading the Organizational Change

Every company has its own particular, distinctive corporate culture. I discovered the finest way to uncover the culture is to uncover the *story* every employee knows and tells (and retells!) to other employees. Usually, a new employee will hear the story within the first week on-the-job. With this in mind, what is the story that conveys the corporate culture of Outback Steakhouse, Inc.? Gannon explained this is an on-going story that every employee learns the first day on-the-job in an Outback Steakhouse restaurant.

"Fanatical Commitment to Flavor"

Outback's three founders – Gannon and the other two founders – always made every decision on food by blind taste-testing. Specifically, they evaluate ingredients based solely on the taste – before looking at how the ingredient appears. This is somewhat akin to orchestras choosing musicians by having the conductor hold a "blind listening" of each musician, listening only to the sound of the musician's playing, without seeing the musician face-to-face.

For Outback, the blind taste-testings result in Outback picking only the very best ingredients, regardless of cost. In fact, this tradition continues. To this day, many years after founding Outback Steakhouse, each and every food decision still is based on the three founders blind taste-testing ingredients that go into preparing Outback's food.

Doing this is crucial, because of Outback's "fanatical commitment to flavor" Gannon revealed. "Everything is made from scratch in our kitchens. And all our employees are involved in making this fantastic, flavorful food."

Culture – or Main Focus – of Outback Steakhouse, Inc.

The Outback Steakhouse story perfectly conveys the corporate culture. This culture has two main elements.

Focus 1: Quality – & Commitment to Taste

As the story communicates, Outback intensely focuses on serving only fantastically flavorful food made with only the most flavorful ingredients. It is the flavor – not the cost – of each ingredient that produces the culinary treats that keep Outback diners returning over and over again.

Focus 2: "No Rules – Just Right"

Actually, *"No Rules – Just Right"* is an Outback slogan. This means the goal of all employees is to do whatever is needed to make a customer happy.

For example, Gannon said customers conjure up all sorts of requests, such as (A) splitting steaks or (B) putting cheese on a filet. What do waitpersons do with these quite unusual requests? They (A) split the steak or (B) put cheese on a fine piece of meat which – all culinary experts would agree – definitely is not meant to include cheese!

Another example: If a customer requests that food be re-cooked or sent back to the kitchen, the proprietor almost always will talk to the customer to see how to make the customer's dining experience happy. Then, after the food is prepared again, the proprietor typically delivers the re-done meal to the customer, and asks what else the customer would like to create a satisfying dining experience.

Given Outback's emphasis on helping every customer experience a wonderful dining adventure, I asked Gannon for a copy of the company's guidelines for how to put into action its *"No Rules – Just Right"* path to customer satisfaction. I figured Outback printed guidelines to help its 40,000 employees make everything *"Just Right"* for its 100-million customers per year.

However, Gannon cheerfully informed me that Outback's headquarters never publishes such guidelines. Reason: Doing so would rob each of Outback's hundreds of proprietors of their jobs

– namely, managing their own restaurant in the way that maximizes each restaurant's business. Or, to put it another way, if Outback published such *"No Rules – Just Right"* guidelines, it implicitly would put power into the hands of people in corporate headquarters. Gannon is so incredibly right. Since Outback excels by, in effect, making proprietors owners, such dictates from corporate headquarters staff would rob proprietors of their job running the restaurant like their own place of business.

Big, Exciting Vision of Outback Steakhouse, Inc.

Many companies think their corporate vision is the puffy, cliché-filled mission statement hung in the headquarter's waiting rooms or appearing in its annual report. But that is not true. Instead, a company's actual vision is the really big, ultra-exciting goal the organization aims to accomplish.

In this light, Gannon revealed Outback's corporate vision is the following:

Our key goal is to create a
world-class casual dining company that endures.

As with the exciting vision of all successful businesses, Outback's vision is as big as it gets: *"world-class."* And that is not all. Gannon also pointed out to me that the word *"endures"* is crucial and vastly separates Outback from other restaurant chains.

He explained most restaurant companies have only a 10 - 15 year life-span. Most diners see this when a restaurant with a new "concept" or "theme" (A) opens up, (B) generates brisk business for a number of years, and then (C) vanishes off the face of the earth – or greatly downsizes – as the restaurant's "concept" or "theme" loses fans. For instance, a number of restaurant chains opened up with entertainment-oriented themes. They produced a big splash for a number of years. But then, customers tired of those restaurants' concepts, and moved on to other dining establishments.

As such, Outback's vision to *"endure"* or exist for a long time dramatically separates Outback from the pack. Its big, exciting vision to *"endure"* makes Outback a business that proprietors, employees, customers, vendors and stockholders can count on for the long-term.

Ways the Organizational Change Fits into Outback's Vision

Indeed, Outback organized the company to fulfill the vision. Gannon explained, "Our Partnership Program creates the mechanism for how we achieve our company's vision. Our proprietor and incentive programs propel our growth. Outback is dependent on its people to make the company a *world-class* casual dining company that *endures*." It would be hard to accomplish this without Outback's approach to having proprietors with a vested interest in their restaurants, rather than managers who can come and go whenever the mood strikes them.

Goal-Setting to Accomplish the Company's Major Organizational Change

Outback's goal-setting mechanism is twofold. First, at each restaurant, the proprietor sets goals related to running his or her business. These restaurant goals include budgets and sales goals.

Second, at corporate headquarters, executives focus on big picture goal-setting for growing the company as a whole. One of the executive team's primary goals "is to uncover dining concepts that attract the quality of proprietors that we have today," said Gannon. For example, Gannon mentioned to me that the executive team was exploring four dining concepts it could develop to expand Outback using its enormously successful proprietor system.

Teamwork to Accomplish Goals

Teamwork automatically flows from Outback's Partnership Program. This starts at the company's top level. "After all, you'd much rather work with someone who is your partner, rather than an employee," commented Gannon. This philosophy spreads down to employees, because each partner has a vested interest in developing a winning team that produces large sales volumes and profits.

I also think a key reason Outback excels at teamwork is because it is operated by incredibly friendly, gregarious people. These are people who value socializing with each other at work and outside of work. And that high level of friendliness translates into

 ◆   managers who enjoy working together

◆   restaurant staffs who enjoy collaborating
◆   customers who value the cordial environment proprietors
    create in the restaurants

In fact, Gannon even went on a two week trip to Australia –
after all, Outback is an Australian-themed restaurant – with the
company's most successful proprietors. This is a delightful
blending of friendliness on and off the job that promotes
enjoyment, collaboration, and teamwork.

This teamwork also comes out in the daily operation of each
Outback restaurant. For example, as mentioned earlier, if there is a
"re-cook" or re-doing of a customer's order, the proprietor brings
out the re-cooked food to directly participate in the solution. This
vastly differs from most other restaurants where the customer only
deals with the wait staff. But, at Outback, the proprietor, wait staff
and other employees possess incentives to work together as a team
to create magic moments of dining pleasure. This effective
teamwork keeps customers coming back for more.

Organizational Change Ingredient 2:

Successfully Handling Employee Problems during the Organizational Change

Most organizations – including most in the restaurant business
– run into resistance and roadblocks from employees who do not
want to implement changes.

But, Gannon finds Outback's Partnership Program receives
very little resistance from employees. Why? Because a key concern
of restaurant employees is to know who makes decisions affecting
them, especially promotions and salary. At Outback, employees
see their restaurant's proprietor as the final decision-maker. This
builds teamwork and employee confidence.

Due to Outback's unique Partnership Program, employees do
not have reasons to worry about organizational changes like
employees at other companies. At other companies, employees
live in fear that decision-makers far from their immediate
supervisor or general manager could make organizational changes
that profoundly alter or do away with their jobs.

However, in the Outback restaurants, all employees see seven
days a week that the overriding goal of the final decision-maker –
the proprietor – is to create fantastic dining experiences for

customers so they come back again and again. This clearly prominent goal does away with anxiety about far away powers-that-be that employees in other companies always wonder about. If it is reasonable for most employees to feel a tad paranoid about who makes decisions impacting their careers, at Outback such paranoia is not needed. As such, employees can focus their energies on doing their jobs with the proprietor as their highly motivated and 100% dedicated team leader.

Recommendations to Help Each Outback Employee Succeed

At Outback, Gannon explained if an Outback employee understands *and* constantly acts on two elements, then the employee is bound to succeed in a big way:

Recommendation 1: Commitment to Quality

"We only serve high quality food," said Gannon. "So, clearly, we value every employee who participates in this."

Recommendation 2: Commitment to Service

Employees simply need to follow Outback's unbreakable *"No Rules – Just Right"* approach to delighting diners. I frequently notice when I consult to companies that if a company has a catchy slogan about customer service – one that employees immediately can understand and act on – then customer satisfaction flourishes. Outback's *"No Rules – Just Right"* is one such catchy slogan that each employee can act on every hour on-the-job.

Outback's Magnificent Hiring Method

Outback Steakhouse, Inc. does so many things right. Another arena that makes the company succeed is its hiring methods. Importantly, 80% of proprietors come from among Outback's 40,000 employees. So, the company already knows them well. Most proprietors worked two or three years as hourly employees in an Outback restaurant *before* being accepted to contribute $25,000 and become a proprietor of an Outback restaurant.

"That's another beauty of our Partnership Program system: We grow our own talent internally," Gannon remarked. "In this way, our possible partners/proprietors know exactly how Outback Steakhouse works, what to expect, and how much they can achieve in this company."

From my expertise as the developer of two pre-employment tests and author of *Hire the Best – & Avoid the Rest*™, I know

Outback's method is based on two sound hiring principles.*

First – as I say in my *Hire the Best – & Avoid the Rest*™ book and workshops – "past behavior is the best predictor of future behavior." By finding future proprietors among its current employees, Outback definitely knows the actual on-the-job behavior of proprietor candidates. So, there should be no surprises, since Outback has observed the person for a number of years.

In fact, a key reason many companies use pre-employment tests is because they must predict how a job applicant will perform on-the-job, but they never observed the applicant actually working. Tests – such as the *Abilities & Behavior Forecaster*™ test – (1) readily are customized for each job in a company plus (2) provide an *objective* comparison of a job applicant to *successful* employees who already work in the company.

In sharp contrast, interviews of job applicants (A) tend to be *subjective* – not objective – and (B) most interviewers do lousy at predicting how an applicant, if hired, would perform on-the-job! Also, reference checks unfortunately often do not provide an accurate, objective prediction of an applicant's possible success or failure on-the-job.

Second, a "realistic job preview" (RJP) proves incredibly useful when hiring people, especially for a very intense job, such as an Outback proprietor position. An RJP for an outside job applicant entails totally candidly showing and telling the job applicant exactly what work really is done on-the-job. Research shows applicants who get a candid RJP of a job are (1) less likely to take the job and (2) if they do accept the job, they are less likely to quit or turnover.

Since Outback usually finds proprietors among employees who already work for the company, prospective proprietors already spent years observing how a real Outback proprietor operates. In effect, Outback's prospective proprietors already have had a lengthy "realistic job preview." As such, they know precisely what they are getting into if they become proprietors.

---

*Information about Dr. Mercer's *Forecaster*™ tests and *Hire the Best – & Avoid the Rest*™ materials are available in the Materials You Can Order section in the back of this book.

Outback Steakhouse65

Organizational Change Ingredient 3:
Successfully Managing Yourself during the Organizational Change

When I consult to highly effective leaders, I always notice they bring important personal traits to their job, which they apply to produce big successes for their companies and careers. Among other traits, I find stellar managers and executives possess an ingrained sense of optimism, exude buoyant attitudes, and repeatedly use certain helpful phrases. They also bring profound lessons learned from role models and life experiences to their work.

Optimism Helped This Executive Succeed in Implementing Major Organizational Change

"My mother says I'm an optimist to a flaw, so that I'm out of balance," Gannon grinned.

He continued, "Optimism is not only about what you can get done in business – but also in all of life." For example, "I started playing polo at age 40 years old. I didn't just want to play polo. I wanted to win the U.S. Open Championship in polo. This is the highest, world-class level competition in polo. I've played on our team that won the U.S. Open in three out of four attempts." In fact, Gannon's polo team has been ranked #1 in the entire world!

Gannon's playing on the polo team truly is extraordinary. Most millionaires who own part of a sports team watch from the sidelines as professional athletes perform their feats on the playing field or, in this case, polo field. But staying on the sidelines is not in Gannon's nature. Instead, he actually plays on the polo team, while still performing his heavy duties as an Outback co-founder and senior vice president. Note: All the other polo team members are full-time professional polo players.

Primary Attitude of This Executive that Most Help Him Succeed

Gannon credits his success to *envisioning* what he wants to achieve – and then going out and actually achieving it. Or, as he puts it, "To achieve great success, you have to *envision* it."

This rests in sound psychological principles. Indeed, in the book and audiobook entitled, Spontaneous Optimism™· *Proven*

Strategies for Health, Prosperity & Happiness, my co-author and I showed how a person tends to achieve what he or she focuses on the most. And part of this focus is to *see* yourself as successful – in whatever you want to achieve – before you actually achieve your success.*

This technique can be seen in highly successful people. For example, Gannon offered Mohammed Ali as an example. He explained, "Mohammed Ali did not see himself as the greatest *prizefighter* in the world. Instead, Ali saw himself as the greatest *athlete* in the world. He gets respect because of the way he saw himself which, in many ways, he turned into reality."

In business, first Gannon envisioned starting a business. Then, he envisioned creating a successful international restaurant chain that creates strong, passionate, emotional responses in customers. For example, "I always wanted to walk down the halls of the National Restaurant Association conference, and have people poke each other and say, 'Hey, that's Tim Gannon!'" Indeed, Gannon accomplished this, also.

Phrases This Executive Says to Keep Focused & Optimistic

He especially likes two phrases.

Phrase 1: "Intimidate, Dominate, Celebrate"

In polo and in business, Gannon says he borrows a phrase used by the Chicago Bulls basketball team: "Intimidate, Dominate, Celebrate."

He explains:

◆ Intimidate – "Be the best"
◆ Dominate – Dominate your industry
◆ Celebrate – "Celebrate as a *winning team*."

Gannon emphasizes the importance of celebrating victories with team members on the polo field and in business. For example, as mentioned earlier, Gannon took a two week trip to Australia with 30 partners/proprietors to celebrate their business success.

Phrase 2: "Essentially, a leader is one who makes things happen."

This phrase comes from an idea Gannon learned from Norman Brinker, his former boss and the founder of Steak & Ale and Chili's

---

*For information on *Spontaneous Optimism*™, you can refer to the Materials You Can Order section in the back of this book.

restaurant chains. He explains, to lead people, you have to do two things:

♦ generate excitement
♦ make things happen

For Gannon, "making things happen" includes creating new restaurant concepts and new dishes to delight customers.

How This Executive Gets People to Focus on Solutions – Not Problems

Optimists overwhelming focus on solutions, while pessimists overwhelmingly focus on problems. As a leader, Gannon must set the tone for people at Outback that they need to act like optimists and focus on solutions. How does Gannon do it? He explains:

> *I get people to think about problems that may arise before they occur. For example, if onions – Outback's most successful appetizer – are going to be a bad crop, then be aware, communicate the problem, and get people involved in solving the upcoming challenge.*
>
> *In short, if you see a problem, then rally your troops. If there is a problem coming, ring the bell and don't sit on it. Incredibly open lines of communication to help people focus on solutions, not problems.*
>
> *For example, when we started using a new meat company, I asked that company to teach its fine meat cutting methods to a second meat company. Why? Because we anticipated so much growth, we knew we would need more than one company supplying meat. Now, our various meat suppliers share information about how to best serve their Outback Steakhouse account.*

This Executive's Favorite Story

Ever since I started consulting to companies – shortly after earning my Ph.D. to become a business psychologist –- I discovered that a person's favorite story provides a sort of telescope to clearly see the individual's personality. The story reveals a lot about what makes that person tick. So, what is Gannon's favorite story?

The Saddle Story

Gannon landed a job in Tampa. But, he was so broke that he did not even have money to pay for gas for his long drive to Tampa.

So, he sold his cherished saddle for exactly $250 to get gas money.

But, he never forgot how broke he was. And he never forgot the saddle.

Eleven years later – after achieving tremendous success in the restaurant business – Gannon bought back that same saddle. Now, that saddle sits in his bedroom – next to his U.S. Open Polo Championship trophy.

Gannon explained, "Every time I look at my saddle, I see how far I've come."

This story illustrates a number of Gannon's key traits that make him successful. First, he does what he must to get where he wants to go. This even includes selling a cherished possession, such as his saddle. Second, he enjoys and celebrates how much he accomplishes. Upon achieving success in business and in polo, he bought back his saddle, and keeps it next to his trophy that shows he literally made himself into a world-class success in many ways.

Formative Childhood Events of This Executive

Some people remember only the good, some people remember only the bad, and some people remember only the ugly. People who make it big do not just have experiences. Instead, they learn from their experiences. And they take their developing knowledge with them as they progress toward their goals they envision for themselves.

For Gannon, this included a number of formative events that helped shape him. For example:

At age 12 years old, I sold newspapers in the street – and from that I knew that although I came from a poor family, I could go out and make as much money as I want.

At age 14 years old, I had 900 customers and two employees. The average newspaper seller had only 150 customers and no employees. I was riding high, earning about $75 per week – which was a lot of money for a 14 year old to earn.

So, I had all the money I wanted – and I never knew I came from a poor family.

From his incredibly formative childhood experiences, Gannon offered this advice:

How hungry are you and how deep is your hunger? If you don't have deep hunger, then you'll never achieve great success.

This Executive's Most Important Role Model – & Lessons He Learned

Gannon's top role model is Norman Brinker. This person founded two large restaurant chains, Steak & Ale and Chili's. Brinker also won the U.S. Open Championship in polo – just like Gannon also won. Importantly, Gannon admires that Brinker is a "self-made man."

From working and socializing with Brinker, Gannon learned this vital lesson: "You have to be totally dedicated to honesty. Your word needs to mean everything. For example, if Steak & Ale got an extra case of meat from a supplier, we'd send it back to the meat supplier."

Gannon carried this lesson to people who work for Outback Steakhouse, Inc. In fact, in effect, the amazingly transparent Partnership Program is an example of honestly revealing and financially sharing the profits of the well-run Outback business.

In fact, as Gannon looks into his future, he feels most enthused about *"creating an environment in which lots of people working with us can achieve tremendous success because of their relationship with Outback. At the end, what you take is the job of relationships."*

7

EGGHEAD.COM
Hatching A Brand New Business

Egghead.com's *Vision:*
Our key goal is to be the
leading Internet destination for
buying technology products, services, and related categories.

Imagine the dizzying array of business growth possibilities for a company that expertly combines the potential of

◆ mushrooming e-commerce
◆ the most recognizable brand name in its industry niche
◆ selling tremendously sought after products (in fact, sold in two appealing ways!)

If you feel lightheaded drooling at the burgeoning potential of this business, then you need to realize the company's name is famous – Egghead.com. It emerged from the combination of Onsale with Egghead to form a powerhouse in the online business world – *"Egghead.com – the computer store inside your computer"* as its advertisements help blaze into our consciousness. This company markets technology products – especially computers and computer-related gear via both online

◆ auctions
◆ e-tailing

Jeff Sheahan, President and Chief Operating Officer, revealed the major organizational change done by the company. Jeff started with Onsale and continued with the company after it merged with, and was renamed, Egghead.com.

Egghead.com's Major Organizational Change

In a very short period of time, less than a half-year, Onsale.com made three far-reaching organizational changes. Since the first major organizational change – adding e-tail business to Onsale's existing online auction business – is such a monumental organizational change, this chapter focuses on that highly profitable change.

Note: Although the company did change its name to Egghead, it often will be referred to as Onsale in this discussion of the company's absolutely fabulous organizational change. At times, the Egghead and Onsale names will be used interchangeably.

Organizational Change 1: Added E-tailing Business to its Online
Auction Business

President & COO Sheahan considered this the major organizational change: In an incredibly short period of *only three months*, Onsale.com shifted from being the first online auctioneer to being *both* an e-tailer (online retailer) and an online auctioneer of computers and computer-related gear.

"This was a company born and raised on the Web – with the concept of being the biggest auctioneer on the Web," explained Sheahan. "Now, we're shifting to being a Web-based e-tailer, also. Doing this requires a new business strategy." Some ingredients of this new business strategy are shown in Diagram 1.

Diagram 1. **Onsale's Core Strategies**

✓ Build Onsale's brand awareness and traffic through an integrated multimedia advertising and public relations campaign.

✓ Become the leading e-commerce site for "ease of use" by significantly upgrading our features, functionality, services, and content, addressing the needs of our customers, suppliers, business partners, and clients.

✓ Provide world-class, highly automated and personalized, customer service both pre- and post-sales, by delivering a single call/request resolution and a high-touch customer care experience, which benefits our customers, suppliers, and business partners.

✓ Become the most efficient transaction processor on the Web by continuously improving our systems and processes and leveraging our world-class technology.

✓ Create a value proposition based on service.

Source: Onsale/Egghead.com

Organizational Change 2: Acquired Business with Famous Brand Name
Onsale.com acquired Egghead.com, which is a well-known brand name. Egghead previously operated actual "brick-&-mortar" stores selling computer products. It transformed itself into an online retailer of computer items, and then Onsale acquired it.

Onsale's rationale for combining with Egghead.com was fourfold, according to Sheahan:

◆ Create a clear market leader in the largest e-commerce category: technology products
◆ Realize significant benefits of increased size and scale
◆ Combine complementary customer bases with minimal overlap
◆ Position as industry consolidator

Organizational Change 3: Changed Company Name to Famous Brand Name

Onsale changed its name to Egghead.com. Reason: Marketing research showed the brand name "Egghead" was five times more widely known than the brand name "Onsale." Specifically, 32% of online buyers of computer-related items recognized the Egghead brand name, while only 6% knew the Onsale brand name. So, in addition to approximately doubling its business, Onsale also picked up a significantly valuable and strongly bankable brand name for itself.

How This Change Was Crucial to Egghead's Growth

Sheahan emphasized the development of the e-tailing business was essential to the company's growth for four key reasons:

Reason 1: Limits to growth in the auction market

Why? It is a hard and oftentimes uphill battle continually to get refurbished and used equipment that customers definitely want to buy. Possible result: The unevenness of supply and the uncertainty of margins.

Reason 2: Reliable place to shop with a steady, consistent supply of new goods

Adding e-tailing to Onsale makes it a reliable place for customers to find and buy over 35,000 computer and computer-related products.

Reason 3: Improve conversion rate

Offering e-tailing improves the conversion *rate* at which visitors to Egghead transform from being visitors to the site to being actual buyers of Egghead's products.

Reason 4: Extends Customer Lifetime Value

The company greatly extended the *customer lifetime value* by providing customers with more opportunities to buy from the company. Previously, customers only had one option, namely, seeing if Onsale happened to have auction items they wanted to purchase. Now, customers are greeted at the company's Web site with two options to buy: (A) auctions of used, refurbished, or overstock items and (B) e-tail sale of new products.

Importantly, Sheahan pointed out that extending the *customer lifetime value* proves crucial to the company's ultimate profitability and growth. Sheahan explained the cost of acquiring customers is expensive. The costs are the following:

1. Drive traffic to the company's Web site, using advertising and other media.
2. Provide good values so visitors to the Web site actually buy something.
3. Keep customers coming back to buy more.

Of course, the more customers return to buy more from the company, the more extended – and profitable – is its *customer lifetime value.*

Steps Used to Implement This Crucial Organizational Change

Sheahan's rapid addition of e-tailing to the company's arsenal of sales methods entailed three main steps.

Step 1: Create Innovative Value Proposition for E-tail Side of the
         Business

The company launched the e-tail business, calling it "At Cost." Sheahan – whose experience includes strong expertise as a retail marketing executive – explained the "At Cost" retailing concept was essentially (A) offering a reasonable price and then (B) adding on a fee to process the order. Onsale, and now Egghead, does this in such a way that customers confidently know they get great prices for quality merchandise.

Step 2: Choosing the Right Distribution Partner

Over 60% of Egghead's transactions are for goods shipped by third parties on behalf of Egghead. One way to understand this is through the following four ingredient diagram of the flow in a retail business:

Manufacturers → Wholesalers → Retailers → Customers

Manufacturers are makers of products and goods. In the case of Egghead or Onsale's business, relevant manufacturers are makers of computers and computer-related gear. Manufacturers ship products to *wholesalers*. The wholesaler, such as Tech Data or Ingram Micro, keeps the products in inventory in its warehouse. Typically, the wholesaler ships products to bricks-&-mortar stores or warehouses of a *retailer* that, in turn, sells the products to *customers*.

In contrast, Egghead.com – although it is a retailer (or "e-tailer") – only takes possession of the goods on less than 40% of its sales. In the main, Egghead.com (A) obtains orders from customers on its Web site and then (B) transmits orders to the distributor it uses which, in turn, ships the products directly to Egghead.com's customers.

As such, this company does business without many costs woven into traditional retailing, including the need for stores, company warehouses, sales clerks, and other store staff. In fact, this works so well that just a few hundred employees at the company obtain and process many hundreds of millions of dollars of customer orders for products. In extremely sharp contrast, any traditional storefront retail chain would need thousands of employees to obtain and transact such a high sales volume.

Step 3: Communicate to Employees & Wall Street

Sheahan realized that all the wonderful changes required the company to make sure key stakeholders – the investment community and people working at the company – knew and understand how and why adding the e-tail business proved crucial to the company's evolution, profitability, and growth.

Measurable Improvements Produced by the Organizational Change

Sheahan proudly pointed to a number of strong trends which are the result of the company's addition of its e-tail business (also summarized in Diagram 2):

- 10 - 15% quarter over quarter sales *growth* in the first three quarters since launching the e-tail business
- An absolute increase in *gross profit dollars*
- High service levels in the new goods superstore business, including

✓ 2 - 3% *return rate* –
this is well below the average in traditional storefront-type retail businesses; and it is half of catalogs' 5% return rate
✓ 75 - 85% *fill rate* –
shipping complete orders (no back-orders or missing items) within 24 hours; this is consistent with many catalogers' fill rate

Diagram 2. **Results of Onsale's Absolutely Fabulous Organizational Change of Launching E-Tail Business**

Category	Results
Sales growth	10 - 15% quarter over quarter
Margin dollars	Increase
Return rate	2 - 3%
Fill rate	75 - 85%

Note: Fill rate = Shipping complete orders (no back-orders or missing items) within 24 hours; this matches fill rate of catalog companies

Unmeasurable or Qualitative Improvements from the Organizational Change

"We feel impressed with ourselves. We proved we could do it. *We went from concept to execution in less than three months,*" exclaimed Sheahan. In fact, Sheahan implemented establishing the e-tail business in his first 90 days of working at Onsale.com. Importantly, he credits creating a hard-charging, teamwork-oriented, collaborative environment as crucial to this rapid organizational change.

Sheahan explained, "In Internet businesses, expansion is compressed. This is because there is normal time and there is hyper-fast Internet time. This compelled us to move fast to diversify from being only an auctioneer to being an auctioneer *and* e-tailer. You need to be the first mover in e-commerce. So, we needed to move hyper-fast. The space was open for us to jump into e-tailing of computer goods and assume the leadership in that business category. If we had waited three to six months, we may not have been first into this business category."

Organizational Change Ingredient 1:
Successfully Leading the Organizational Change

As I consult to companies, I continually observe an extremely vital fact of business life: Changes that logically flow from the company's corporate culture and big, exciting vision are quite likely to achieve desired results. This holds especially true in companies that also wisely use goal-setting and teamwork to advance the organizational change from planning to actual implementation. Sheahan and his staff did a superb job in all this.

Onsale's Corporate Culture

From consulting I do, I found the finest way to pinpoint a company's culture is to find out what story the employees all know and repeatedly tell. The story's theme conveys the corporate culture. Interestingly, the story usually centers on the company's founder, as is the case at Onsale. Sheahan told me this is the story the company's employees all seem to know and retell:

> *Onsale.com was the first company to bring online auctions to the Web. Our founders – CEO Jerry Kaplan and Chief Technology Officer Alan Fisher – invented a whole new way of retailing which is online auctions. In fact, they developed the software without which online auctions would not be possible. So, we are – in essence – a company that birthed a whole new way to do business. This story is about the birth of a new idea – a company that is first in an extremely innovative way.*

Culture – or Main Focus – of Onsale.Com

The story conveys the corporate culture which includes two key components:
1. Innovation
2. Superb service

Or, as Sheahan summed it up, "Let's deliver a unique shopping experience that is convenient, informative, and low cost. Let's deliver goods in an innovative way, and always add world-class customer service."

For instance, Onsale started by taking used, end of life and re-manufactured goods and sold them through auction with something revolutionary, namely, the back-up of a "retailing" approach to customer service, including returns privileges.

This was a revolutionary step. Why? Because prior to Onsale.com, auctions in the physical world were a *caveat emptor* – buyer beware! – business. That can make buyers wary. Realizing this concern of consumers, Onsale added *trust* to its auction business with its sensible return policy and customer service. These are services auction buyers in the physical world very seldom or never found elsewhere.

In fact, to this day, company co-founder and CEO Jerry Kaplan is online each day with customers. He does this to make sure they get what they want in both products and service.

Links between Onsale's Corporate Culture and Its Major Organizational Change

Onsale.com offered two options to visitors coming to its Web site:
1. Onsale At Cost
2. Onsale At Auction

Sheahan noted how the e-tail business links the company's innovativeness with its good service. "The e-tail At Cost is done in an *innovative* way -- true to our innovative roots. These *innovations include great service*," such as the following:

1. *Added "800" phone number.* The company added an "800" phone number which Onsale.com did not have before. And the "800" number is very visible. Sheahan explained, "This builds tremendous trust, because customers know they easily can talk to a real person at our company."
2. *Additional pre-sale information.* Additional pre-sale information was made readily available. This conveniently provided information helps buyers learn about products, compare goods, and make informed buying decisions.
3. *Added shopping cart to Web site.* This enables customers to group their products together.
4. *Onsale buyers became merchandisers.* Sheahan purposely worked to transform the buyers working for Onsale.com into merchandisers. How? Like traditional retailers, they must display products in an appealing way that entices customers to buy.

Big, Exciting Vision of the Company

Behind every successful company is an alluring vision of the company achieving something truly monumental on a grand scale, often on a nationwide or worldwide basis. Employees at the successful company know this big, exciting vision. They realize that each day they come to work to play a role in advancing the organization toward realizing its vision.

According to Sheahan, the company's vision is the following:

*Our key goal is to be the
leading Internet destination for
buying technology products, services, and related categories.*

"We want our corporate vision emblazoned across everyone's mind," said Sheahan. A main method to accomplish this is through captivating phrases the company uses in its promotional endeavors. For instance, Onsale.com used the catchy phrase, *"If it's computers, it's Onsale."* After Onsale acquired Egghead.com, and changed its name to Egghead.com, it unveiled another entrancing slogan: *"Egghead.com – the computer store inside your computer."* Such slogans or phrases play a crucial role in making a company's brand identity and image stick in consumer's minds. They also provide employees with a ready slogan to keep them on-track with the company's vision.

Importantly, Sheahan explained the company's vision and advertising slogans also continually reinforce employees' perceptions that they are working in a monumentally special company. Sheahan commented, "Cybershopping provides you with more breadth, depth, and an almost limitless supply of products. Catalogs and stores are limited in how much they can offer. In contrast, online e-tailers like Onsale.com can offer an endless supply of products consumers can get everyday, 24 hours a day, 7 days a week. Onsale.com is not constrained by its physical location like stores or catalog companies." This business model makes it possible for *"the computer store inside your computer"* to reach its vision to *"be the leading Internet destination for buying technology products, services, and related categories."* And everyone – employees and customers – readily can share in Egghead's big, exciting vision.

Ways the Major Organizational Change Fits into the Company's Vision

President & COO Sheahan pointed out that Onsale adding an e-tail business to its existing auction business smoothly fits into the corporate vision in four key ways. First, starting the e-tail business changed the company's purchasing agents from buying for auctions to buying for retail-type sales. This forced buyers to think and act like merchandisers who have a bottom line need to think constantly about what products customers want presented to them – plus how to present those products in an appealing manner.

Second, the change necessitated more online and offline customer services to provide customers with increased help, support, and trust in purchasing goods from the company. Third, the company launched a branding campaign through television ads, radio ads, and online banner ads. "The purpose of the branding campaign is to plant in the minds of consumers that we are the *'computer store inside your computer'* – the leading place to buy computer products online," remarked Sheahan. Fourth, the major organizational change requires the company to "recruit employees who will provide the people power to create a $1-billion business in only 18 - 24 months," Sheahan said.

Goal-Setting to Achieve the Company's Major Organizational Change

As President & COO, Sheahan spends quite a bit of time on goal-setting, done in a very organized manner with "metrics" or measures and deadlines that each function needs to achieve. This is done bottom-up.

First, merchandisers in the company determine product categories. Second, marketers pinpoint how to advertise the product categories – on TV, radio, and online – to attract visitors to the Egghead.com site. Also, marketers must work toward specific *Customer Lifetime Value*, which is a goal of how much an average Egghead.com customer buys each quarter.

To implement the major organizational change, Sheahan set four goals for himself, namely, two sales and marketing goals, one customer service goal, and one human resources goal. His goals were the following:

Goal #1: Improve visitor to buyer conversion rate by 20%.

Goal #2: *Increase quarterly average amount of money spent per quarter by existing customers (also called Customer Lifetime Value) by 25% within 1 year.*
Goal #3: *Reduce the number of "touches" to resolve a customer issue by 30%.*
Issues include returns, problems with order, and pre-sale questions. "Touches" are interactions with customers either online or offline by phone.
Goal #4: *Reduce employee turnover by 25% within 1 year.*
Sheahan realized reducing turnover is tough in Silicon Valley due to the huge number of exciting companies people can work for.

Teamwork to Accomplish Goals

President & COO Jeffrey Sheahan and CEO Jerry Kaplan cleverly package two Tuesday and two Friday activities to assure (A) teamwork, (B) interdepartmental cooperation, and (C) achievement of business goals.

Teamwork Activity 1: Tuesday, Noon - 2:00 p.m. over lunch - Executive Staff Meeting
The company's top executives participate in this weekly meeting: (1) CEO Jerry Kaplan, (2) President & COO Jeffrey Sheahan, (3) Chief Financial Officer, (4) Chief Technology Officer, (5) Vice President of Human Resources, and senior vice presidents of the various functions. The meeting focuses on strategic as well as operational issues. The overwhelming chief focus is on strategy, but on-going significant business issues are addressed as well.

Teamwork Activity 2: Tuesday - Weekly Key Data Pack
Each manager submits a *"5 - 15 Report."* This report takes a manager 15 minutes to write, and it takes Sheahan 5 minutes to read. Each *"5 - 15 Report"* shows precisely how the manager is progressing on his or her key performance "metrics" or measurable goals the manager is working to accomplish. Also, every *"5 - 15 Report"* is brought to the weekly Friday Senior Staff Meeting to help focus the discussion about operational issues and how the company can improve.

Teamwork Activity 3: Friday morning - Weekly Senior Staff Meeting
Participants are all the company's middle managers. These are managers who report directly to the top five executives, namely, the CEO, COO, CFO, CTO, and VP-HR.

Each middle manager communicates how he or she is progressing on achieving the measurable goals. This proves crucial. As Sheahan points out, "When you're moving at e-speed, this gives us a chance each week to get together and keep each other on track."

Teamwork Activity 4: Friday - 3:30 - 3:50 p.m. - "Social"

All employees get together for a 20-minute stand-up meeting (no sitting allowed!). Ice cream and cake are served. People sing praises about – and also reward – individual employees who accomplished wonderful things for the company.

Organizational Change Ingredient 2:
Successfully Handling Employee Problems during the Organizational Change

It never ceases to amaze me how imaginative employees are when it comes to trying to derail organizational changes. When I consult to companies – or in my previous career as a corporate manager – I witnessed many ways employees resist or otherwise fail to help the change progress in a timely manner.

Employee Problems Affecting the Major Organizational Change

Fortunately, Onsale did not encounter much overt resistance. However, Onsale did encounter a few employee problems that required surefooted attention. First, some employees who started with the company did not understand the change from an auction business to an e-tailing business. This had to be addressed.

Second, more structure was needed that employees were not used to. For example, with the advent and growth of the e-tailing business, Onsale made (A) each employee more accountable and (B) more inspections to see how well employees met or surpassed their work goals. Some people recoiled at being watched and evaluated more carefully and consistently than before.

Third, some employees utterly treasured the thrill of working in a start-up company. But as Onsale grew and expanded into e-tailing, some original employees needed to start managing. In contrast, previously Onsale employees could work as individual contributors – and receive massive recognition for their individual contributions to the company's growth. Then, very quickly, those same employees were thrust into managing people. This suddenly made them responsible for their own results plus the results of employees working for them.

This triggered a common concern: A tremendously valuable individual contributor in a company may not make a good manager of people. Managing often is not part of their skill set – plus managing just does not give them the same thrill as serving as an individual contributor. Given Onsale's rapid initiation of its e-tail business, this became a sticky concern that Onsale needed to address quickly.

Comparing the Company's *"Old-Style"* Employees with Its *"New-Style"* Employees

As companies change their business strategy and tactics, the *old-style* employees who did fine before the change sometimes do not provide the new talents the company needs. Then, so-called *new-style* employees with different talents are needed to carry forward with the organizational changes.

At Onsale, Sheahan mentioned two distinctions between the company's old-style and new-style employees, as shown below:

Old-Style Employees	New-Style Employees
Top executives make most decisions	Pushing decision-making down to middle managers and line supervisors
Individual contributor	Managing and developing employees

"De-Employment" to Help the Organizational Change Succeed

Much of the turnover has been the result of a shift from a first-stage company to a mid-stage company. Specifically, Onsale

◆ turned buyers into merchandisers, either through re-training or replacing

◆ brought in an experienced, large site customer service leader who could combine technology with call center dynamics

Improvements in Hiring Methods

In my consulting and seminars on *Hire the Best – & Avoid the Rest*"™ methods I developed, I help companies improve their hiring methods.* Often, hiring improvements are required for a company to find and hire people who are likely to help the company grow in its new or improved way of doing business.

Egghead.com, and its predecessor Onsale.com, started looking for people who want the excitement of an entrepreneurial environment yet enjoy working in a company with sales rapidly approaching $1-billion. To do this, the company found it best to look for job candidates who work for large companies in mature businesses who crave the thrill of working in an exciting post-start-up company whose business certainly is not mature. The applicant pool for such people is not huge. Nevertheless, it has proven crucial for the company to hire the type of person who wants the exhilaration of working in a fast-moving organization with remarkable growth prospects.

Organizational Change Ingredient 3:
Successfully Managing Yourself during the Organizational Change

It definitely is not enough to provide organizational leadership and also handle employee problems during times of change. The executive who successfully navigates a company through organizational change needs to be – himself or herself – a magnificent role model for employees to watch and, in some ways, model themselves after at work. What do employees look for? Employees pick up cues about the leader's optimism, attitudes, expressions, and way of handling situations. In fact, this is addressed in two of my books and audio-books: (1) *Spontaneous Optimism™; Proven Strategies for Health, Prosperity & Happiness* and also (2) *How Winners Do It: High Impact People Skills for Your Career Success.* My books and related business tools and speeches even delve into research and practical tips on how

---

* For details on Dr. Mercer's tests, seminars, tool kit and book on *Hire the Best – & Avoid the Rest™*, you can refer to (A) information in other chapters and also (B) the Materials You Can Order section in the back of this book.

optimists tend to achieve much more career success than pessimists*.

Optimism Helped This Executive Succeed

Sheahan credits his optimism with helping him in many ways:

> *Optimism plays a huge role in my life. Optimism is the only way to approach life.*
>
> *I bound out of bed in the morning, and can't wait to get to work.*
>
> *Let's focus on solutions and how we can make things work for our benefit.*
>
> *For me, I focus on how I can make things work, make things happen. I play to win, and I play fair.*
>
> *For example, when an obstacle pops up, I often say, "We can figure this out. Let's put our heads together to figure this out."*

His approach to life and work proves remarkably optimistic – which, in turn, makes Sheahan a great role model for Egghead employees.

How is Sheahan an optimist? Among many things, I find optimists focus on doing things with *enthusiasm* – and Sheahan likes to "bound out of bed in the morning." That is enthusiasm in action. Also, optimists focus on solutions. And that is exactly what Sheahan does. He always aims to *"make things happen"* and *"figure this out."*

Attitudes of This Executive that Most Helped Him Succeed

This executive prizes four of his attitudes he uses each day:

Attitude 1: *Complete Honesty*
"You never lose when you're honest with people and suppliers. Bad news doesn't get better with time."

Attitude 2: *Air It Out*
"I am not an authority on all good ideas. Check your title at the door. When we get together, it's about teamwork."

Attitude 3: *Hard Work*
"You only make things happen when you combine commitment with hard work."

---

* For information on *Spontaneous Optimism*™ and also *How Winners Do It,* you can refer to the Materials You Can Order section in the back of this book.

Attitude 4: *Treat Everyone with Respect*
"Show respect toward everybody, from the warehouse employee to the CEO."

Favorite Phrases of This Executive

Sheahan particularly likes three phrases that help him keep focused on his goals and maintain his optimism.

Phrase 1: *"Make it happen."*
           "In fact, the phrase 'Make it happen' is so important that I display it on my door."

Phrase 2: *"Let's make this a learning experience."*

Phrase 3: *"Be an initiator."*

It appears noticeable that each of Sheahan's three favorite phrases is an exciting call to action. They convey enthusiasm and a let's-get-things-done approach that sets an upbeat tone for everybody around him.

How This Executive Got Employees to Focus on Solutions – Not Problems

Pessimists love to wallow in problems and complaining. In sharp contrast, optimists – including markedly effective leaders – focus on solutions. In fact, I discovered one of the chief lessons leaders instill in their employees is that it is imperative to focus on solutions, not problems. Sheahan certainly does this quite well. He illustrates this point when he said:

> *To get employees to focus on solutions, I do that myself so they can observe how it's done. Also, I play a facilitator role with employees and in meetings. It's like being a conductor of an orchestra in business.*
>
> *I continually press people to come up with how to make things happen. I don't let people get mired down in how things may not work.*
>
> *For example, we sell banner ads that appear on our Web site. So, the advertising salespeople want to sell ads. But, our key revenue source is our products we sell – not ads we display. So, we always need to figure out how we can make money selling ads while not distracting visitors from buying goods from us while they are on our Web site.*

Favorite Story of This Executive

A person's favorite story reveals a lot about his or her outlook on life and, by extension, leadership abilities. Here is Sheahan's favorite story:

> I was an executive for five years in Europe. In that time, my company acquired five other companies.
>
> I especially like the story of Alexander the Great. His philosophy when he conquered a land was to focus on getting its residents involved in creating a great nation. Doing so defused anger at having been conquered, and also got residents onto Alexander's team. His philosophy worked vastly better than if Alexander just brought in his own people and subjugated the residents.
>
> The approach used by Alexander the Great differs greatly from the methods used by Genghis Khan. When Genghis Khan conquered a land, he fought and killed many people and oppressively subjugated its citizens. The Genghis Khan method draws attention to the fact that managing through fear is a very short-term motivator.

His story illustrates Sheahan's heartfelt point-of-view that it proves vitally important to use collaborative teamwork to bring people on board. This approach boosts the likelihood the organization will advance toward its vision to build a bigger and more dynamic company.

Role Models of This Executive – & Lessons Learned from Each One

Each person picks up valuable lessons from the individuals he or she views as role models. Some role models are people in the person's life. And other role models are individuals the person observes from a distance, perhaps through reading about the person or seeing the person in the media. Sheahan's role models include two with whom he had very close relationships, and a third one he observed from media reporting.

Role Model 1: Mother. *Lessons Learned:* "Fight for what you believe in. Find a solution that makes sense for both parties. Don't give up until you try. Power of hard work: She worked 2 - 3 jobs to support her family."

Sheahan was raised by his mother. One powerful experience for him occurred when he was in grammar school. He was told he needed to change schools, because the boundary lines for the school districts were redrawn. But, he wanted to stay at the same grammar school. He did not want to go to the new school. So, his mother met with school bureaucrats, and worked out a solution in which Sheahan could continue at his same grammar school.

Role Model 2: Martin Luther King. *Lessons Learned:* "Bravery and courageousness. His way of communicating inclusiveness and collaboration to build a following."

Role Model 3: Mel Braveman – Sheahan's boss at his first job after earning his bachelor's degree. *Lessons Learned:* "Sell ideas, not products. Listen to people, because when you listen you'll find out what people really need. He didn't launch into selling until he really understood the prospect's business. Also, he had great ethics and morals."

In looking back over everything discussed here about Sheahan's magnificent leadership, it appears obvious that he put into action the vital lessons he learned from his three role models.

8

The Ritz-Carlton Hotel Company

Profiting from Creating the Ultimate Luxury Hotel Experience

The Ritz-Carlton Hotel Company's *Vision:*
Our key goal is to be the
premier worldwide provider of luxury travel and
hospitality products and services.

I deliver 80 - 100 speeches and workshops annually, plus I do a lot of consulting to organizations. So, I spend a lot of nights in hotels – all sorts of hotels in many, many cities.

Let me tell you something I say each and every time I stay in a Ritz-Carlton hotel. I always say the exact same thing: "I would like to live in a Ritz-Carlton hotel!"

In all my experiences, Ritz-Carlton hotels consistently are

◆ beautiful
◆ charming
◆ delightful

The service always proves incredible. The employees provide magnificent customer care. Plus, each Ritz-Carlton looks splendid. The decorating always appears sophisticated, elegant, and supremely comfortable.

This group of luxury hotels creates a consistently absolutely fabulous ambiance. In fact, I have stayed in and dined in so many Ritz-Carlton hotels that as soon as I enter the front door, I automatically expect a magnificent experience. Indeed, a superb experience is precisely the goal expressed in the company's formally published *Credo* which states:

The Ritz-Carlton Hotel is a place where the genuine care and comfort of our guests is our highest mission.

We pledge to provide the finest personal service and facilities for our guests who will always enjoy a warm, relaxed yet refined ambience.

The Ritz-Carlton experience enlivens the senses, instills well-being, and fulfills even the unexpressed wishes and needs of our guests.

For insight into how The Ritz-Carlton Hotel Company does it, I will provide you with perspectives from Leonardo Inghilleri, senior vice president of human resources. The company's over-16,000 employees can make-or-break each customer's experience with this ultimate luxury hotel company. As such, the chief human resources officer certainly plays an incredibly important role in guaranteeing the ultra-special Ritz-Carlton experience for all customers entering these hotels.

The Ritz-Carlton Hotel Company is a hotel management company that develops and operates luxury hotels for others. The owners are individuals, investor groups, banks, and insurance companies. These hotels are in a wide array of locations where travelers desire luxury accommodations. Locations include the United States, Canada, Mexico, Spain, Germany, Singapore, Japan, Indonesia, Malaysia, Hong Kong, and the Virgin Islands.

The Ritz-Carlton Hotel Company's Major Organizational Change

"The company's major organizational change is becoming super-responsive to customers through an extremely empowered, carefully selected, and highly trained workforce," explains Inghilleri. Or, as the Ritz-Carlton motto charmingly instills in its employees, *"We Are Ladies and Gentlemen Serving Ladies and Gentlemen."*

"The focus is on satisfying the individual needs of all our customers," says Inghilleri. "The more a person stays in a Ritz-Carlton hotel, the better the company and its employees know the customer – and the better employees get to know and service guests' personal preferences."

I can verify this from personal experience. One time when I stayed in a Ritz Carlton, I requested four bath towels plus an extra blanket. Those items were brought to me. Now, when I stay at a Ritz-Carlton hotel, as soon as I walk into my room, I look around and – lo and behold – I find four bath towels and an extra blanket. This is enchantingly delightful, individualized customer service. My preferences for extra towels and a blanket are in the company's computer, so each Ritz-Carlton hotel automatically fulfills my preferences – without me needing to call the front desk to make my special requests.

Inghilleri emphasizes the importance The Ritz-Carlton Hotel Company places on providing personalized or individualized service to create its magical luxury hotel experience:

We don't want our guests to keep repeating their requests. We aim to satisfy guests' requests before they ask for items. We convey a message of great appreciation for customers' needs. For example, if a diner in a Ritz-Carlton restaurant takes out some vitamins or pills, a waitperson or the host usually will notice and immediately bring a glass of water so the diner can take his or her vitamins or pills.

Importantly, it is our employees who create the luxury hotel ambiance that is synonymous with the Ritz-Carlton name. Their purpose is to fulfill our dream as a corporation that wraps guests up in a cocoon of luxury. The luxury experience starts the moment a guest steps into a Ritz-Carlton hotel – and it continues until the moment the person leaves the hotel to re-enter the rest of the world.

Indeed, the Ritz-Carlton approach contrasts sharply from the typical hotel in which employees generally

♦ show up because it is a job
♦ receive limited training
♦ are not encouraged to be responsive to customers' needs
♦ have high turnover – often over 70%

In fact, in my business travel to deliver speeches, workshops and consult, I stay in many hotels. Based on my extensive business travel, I now classify each hotel as falling into one of two types, namely, (1) hotels run by "adults" and (2) hotels run by "children." My terms of "adults" and "children" do not refer to hotel employees' ages. Instead, I mean truly fine hotels – especially Ritz-Carlton hotels – are run by "adults" who take a mature, active role in assuring guests feel delighted and somewhat pampered. In contrast, a hotel run by "children" which includes most non-Ritz-Carlton hotels – are staffed by employees who show limited or no concern about how guests feel about their stay.

It is so wonderful there are Ritz-Carlton hotels to stay in!

How Was This Change Crucial to Ritz-Carlton's Success?

Senior vice president Inghilleri says this organizational change contributes three key factors to Ritz-Carlton's business growth:

1. *Personalized service* is a core element in the company's position in the marketplace as a luxury service provider
2. *Self-directed workforce* reduces operating costs
3. *Management takes a visionary, standard-setting, and cheerleading role* – so front-line employees can operate with authority and responsibility

Steps Used to Implement This Crucial Organizational Change

The Ritz-Carlton Hotel Company used a few steps to develop ultra-responsiveness to customers through an extremely empowered, carefully selected, and highly trained workforce.

Step 1: List Actions Needed by Front-Line Workers

Determine specific activities front-line workers *must* carry out to create a luxury hotel experience for guests. These crucial front-line workers serve in a variety of jobs that are highly visible to customers. The jobs include front desk staff, bellhops, house-keepers, waitpersons, and restaurant hosts. In many respects, these front-line employees can make-or-break a customer's experience in a hotel or restaurant in the hotel.

Step 2: Stabilize the Workforce

For example, The Ritz-Carlton Hotel Company determined it cannot deliver excellent service to customers if it has high turnover. Lower turnover means the Ritz-Carlton hotels always have employees with superb skills and abilities to help customers.

Step 3: "The Line-Up" Meeting Each & Every Day

To assure on-going communication, at the start of every shift, each employee participates in a five to seven minute meeting called "The Line-Up." This meeting includes

1. review of one of the 20 "Basics" on the Ritz-Carlton's *Gold Standard Card*
2. some training
3. discussing guests in the hotel, such as specific customers or VIPs staying on the property
4. recognition for good work or an employee's birthday

The company lists 20 "Basics" in a fold-up *Gold Standard Card* all employees keep in their pockets to remind them of what to do to provide spectacular service. In fact, one time when I complimented a Ritz-Carlton employee, I asked her how the company makes sure employees consistently provide fantastic, personalized service. She proudly handed me the *Gold Standard Card* she kept in her pocket, and told me the employees live and breathe the guidelines printed on the card. Diagram 1 shows some of these 20 "Basics."

Diagram 1. **Selected Ritz-Carlton "Basics" from the Company's** *Gold Standard Card*

Every Ritz-Carlton employee carries a pocket-sized card called the *Gold Standard Card*. This card contains key ideas and techniques each Ritz-Carlton employee needs to use all the time. Here are some of the 20 "Basics" that assure Ritz-Carlton employees provide spectacular personalized service for each and every guest:

10. Each employee is empowered. For example, when a guest has a problem or needs something special, you should break away from your regular duties to address and resolve the issue.
12. To provide the finest personal service for our guests, each employee is responsible for identifying and recording individual guest preferences.
13. Never lose a guest. Instant guest pacification is the responsibility of each employee. Whoever receives a complaint will own it, resolve it to the guest's satisfaction and record it.
14. "Smile – We are on stage." Always maintain positive eye contact. Use the proper vocabulary with our guests and each other. (Use words like - "Good Morning," "Certainly," "I'll be happy to" and "My pleasure.")
16. Escort guests rather than pointing out directions to another area of the Hotel.

Source: The Ritz-Carlton Hotel Company. Copyright The Ritz-Carlton Hotel Company. Reprinted with permission.

This daily Line-Up Meeting brings each employee into the "fabric of the Ritz-Carlton experience," points out Inghilleri. And, importantly, employees are not allowed to skip a Line-Up Meeting.

The core topic of each Line-Up Meeting is determined by top management. For example, for one week employees in Line-Up might focus on telephone etiquette, divided into seven segments, with one segment covered each day of the week. Inghilleri emphasizes, "Unless workers are involved daily in discussing individualized service, they could forget their crucial role of being *"Ladies & Gentlemen Serving Ladies & Gentlemen."*

Measurable Improvements Produced by This Organizational Change

In just four years of intensely focusing on training and empowering employees to provide absolutely fabulous *personalized service*, Ritz-Carlton achieved many measurable improvements. These improvements include the following tremendous results:

◆ Increased gross operating profit from 25% to 36%

◆ Cut turnover in half, from 50% down to 25%

The low turnover is quite remarkable. Many hotel chains have turnover of 70% or more. Importantly, the Ritz-Carlton's low turnover proves crucial for business growth. Why? Because the company discovered that only with low turnover does it have employees who know how to do a consistently stellar job providing luxury personalized service.

Unmeasurable Improvements

Inghilleri credits the organizational change with bringing four qualitative enhancements.

Qualitative Improvement 1: Pride & Joy in the Workers

This feeling of pride and joy allows the Ritz-Carlton to reap the benefits of workers planning and executing significant aspects of their jobs serving customers. This gives workers a sense of belonging and affiliation with the company. This feeling of affiliation and belonging allows Ritz-Carlton to concentrate on improving its business in myriad ways.

Qualitative Improvement 2: Anticipation of Customer Needs

For example, as mentioned earlier, if a customer in a Ritz-Carlton restaurant takes out vitamins or pills, a waitperson or host knows to give the customer a glass of water – immediately. After all, vitamins or pills necessarily go with water! In contrast, most hotel restaurant employees never notice nor care about providing such non-requested service.

Qualitative Improvement 3: Employees Do Not Have A Job – They Have A Profession

Most hotels that are not Ritz-Carlton, it seems to me, are staffed with employees who are not deeply and personally attached to their work nor the hotel. In sharp contrast are Ritz-Carlton staff members. They overwhelmingly perform like professionals carrying out crucial duties, rather than just regular employees solely "doing their jobs."

Example: One time I was at a Ritz-Carlton Hotel for a business conference where I delivered the keynote speech and also a workshop. In the morning, one employee graciously helped me set-up my audio-visual equipment before my speech. That was not all. During my speech, that same employee came into the room many times and stood at the back of the room to see if I needed anything. At one point, the employee even tweaked my microphone's volume control to enhance the sound quality. Then, after I finished my speech, that same Ritz-Carlton employee walked up to me and asked, "How can I help you?" Note: I had not asked the employee to do any of this.

I mentioned I would deliver a workshop at the conference at 2:00 p.m. that afternoon. Lo and behold, as I checked my audio-visual equipment before delivering my 2:00 p.m. seminar, that wonderful employee again showed up, and asked, "Can I help you with anything?" Note: I did not ask the employee to do this!

During the workshop I conducted in the afternoon, the employee showed up a number of times and stood at the back of the room to see if my audio-visual equipment was working properly. Interestingly, the employee noticed I drink water when I deliver speeches and workshops. During my workshop, the employee even brought me an extra glass of water – although I did not ask for it.

After my seminar, I asked her how she learned to provide such amazingly wonderful service. With a proud smile, she looked me in the eye, as she told me something I always will remember. She said, *"I love helping our guests. After all, here at the Ritz-Carlton we are ladies and gentlemen serving ladies and gentlemen."* I must say I have come to expect – and cherish – such personalized service and attention to detail provided by Ritz-Carlton employees.

Qualitative Improvement 4: First Hotel Company To Win the Coveted Malcolm Baldridge National Quality Award (plus win it twice!)

To grasp how spectacular this feat is, realize The Ritz-Carlton Hotel Company is the

- first and only hotel company to win the award!
- first and only service company to win the award two times!!

Organizational Change Ingredient 1: Successfully Leading the Organizational Change

Based on consulting I provide to many companies, I continually find that the only organizational changes that take hold and produce fabulous results are those that

- logically flow from the company's culture and big, exciting vision
- are achieved using an organized goal-setting method
- rely on teamwork and interdepartmental collaboration

The Ritz-Carlton Hotel Company's major organizational change – *"becoming super-responsive to customers through an extremely empowered, carefully selected, and highly trained workforce,"* as phrased by Inghilleri – superbly used all these elements.

Ritz-Carlton's Corporate Culture

From my consulting experience, as well as my previous work as a corporate manager, I discovered the best way to uncover a company's culture is to discover the story every employee tells and re-tells. The principle or underlying point of the story conveys the company's culture, which are the guidelines and actions the company most values. Inghilleri told me this story which is well-known among employees of The Ritz Carlton-Hotel Company:

"Ladies & Gentlemen Serving Ladies & Gentlemen"
When he was 14 years old, Horst Schulze – currently president of The Ritz-Carlton Hotel Company – worked as an apprentice waiter in a very fine restaurant in his native Germany. Initially, he saw himself as a "servant."

Then, he realized the fine restaurant was staffed by highly skilled professionals. For example, he looked in awe as he repeatedly saw the maître d' chat with and entertain the diners. In fact, the maître d' spoke many languages. So, he spoke German to the German diners, French to the French guests, and English to the English customers. He also expertly helped diners with their food and wine choices.

From this experience, it dawned on Horst Schulze that a

luxury establishment is composed of ladies and gentlemen serving ladies and gentlemen. He instilled this insight into The Ritz-Carlton Hotel Company where he now is president.

Culture – or Main Focus – of The Ritz-Carlton Hotel Company

Horst Schulze's experience gives rise to The Ritz-Carlton Hotel Company's motto which perfectly expresses its corporate culture: *"We Are Ladies and Gentlemen Serving Ladies and Gentlemen."* This motto expressing the corporate culture provides an on-going reminder to each employee that he or she is vitally important.

Link between the Corporate Culture & the Major Organizational Change

It is readily apparent that the company's increased and intense focus on *personalized service* grows directly out of its culture of *"Ladies and Gentlemen Serving Ladies and Gentlemen."* The company created a perfect fit between its major organizational change and its delightful luxury corporate culture.

Big, Exciting Vision of The Ritz-Carlton Hotel Company

I always find that companies that succeed in huge ways have a clearly laid out vision that is both big and exciting. The Ritz-Carlton's vision definitely is very big and very exciting. It is the following:

To be the premier worldwide provider of luxury travel and hospitality products and services.

Specifically, the company plans to accomplish its dominance in the luxury travel and hospitality business through consistently providing

- ◆ excellent personalized service, especially anticipating each guest's needs
- ◆ excellent meals
- ◆ reliable rooms
- ◆ best amenities available anywhere

Ways the Organizational Change Fits into the Company's Vision

It is easy to see The Ritz Carlton Hotel Company's major organizational change perfectly coincides with the company's big, exciting vision. Indeed, as anyone who has had a Ritz-Carlton hotel or dining experience can verify, the company totally gears everything it does to being *"the premier world-wide provider of luxury travel and hospitality products and services."*

Goal-Setting to Accomplish the Company's Major Organizational Change

Inghilleri used only three words to summarize the company's highly effective goal-setting method: *"We measure everything."* Here are key measures Ritz-Carlton uses.

Measure 1: J.D. Power Surveys

The company uses J.D. Power to survey the satisfaction of two types of customers. First, it surveys the satisfaction of hotel guests. Second, the company surveys meeting or event planners; these are people who hold conferences, parties, or business events in Ritz-Carlton hotels.

Measure 2: Employee Satisfaction

Measure 3: Count Defects in Ritz-Carlton's Service Quality Index

The Ritz-Carlton's *Service Quality Index* (SQI) records defects in 12 categories or "indicators" that prove most important to Ritz-Carlton customers. The 12 SQI categories are show in Diagram 2.

Diagram 2. **Categories & Points in Ritz-Carlton's Service Quality Index**

The Ritz-Carlton Hotel Company prides itself on providing extremely high quality customer service to produce superb guest satisfaction. To measure quality each day, points are deducted for each mistake. Here are the 12 categories or "indicators," with possible point deductions in parentheses.

1. *Missing Preferences* (10)
   Regular guest arrivals whose "profile" lacks any actionable preferences beyond room type, smoking preference or title.
2. *Unresolved Difficulties* (50)
   Any difficulty discovered during the J.D. Power survey process for which there was inadequate resolution.
3. *Housekeeping* (1)
   A total score of housekeeping defects, identified during five random inspections each day.
4. *Abandoned Calls* (5)
   Reservation calls that are not answered and the customer hangs up.

5. *Room Changes* (5)
   Customer requests for a change of room after Check-In.
6. *Guest Room Condition* (5)
   Customer requests for repairs to their guestroom.
7. *Unready Guestroom* (10)
   Any guestroom that is not immediately ready for the guest when they arrive to register, regardless of time of day.
8. *Hotel Cleanliness* (5)
   Any unacceptable appearance of a public area, identified during the morning process.
9. *Meeting Event Difficulties* (5)
   A total score of difficulties, stated by the Event Planner during the post-event conversation.
10. *Food & Beverage* (1)
    A composite score of measurements from Food & Beverage Operations which consist of
    A. Each Outlet (1)
       Customer dissatisfaction, any type/any outlet restaurant or lounge.
    B. Room Service (1)
       Room Service Orders which are either delivered past the commitment time and/or are delivered incomplete.
    C. Banquet (1)
       Each banquet event difficulty recorded on the Banquet Captain's report.
11. *Missing/Damaged Guest Property* (50)
    Number of claims/incidents for the disappearance or damage of guest property (i.e., vehicles, vehicle keys, luggage, clothing, jewelry, valuables, etc.) or accidents requiring care from a medical professional involving a guest or employee.
12. *Invoice Adjustment* (3)
    Customer requests for a credit or refund for real or perceived deficiencies.

Source: The Ritz-Carlton Hotel Company. Copyright The Ritz-Carlton Hotel Company. Reprinted with permission.

For example, Inghilleri explained, "We subtract points for each mistake. So, the closer the score is to zero, the better the individual Ritz-Carlton hotel has done. This allows each Ritz-Carlton hotel to understand how well it is running its business. Every employee sees the latest SQI scores. So, when employees show up for work, they immediately see how the hotel did in service the previous day."

Talk about immediate feedback! It would be hard to get detailed feedback on the quality of service any faster than 24 hours later!! With this information, employees readily know what services need improvement. For example, if the previous day's SQI shows defects in room service or cleanliness or laundry, then the employees responsible for those services know they need to improve.

Inghilleri emphasized that all Ritz-Carlton managers work on aspects of six principal long-term objectives. For example, sales managers work on sales and marketing aspects. Likewise, managers in charge of food service, finance, housekeeping, front desk, human resources or other departments, each focus on facets of these long-term objectives their respective department can impact.

Objective 1:Be the employer-of-choice for people who crave to work in a highly empowered atmosphere in which they provide extremely individualized service to each customer

Objective 2:Improve customer loyalty in 3 ways –
  A. Improve individual guest satisfaction (measured by J.D. Power surveys)
  B. Improve meeting event satisfaction
  C. Improve guest satisfaction with the value they get for the price

Objective 3:Reduce customer difficulties

Objective 4:Increase revenue per available room in each hotel

Objective 5:Increase hotel profitability

Objective 6:Develop valuable new products – especially in service, meals, rooms, and amenities

Teamwork to Accomplish Goals

"We are a culture of collaboration with an empowered workforce," explained Inghilleri. "This includes lateral participation, involving people, and working across departments to provide world-class services and products."

For example, one Ritz-Carlton hotel received many complaints that room service constantly was late. So, the room service manager bought more serving carts. But, room service still was consistently late.

So, the hotel put together a group of employees from various departments to look into this continuing glitch. This interdepartmental group realized using elevators for room service was slow. So, employees spoke to the hotel's engineers who are in charge of the elevators.

The engineers realized the elevators made lots of stops, because housekeepers used the same elevators. The housekeepers, in turn, said they excessively used the elevators because the hotel was short on linen on some floors. To accommodate for this, the housekeepers used elevators a lot to "borrow" linen from other floors.

So, the solution was not to buy more room service carts, after all! Instead, the solution the interdepartmental team discovered was to buy more linen!! The hotel bought more linen. Doing so freed up the elevators, because the housekeepers were not using the elevators to travel to other floors to "borrow" linen. Without this interdepartmental teamwork of employees empowered to investigate and solve this nettlesome problem, the hotel never would have discovered late room service was caused by not having enough linen.

Organizational Change Ingredient 2:
Successfully Handling Employee Problems during the Organizational Change

From consulting to many organizations undertaking change actions, I repeatedly find there always are some employees who try to "shoot a hole in the boat." To resist the organizational change, they throw up subtle – and sometimes not too subtle – roadblocks. While they mean to protect themselves, they also harm the improvements the organization is making. As such, it proves vitally important for executives and managers who lead change to take action so no employee problems subvert the improvements being implemented.

Actions of Employees Who Resisted – or Undermined – The Ritz-Carlton Hotel Company's Organizational Change

Inghilleri discovered two types of employees defied the major organizational change.

Defiant Employee 1: Cynics

These are employees who undermine and sabotage. Inghilleri explained a cynic says, in effect, "You say you want to do this for the customers and workers, but that's not true. You just want to line your pockets with more money!"

Defiant Employee 2: Skeptics

"Skeptics are turned-off to the vision of the organization," said

Inghilleri. He described a skeptic as someone who says, in effect, "I don't think it'll ever work!"

Methods Used to Handle Employees Who Resisted Ritz-Carlton's Organizational Change

Inghilleri emphatically stated, *"If leaders do not isolate cynics or skeptics, then they can poison the atmosphere."* As such, the company needed either to convince cynics and skeptics of the wisdom of the Ritz-Carlton's goals and vision – or isolate them. He also observed cynics and skeptics tend to leave the company.

How does this extraordinary company isolate cynics and skeptics – or somehow encourage them to leave? The Ritz-Carlton Hotel Company developed a four part solution that works exceedingly well:

1. *Selection* of great employees
2. *Orient* employees intensely in their first hours on-the-job
3. *Train* employees a large amount in Ritz-Carlton work methods and philosophy
4. *Line-Up Meeting* every day

First, the company is very careful in its employee selection process so it hires the right people. These are individuals who desire empowerment, enjoy thinking on their feet, and cherish working as *"Ladies and Gentlemen Serving Ladies and Gentlemen."*

Second, the company orients all new employees to the Ritz-Carlton's values and philosophy during their very first day of employment. Inghilleri wisely points out that people really change and improve when they have a "significant emotional experience, such as death of a loved one or a big loss. Also, the first day on a new job is a significant emotional experience." So, in the first few hours of employment, the company orients every new employee to the Ritz-Carlton operating system and philosophy.

Inghilleri observed new employees are open to incorporating these core Ritz-Carlton values and methods in the first few hours of their first day on-the-job. He also points out that any company that fails to promptly and deeply orient new employees misses the fastest and most powerful method to instill the company's way of operating into the new employees.

Third, Ritz-Carlton trains employees in how to do their jobs the Ritz-Carlton way. This includes a strong training, certification, and mastery program. How much does the Ritz-Carlton train employees? Let the numbers speak for themselves. In the first year

on-the-job, training averages
- ◆ 250 hours/year for line employees
- ◆ 310 hours/year for managers

Let's put it another way, assuming about 2,000 hours in a work-year (50 work-weeks/year X 40 hours/week = 2,000 work-hours/year). First year training hours mean line employees get training one of every eight hours. Managers obtain training one of every 6.5 hours. That is a big – and obviously very profitable – commitment to training Ritz-Carlton employees to provide stellar service.

And training does not stop after the first year on-the-job. After the first year, training averages
- ◆ 95 hours/year for line employees
- ◆ 110 hours/year for managers

Apparently, all this training greatly helps each Ritz-Carlton hotel be a luxurious property. Or, as Inghilleri colorfully put it, *"A successful organization will not tolerate mediocrity."*

This reminds me of a wonderful quote from W. Somerset Maughn: "The mediocre always are at their best." Every Ritz-Carlton customer realizes The Ritz-Carlton Hotel Company never tolerates mediocrity.

Fourth, the company talks to employees about how to perform on-the-job seven days a week in its daily Line-Up Meetings at the start of each shift. What does this accomplish? Inghilleri points out the daily Line-Up Meeting offers each department a 365 days/year place to "Repeat, repeat, repeat and repeat Ritz-Carlton methods every day."

Also, Inghilleri notes the daily Line-Up Meeting in each department serves an additional vital purpose: "It isolates cynics and skeptics. By repeating Ritz-Carlton's key messages, we make sure every worker knows how to contribute to Ritz-Carlton's *vision* in their own job." For example, every housekeeper knows how to contribute to the company's *vision* in the way he or she cleans rooms. Each of the company's restaurant workers, front desk staff, bellhops – and everyone else – knows exactly how to contribute to the company's *vision* in how they do their job.

Comparing Ritz-Carlton's *"Old-Style"* Employees with Its Needed *"New-Style"* Employees

Invariably, some employees who performed fine on-the-job

before the organizational change may not do well *after* the change is implemented. I refer to these as "old-style" and "new-style" employees. For this reason, after implementing an organizational change, a company is wise to pinpoint exactly what talents the "new-style" employees need to possess.

In the case of The Ritz-Carlton Hotel Company, the table below compares its "old-style" employees with the "new-style" employees needed after its major organizational change.

Old-Style Employees	New-Style Employees
Works in 1 department	Interdepartmental
Solo work	Teamwork
Likes receiving direction	Likes independence
Prefers to be told what to do	Prefers shared leadership
Planning done by managers & execution by workers	Participative management
No passion for the work	Pride in their job

Inghilleri explained the last two comparisons with these comments. He said "planning done by managers and execution by workers is Taylorism," named for Frederick Taylor, founder of "scientific management" during the industrial era of business. In contrast, "participative management," states Inghilleri, allows workers to plan and execute their work. For example, Ritz-Carlton would not plan housekeeping changes, unless it first involved housekeepers and other employees who deal with housekeepers.

Importantly, the "new-style" employee trait of "pride in their job" also is crucial. Due to the way Ritz-Carlton operates its business, Inghilleri emphasizes, *"Employees feel they have a profession, not just a job."*

Recommendations to Employees Who Work in Companies Undergoing Major Organizational Change

Executives who lead successful organizational change are incredibly qualified to advise employees of any company on how to survive and thrive when their employer implements organizational change. As such, Inghilleri possesses first-hand knowledge about what an employee needs to do to come out ahead.

Inghilleri emphasized that when a company offers an employee the opportunity to help put an extraordinary vision into action, it proves crucial for the person to accept this fact: *"Desire is*

fundamental, because extraordinary things can only happen with extraordinary efforts. Ordinary efforts only create ordinary results." As such, Inghilleri offers three building blocks to help people whose organizations are implementing major organizational change:
Recommendation 1: Affiliation
Each employee needs to make sure he or she feels like part of the enterprise. If not, then Inghilleri recommends the employee find another job.
Recommendation 2: "Accept change is a must to make continuous improvements"
Recommendation 3: Leaders must "hold the course"
By this, Inghilleri insists leaders must stay focused and loyal to implementing the company's *vision*.

Organizational Change Ingredient 3: Successfully Managing Yourself during the Organizational Change

Everyone needs role models. And during organizational change, employees look to the executives leading the change to provide – through their actions and words – examples of how to act, react, and deal with the changes. Based on consulting I provide to many companies, I found ideal leaders exude optimism in their mood, attitudes, and phrases they use.*

Also, astounding leaders typically had life experiences as they grew up that helped them develop into high-achieving individuals. For these reasons, I spoke with Inghilleri about his optimism and life experiences that help make him an outstanding leader.

Optimism Helped This Executive Succeed in Implementing Major Organizational Change

Inghilleri displays optimism. He emphatically states,
Optimism is absolutely significant. I'm an optimist in life – both my professional and personal life. You have to be positive. Nothing positive is created through negative thinking.

---

*Relevant materials from Dr. Mercer include (1) *Spontaneous Optimism™: Proven Strategies for Health, Prosperity & Happiness* and also (2) *How Winners Do It: High Impact People Skills for Your Career Success*. For information, you can refer to the Materials You Can Order section in the back of this book

Starting when I was a teenager, I always have had a personal mission statement to help me in my life. It helps me know where I'm going even when I am challenged.

Knowing where he is going professionally and personally proves vital to Inghilleri. This executive also explains how it is a moral imperative for every leader. He powerfully observes, "Leadership is linked to providing direction to determine where an organization is going. And I think it's immoral to lead other men and women if you don't have a clear direction for your own life."

Attitudes of This Executive that Most Help Him Succeed

Inghilleri credits his optimistic, upbeat disposition to four key attitudes he holds near and dear.

Attitude 1: Be a positive person
Attitude 2: Believe in self-reliance
Attitude 3: "Clarity of thought about what I want to accomplish"
Attitude 4: "Don't suffer in silence – share the burden"

He explains, "I share my difficulties with others to draw on their wisdom, energy, and advice."

Phrase This Executive Says to Keep Focused & Optimistic

This Ritz-Carlton senior vice president especially likes using this phrase: *"Nothing happens until it happens."* By this, he means, "Initiate action so work actually gets set in motion and delivery of results takes place."

Highly successful executives focus on achieving results in a timely fashion. As such, Inghilleri's "Nothing happens until it happens" phrase conveys this critical sense of speed and results-orientation. It also keeps people around him on their toes making sure needed work gets done.

How This Executive Gets Employees to Focus on Solutions – Not Problems

A key characteristic of optimists – including highly successful executives – is they overwhelmingly focus on solutions. In contrast, pessimists – and people my research found are less-than-successful in their careers – tend to focus on problems and complaining. Important: An executive is a role model for employees. If the executive focuses on solutions *and* insists his or her employees focus on solutions, the outcome is a solution-focused, results-oriented team.

How does Inghilleri make sure Ritz-Carlton employees focus on solutions? He uses three methods.

Method 1: Do not allow complaining
> "I don't accept complaining. Period! Complaining is an attitude I refuse to accept. Instead, I ask people to contribute. And when a person contributes, they have no reason to complain."

Method 2: Uncover the cause – & fix it
> "If someone complains, I go to the root cause of the problem right away. And we focus on fixing it right away."

Method 3: Make the organization terrifically solution-oriented
> "As an organization, we are a positive, solution-oriented company. It's exciting to be in an exciting company."

This Executive's Favorite Story

I discovered that the significant point or theme of a person's favorite story produces clear insight into what that person considers vitally important. Inghilleri feels particularly fond of one very meaningful scene in *Alice in Wonderland*. At a certain point, Alice is lost in the forest. Then, she sees the Cheshire Cat. Inghilleri especially likes the following exchange between the two of them.

Alice: "Which way should I go?"
Cheshire Cat: "It very much depends on where you are going."
Alice: "It doesn't really matter where I'm going."
Cheshire Cat: "Well, then, it doesn't really matter which way you go!"

Inghilleri explains the significant point he finds most meaningful in this scene:

> *Without a clear sense of direction in your life, how do you know what contributions you are making. And without contributions, then what kind of life are you living?*

> *Humans need a sense of purpose. Without a sense of direction, a person is no more than just an animal who spends all its time searching for only basic needs like food, safety, and shelter. Without a sense of direction, you don't know what your purpose is in life.*

This Executive's Role Models – & Lesson Learned from Each One

No one exists alone on an island. Everyone meets many people. And the most noteworthy people are those whom the person considers to be role models. Given the tremendous impact of role models, it is intriguing to find out whom a highly successful leader, such as Inghilleri, considers his top role models. He mentioned three people.

Role Model 1: Father. *Lesson Learned:* "To be a committed, intense, hard-working, very resilient person."

Role Model 2: Lee Cockrell, friend and former colleague, who now is executive vice president of Walt Disney World. *Lesson Learned:* "In my business life, how to produce excellence, have fun, and work with friends."

Role Model 3: Horst Schulze, president of The Ritz-Carlton Hotel Company and Inghilleri's boss. *Lesson Learned:* "Have a passion for both my job and the hotel industry."

9

IBM

Saving $1-Billion

Vision of IBM Accounts Payable Organization:
Our key goal is to be the
best Accounts Payable organization in the world.

When you think of a company that definitely should be at the forefront in using computer technology to streamline operations – you may well think of venerable IBM. Indeed, the name IBM practically is synonymous with computers, information technology, automation, and making business life run smoother through harnessing technology.

Well, believe it or not, IBM used to sink a lot of extra money down the drain in its vendor processing. Just imagine how much money a company like IBM spends each year – a company approaching $100-billion in sales with over 250,000 employees. A lot! And the massive purchasing done by all these employees, for everything from paperclips to machinery, was done without fully taking advantage of IBM's own technology.

Fortunately, a number of executives – including Robert Hughes, manager of IBM National Accounts Payable – came to the rescue. They figured out how IBM could save a ton of money. And they succeeded on a massive scale: *IBM ended up saving $1-billion using improved vendor processing.* Along the way, they helped IBM create new technology and systems IBM now sells to other companies, plus they won numerous highly prestigious awards for their pioneering achievements.

IBM Accounts Payable's Major Organizational Change

IBM dramatically overhauled its vendor processing and, in

doing so, saved $1 billion. That is *billion* with a *b*!!

How did Big Blue (IBM's nickname) do it? As Hughes put it, IBM vastly revamped its process of going from "req to check" – from *req*uisition of a purchase to issuing the *check* to pay for it. This required a shift from looking at accounts payable and purchasing as two fairly separate processes to transforming the system into one seamless process.

While most companies will not save a billion dollars doing anything, the superb methods IBM used to achieve this breathtaking organizational change prove profoundly instructive. Everyone reading about how IBM did it will read a fascinating tale of world-class methods to

◆ lead organizational change endeavors

◆ handle challenges of employees who resist change

◆ serve as a fantastic role model for employees carrying out the organizational change

These absolutely fabulous methods can be applied in most companies to institute a wide array of organizational changes.

How Was This Change Crucial to IBM's Success & Growth?

Hughes emphasized the organizational change proved imperative in three ways. First, IBM recognized its business was changing in the fast-paced technology and services marketplace. So, IBM wanted to use all the tools available, especially the Internet. Second, the change put in place a global – not just North American – vendor processing method in anticipation of IBM's global growth. Third, this major change enabled IBM to maintain cost competitiveness. This, in turn, made IBM's global growth more likely – and much more profitable.

Steps Used To Implement This Crucial Organizational Change

This spectacular organizational change entailed 10 key steps.

Step 1: Formed Team

IBM's Accounts Payable organization hooked up with the Procurement organization to look at "req to check" as one process. Prior to this, vendors dealt with two separate groups: (A) Procurement and (B) Accounts Payable.

Step 2. Mutual Understanding

As the two organizations teamed up on this project, everyone on the team gained better understanding of the other's processes.

Step 3: Concept Stage

After thoroughly thinking through the processes needed to make this project a success, the team entered into what Hughes describes as the "concept stage." This focused the team on picturing or envisioning how to make "req to check" work better for an array of stakeholders:

♦ Procurement Department
♦ Accounts Payable Department
♦ IBM employees as a whole
♦ Suppliers

Step 4: Find Internet Software Tools

Internet tools played a decisive role in transforming the concepts into reality.

Step 5: Test the Internet Software Tools

Importantly, the team focused tremendous attention on testing tools IBM developed internally. Of course, this helped the vendor processing team. A valuable additional benefit was that such testing helped IBM refine its Internet software tools in real world business applications: IBM obtained immediate feedback on what worked and what still needed improvement. This enabled IBM to proceed rapidly in developing proven tools it could market to other companies.

Step 6: "Engaging Enthusiasm"

This entailed dealing with resistance to changing how the Procurement employees and Accounts Payable employees did their jobs. A rallying cry was the excitement of saying, *"We can be the first in the world to do this."*

Also, Hughes put this question to his team when things would seem to slow down: "How will we present this if we are inter-viewed on a major national TV talk show?" The thrill of being *first in the world* and garnering national or worldwide status and recognition helped ignite enthusiasm for this major organizational change.

Step 7: Do 1st Transaction on Internet

Now that the tools were ready and the project team members felt enthused, the next step entailed putting the change into action – to give birth to IBM's ground-breaking way to do "req to check." The first transaction involved a supplier billing IBM with an invoice over the Internet – rather than using the previous method of sending a paper invoice.

Step 8: Celebrate the 1st Success

The first success truly provided an exciting event to celebrate. By celebrating the first transaction on the Internet, IBM stoked the team's enthusiasm and boosted momentum to forge ahead with enhancing IBM's new vendor processing method.

The celebration included giving every employee involved on the project a high quality e-business shirt at a cake-and-coffee party. In organizations – whether it is a company, a social club, a military unit, or a sports team – team members emotionally *"bond"* (feel emotionally closer) and more thrilled to work together when they celebrate a big success. Also, wearing the same article of clothing linked to a big success – such as the high-quality e-business shirt – provided team members with a shorthand, visible symbol to convey they *belonged* to a special group of high-achievers. After all, everyone feels proud to be a member of an elite team.

Step 9: Continue Refining the New Process

This included working out kinks in the system, discovering what was missing, and then plugging those gaps.

Step 10: Publicity

The team looked for both internal and external publicity. Two main internal publicity opportunities included

◆ helping create marketing brochures IBM can use to sell the product the team developed
◆ earning the highly sought-after annual IBM Chairman's Award

External publicity included the prestigious *Electronic Commerce* magazine running a cover story on the vendor processing project's success. This certainly provided a big publicity coup for the project team, as well as for IBM which now could boast a new, field-tested product to offer its customers and prospects.

Measurable Improvements Produced by This Organizational Change

Here are highlights of the amazing quantitative results from the improved vendor processing (also see Diagram 1):

◆ Saved $1-billion over 3 years
◆ Drop in cost to procure goods from 1.8% down to 0.9% for every $100 IBM purchased; previously, when IBM bought $100 of goods, it cost IBM $1.80, but now it costs IBM only 90-cents.

- ◆ Slashed cost to process an invoice from $1.50/invoice down to $1.02/invoice
- ◆ Reduced error rate in procurement from 34% down to 9%
- ◆ Decreased number of computer applications needed for procurement from 12 down to one
- ◆ Better leverage in negotiations with suppliers, because all purchase order and payment information are on an easy-to-access "Business Data Warehouse" for all to see

Diagram 1. **Results of IBM's Absolutely Fabulous Organizational Change**

Category	Result	Before	After
Savings (3 years)	$1-billion		
Cost to procure goods	50% less	$1.80/$100	$.90/$100
Cost to process an invoice	32% less	$1.50	$1.02
Error rate in procurement	74% less	34%	9%
Computer applications needed	92% less	12	1

Unmeasurable or Qualitative Improvements

In addition to the many measurable improvements, Hughes also credits employees with creating two chief unmeasurable enhancements.

Qualitative Improvement 1: Sense of control

The change instilled a feeling of more control over procurement and accounts payable processes. Reason: The new, seamless process enables employees to better anticipate how a modification in procurement processes would change accounts payable processes.

Qualitative Improvement 2: Pride

Hughes noticed employees feel more proud of the work they do. They progressed from transaction *processing* under the old process to transaction *analysis* using the new process. Doing so allows employees to use even more brainpower than before, a motivating factor.

Diagram 2 shows an example comparing the old transaction processing process with the new transaction analysis process. It illustrates the difference in what is entailed in an IBM employee ordering, in this case, a chair.

Diagram 2. **Old Versus New Vendor Processing at IBM**

OLD VENDOR PROCESSING

Step

1 Requestor (IBM employee) wants a chair
2 Requestor calls a Procurement Department employee
3 Procurement employee orders chair from an IBM-approved vendor/supplier
4 Vendor sends chair to the requestor
5 Vendor sends *paper* invoice to Accounts Payable Department
6 Employee in Accounts Payable types in the invoice and matches it to purchase order
7 IBM issues check and mails check to Vendor

NEW VENDOR PROCESSING

Step

1 Requestor (IBM employee) wants a chair
2 Requestor goes on IBM Intranet and clicks on "Chair"
3 Electronically, this order goes to an IBM-authorized vendor
4 Vendor ships chair to requestor
5 Vendor sends *electronic* invoice to IBM for match against purchase order
6 IBM sends funds to vendor's bank using electronic funds transfer

---

Organizational Change Ingredient 1:
Successfully Leading the Organizational Change

From my consulting to many companies – plus my previous work as a corporate manager – I became keenly aware of the following insight into successful organizational change: The changes that achieve or exceed desired results always

♦ help the company move closer to its big, exciting vision
♦ use clearly organized goal-setting
♦ benefit from superb teamwork and collaboration

With this in mind, let's see how Hughes and others at IBM led the tremendous organizational change in the company's vendor processing.

Big, Exciting Vision

The organizations that make the biggest mark on the world constantly strive to achieve a very big, extremely exciting vision. Usually they crave to become the biggest or best in their field. IBM's Accounts Payable department is like that. Hughes illustrated this by phrasing its vision as the following:

Our key goal is to be the
best Accounts Payable organization in the world.

To constantly keep employees sharply focused on this big, exciting vision, as his employees do their work, Hughes frequently asks this question: "Is your idea in alignment with us being the best Accounts Payable organization in the world?" Questions like this – repeatedly asked by the leader – definitely make sure everyone heads in the same direction.

In fact, IBM's Accounts Payable organization established its vision to win the coveted REACH Award given by the influential *CFO* magazine. And Accounts Payable did win this extremely prestigious award! *CFO* also wrote an article about the wonderful work at IBM. This article even included a photo of Hughes.

Goal-Setting to Achieve the Major Organizational Change

In the long run, people hit only what they aim at.
Therefore, they had better aim at something high.

– HENRY DAVID THOREAU

It is one thing to say you want to be the "best ... in the world" at anything – and it is quite another thing to put your money where your mouth is and actually do it. So, Hughes and his team drew up six key goals that – when achieved – would lead to the status of *"best Accounts Payable organization in the world."* They backed each goal with quantifiable measures and deadlines.

These six goals certainly aim high, and they serve as guideposts. They focus team members on spending every minute to be the *"best Accounts Payable organization in the world"* and avoid wasting time on work that does not align with the six goals.

Goal 1: Optimization of human resources via the 3 C's of control, challenge, and connection

Control: Each individual on the team controls his or her destiny at work and also outside of work. So, each individual can decide to settle only for the best.

Challenge: Each manager's goal is to give each employee work that challenges him/her – and eliminate transaction processing work that computers can do.

Connection: This is achieved through teamwork, the cherished Accounts Payable e-business shirt team members can own and wear, and also a connection to IBM's e-business goals.

Goal 2: Best practices

Team members learn about best practices used by other companies from conferences, business magazines, and books.

Goal 3: Controls

This certainly proves important, especially since Hughes' work-group disburses tens of billions of dollars annually.

Goal 4: Continuous learning

"I want people to always have a childlike sense of curiosity and to continue to grow through learning," explained Hughes. For example, one time Hughes taught his team to juggle "to emphasize we can learn anything if we want to and that learning is fun."

Goal 5: Electronic commerce

This major organizational change in vendor processing put IBM at the forefront of using the Internet and eliminating paperwork.

Goal 6: Teamwork

Teamwork to Accomplish Goals

IBM's massive change in vendor processing required massive collaboration by a large number of employees. Hughes cultivated teamwork in four main ways.

Teamwork Method 1: Mentoring

Hughes emphasized, "Experienced employees must help less experienced employees."

Teamwork Method 2: Celebrations – Every Accomplishment Is Celebrated as a Team

For instance, when the team's monstrous accomplishments became the cover story on *Electronic Commerce* magazine, only Hughes' picture appeared on the cover. No one else's photo graced the magazine's cover.

So, at the picnic – complete with disk jockey, karaoke, and plenty of food – to celebrate being the *Electronic Commerce* cover story, two cartoon caricaturists drew each employee's face onto a mock-up cover of *Electronic Commerce* magazine. As such, each team member walked away from the celebration with his or her own 8½ -inch x 11-inch caricature drawing to proudly display on a wall.

Here is another vibrant example of the team's celebrations. When Accounts Payable filed for a patent on one of its processes, it held a big, 150-employee celebration. It included big cookies with Einstein's picture on each big cookie!

The team did something similar when Accounts Payable won the high-status IBM Chairman's Award. For this celebration, each big cookie featured a picture of the chairman of IBM Corporation!

These are fun, playful ways to celebrate – while simultaneously reminding team members that they make ultra-special accomplishments together. Their achievements certainly appear worthy of the magnificent attention of an Einstein – or the chairman of this exceptional company.

Teamwork Method 3: Team Player of the Month

Each month, employees vote on which person will be Team Player of the Month. The winner's name, month and year are engraved on a trophy that the winner proudly displays on his or her desk for a month. The trophy is filled with candy to encourage people to stop by, talk, and share knowledge. Then, the trophy travels to the desk of the next month's Team Player of the Month.

Teamwork Method 4: Peer-to-Peer Gift Certificates

When an employee helps another team member who, as Hughes phrases it, "delights the fellow employee," the person gives the employee a certificate good for coffee and a bagel at either the IBM cafeteria or a gourmet coffee shop across the street.

Organizational Change Ingredient 2:
Successfully Coaching Employees during the Organizational Change

Anytime an organization makes changes, some employees will change at a slow pace. As such, a key responsibility of the leaders is to tackle this challenge and not let them get in the way of achieving the desired results.

Actions of Employees Who Resisted IBM's Organizational Change

Hughes' team focused keenly on *"monthly measurements"* that each employee was expected to attain. This clearly gave each employee specific targets to achieve with only limited room for excuses when a measurement was not met or exceeded. When someone did not live up to the expected monthly measurements, that employee was coached, hand-held, and encouraged.

What employee obstacles sometimes stood in the way of employees performing at their best? Hughes noticed three fears that slowed some employees' progress:

◆ Fear of the unknown
◆ Fear of job elimination
◆ Fear of major job changes

Effective Methods to Coach Employees Who Resisted IBM's Organizational Change

How did Hughes and his direct-reports handle these challenges? He explained the most effective methods encompassed education and communication. The communication component included memos sent to team members explaining the team's direction and progress.

Also, Hughes credits conversations as providing crucial help to employees to understand changes. Specifically, Hughes encouraged managers to walk around and chat with employees to help them understand how their work is in "alignment" with the organization's vision of being the *"best Accounts Payable organization in the world."*

Comparing "Old-Style" Employees with the Needed "New-Style" Employees

Every organization has employees who do perfectly fine – until the company implements major organizational change. Then, all of a sudden, those *old-style* employees no longer fully fit the bill of what is needed. Instead, so-called *new-style* employees – with certain vital talents – become absolutely necessary.

The following table shows Hughes' opinion on the comparison of old-style employees and new-style employees.

Old-Style Employees	New-Style Employees
Works in 1 department	Interdepartmental
Solo work	Teamwork
Likes receiving direction	Likes independence
Prefers to be told what to do	Prefers shared leadership

Focus: Seniority & experience	Focus: Updating & expanding skills
Follower	Leader
Did what s/he was told to do	Childlike sense of curiosity
Paper processor	Systems skills
Status quo	Focus on "Perfect World" way to do work
Controlled	In-control
Did job	Looking for challenge
Focus on doing own individual job	Focus on adding financial value

Hughes pointed out that the new-style employees' "curiosity" included the employees asking questions about how their work aligned with the organization's vision to become the *"best Accounts Payable organization in the world."* "Systems skills" especially included Internet and software knowledge and talent.

Transforming "Old-Style" Employees into "New-Style"

Hughes discovered the two best ways to transform the old-style employees into new-style employees was via "communications and conversations." The secret, Hughes revealed, resided in "getting people to understand how they control their reaction to everything, so they evolve into the new-style by themselves, rather than being told to do so by their manager."

This proves incredibly true. People are more likely to make changes when they decide on their own – without being ordered or told to change. Reason: A person feels great personal "ownership" when he or she comes up with a solution or way to improve. A person feels less enthused or motivated to improve when someone else tells the person to change.

Hiring Methods to Support the Major Organizational Change

In my workshops and book entitled, *Hire the Best – & Avoid the Rest*™, I continually recommend that managers pinpoint the make-or-break, most crucial talents needed to succeed in each job.*

---

*For information on Dr. Mercer's *Hire the Best – & Avoid the Rest*™ book, tests, tool kits and workshops, you can refer to the Materials You Can Order section in the back of this book.

Then, the manager must evaluate each candidate on how well the candidate has – or does not have – these absolutely crucial talents.

For example, Hughes delves into hiring people with a keen emphasis on their attitudes. Specifically, in three to five interviews with different managers, applicants are interviewed to uncover if they have the following attributes:

1. Positive attitude
2. Team player
3. Desire to share knowledge
4. Solid communications skills to share knowledge
5. Technical competence

Organizational Change Ingredient 3: Successfully Managing Yourself during the Organizational Change

A crucial fact of business life is this: *Employees consider the executives who lead them to be role models.* People really do, in many ways, follow the leader. As such, leaders need to be excellent role models to everyone around them. From my experience as a management consultant and business psychologist, I find it is incredibly important for leaders to exude optimism, upbeat attitudes, use uplifting phrases, and bring to the organization an achievement-oriented focus. *

Optimism Helped This Executive Succeed in Implementing Major Organizational Change

"I view myself as very optimistic in every situation," explained Hughes. "I can find the positive in everything."

This also extends to Hughes role modeling how to dig up solutions where most people would not bother. For example, Hughes takes his three sons to basketball games. Near the end of every game

---

*For information on this, you may find it useful to refer to Dr. Mercer's books, audio-books, speeches and seminars on (1) *How Winners Do it: High Impact People Skills for Your Career Success* and also (2) *Spontaneous Optimism*™: *Proven Strategies for Health, Prosperity & Happiness.* For details, you can look at the Materials You Can Order section in the back of this book.

– when the audience is leaving because the game seems out of reach – Hughes asks his kids what the losing team needs to do so it can win. He emphasized, "I want my kids to look for the opportunity in every situation. Thinking through the tough situations as practice prepares you better to handle all situations." This is a great way to teach people – children or adult co-workers – to focus on how to improve, regardless of previous failures or challenges.

Attitudes of This Executive that Help Him Succeed

Optimistic, highly successful people hold certain winning attitudes they carry into everything they do. Hughes considers these to be his most important attitudes.

Attitude 1: Never give up

Hughes emphasized, "Up to the last second, I never give up."

Attitude 2: "Sense that I control everything that happens"

Attitude 3: Find the positive in everything

Attitude 4: Continuous learning

Attitude 5: Always use positive visualizations

Hughes does this by imagining how to respond successfully in various situations he knows he will face. Then, when he is in one of the situations, he already has mentally practiced how to handle it effectively. Doing so greatly boosts confidence and the likelihood of a successful outcome.

Attitude 6: Persistence

All-in-all, Hughes' upbeat attitudes remind me of an insight made by Theodore Roosevelt:

> *The credit belongs to the person who is actually in the arena, who strives valiantly; who knows the great enthusiasms, the great devotions, and spends himself in a worthy cause; who at the best, knows the triumph of high achievement; and who, at the worst, if he fails, at least fails while daring·greatly, so that his place shall never be with those cold and timid souls who know neither victory nor defeat.*

Phrases This Executive Says to Keep Focused & Optimistic

Great role models and highly successful leaders tend to find certain phrases and words keep them aligned with goals they aim to accomplish. Also, their favorite comments consistently convey

to others how they, too, can succeed. Hughes has certain favorites.
Phrase: *"Once you're ripe, you rot."*
This phrase keeps him focused on "continuous learning and growing."
Phrase: *"I want to" versus "I need to"*
When Hughes hears someone say, "I *need* to do" something, he points out, "No, you *want* to." This encourages Hughes and those around him to focus on achieving their goals, rather than bending at what other people expect of them or what they feel forced to do.
Phrase: *"If you only see possible roadblocks, then you've taken your eyes off your real objective."*
In fact, a poster with a phrase like this adorns Hughes' office wall.
Word He Avoids: *"Not"*
For example, in coaching, Hughes never says, "Do *not* strike out." Instead, he says, "Get a hit!" Reason: It proves vastly more useful to suggest what a person should do, rather than what the person should not do.

How This Executive Focuses Team Members on Solutions – Not Problems

A key behavior of optimists and highly successful leaders is they focus on solutions. In contrast, pessimists and under-achieving people tend to focus on problems. As such, it proves crucial for Hughes to focus on solutions and, in doing so, provide a solution-focused role model for his team members.

How does he do this? "I always focus people on the *Perfect World*. For instance, I often ask a person, 'If you ran your own business, how would you do this?' This forces team members to dwell on the best solution, rather than a solution that mainly gets by."

Favorite Story of This Executive

A person's favorite story reveals a great deal about what he or she considers deeply important. Hughes summarized his favorite story as follows:

The Little Train That Could

In this classic story, a little train went on an incredible journey. At one point, it needed to travel up a steep hill, which proved extremely difficult. Throughout this ordeal, the Little Train kept saying, "I think I can! I think I can!!" And, eventually the Little Train did reach its destination.

What makes *The Little Train That Could* such a significant story to Hughes? For him, the story illustrates the importance of persistence. Or, as he puts it, "Anybody can do anything if they put their mind to it."

Also, when Hughes told me his favorite story, he noticeably emphasized the little train used the word "think" – "I *think* I can! I *think* I can!!" This is intriguing. Reason: The placard displayed on the desk of IBM's founder, Thomas Watson, Sr., contained only one word – "THINK." As such, Hughes' favorite story – *The Little Train That Could* – complements the IBM founder's "THINK" motto.

Interestingly, *The Little Train That Could* is an exceptionally popular story among high-achievers. How do I know this? The story came up many times in research I did to develop a pre-employment test. To decide what test questions to ask applicants, I started by asking a long series of questions to groups of high-achievers and underachievers in certain occupations. From their answers, I pinpointed which test questions to use in the final pre-employment test – as well as discovering how high-achievers' answers differ from underachievers' answers.

One question in the test development asked about the person's favorite story. The most frequently cited story among the high-achievers was *The Little Train That Could.* No underachievers chose that story! This classic story conveys universal truths about (A) the value of persistence, (B) focusing on achievement, and (C) how someone can succeed despite all odds.

This makes it all the more interesting that Hughes chose *The Little Train That Could* as his favorite story. In doing so, Hughes joins the long list of high-achievers who love and benefit from this story and the powerful message it delivers.

This Executive's Role Models – & Lesson Learned from Each One

People do not exist in a vacuum. Extraordinary people find role models who, directly and indirectly, teach them important life-long lessons. Putting these lessons into action profoundly influences a person's level of success. Hughes has three main role models who powerfully influenced him.

Role Model 1: Parents and wife. *Lesson Learned:* "You can do whatever you put your mind to."

Role Model 2: High school football coach. *Lesson Learned:* "He helped me get into college through football, even though my grades and SAT scores were not very good. He taught me persistence and to go after what I wanted."

Role Model 3: Father of elementary school friend. *Lesson Learned:* "He always had a positive outlook on everything and a kind word for everyone – and he was an accountant. I respected him, and because of him I got into an accounting career."

10

VF CORPORATION
Unleashing Supply Chain Riches

VF Corporation's Vision:
Our key goal is to be the
world's largest supplier of fashionable apparel for consumers.

You probably have worn clothing manufactured by VF Corporation – and perhaps you never realized it. VF Corporation has the largest market share in the U.S. for jeans, including hugely popular brand names, such as
- Wrangler
- Lee
- Rustler
- Hero (big sellers in Wal-Mart and K-Mart)

The company also produces other apparel, including the famous Jantzen swimwear line. It does well over $5-billion in sales and has about 75,000 employees.

Tom Payne, vice president, business process executive/supply chain, led the company's dramatic improvement of its supply chain management. This produced a profitable array of improvements in VF's business.

VF Corporation's Major Organizational Change

A large organizational change for VF Corporation was its development of a sophisticated, highly successful supply chain management system.

Here is a little history of VF.

Problem: VF used to be a holding company of about 20 companies or business units. Using a hands-off management approach, VF let each of these companies operate as it pleased.

Unfortunately, this led to a large amount of duplication of efforts – with each of the companies planning, sourcing materials, manufacturing and distributing as it saw fit. Obviously, some companies did these activities better than others. Plus, some companies provided what customers wanted better than others. And – by not taking advantage of economies of scale, profits fell through the cracks, like water through sand.

Solution: VF made the strategic decision to simultaneously (A) vastly improve how it helped its customers while (B) decreasing costs. To do this, VF consolidated its approximately 20 companies (each with multiple brands) into six coalition companies. This included VF creating "shared services" groups to service different supply chains and product companies across VF. Specifically, VF consolidated around the supply chains for the six product groups:

1. Workwear
2. Jeanswear
3. Knitwear
4. Playwear
5. Intimate female apparel
6. International

Now, a single supply chain management system delivers the four crucial ingredients needed by a successful apparel company:

Forecasting customer needs & materials management	$\rightarrow$	Planning production	$\rightarrow$	Sourcing manufacturing	$\rightarrow$	Distributing to retail stores

How Was This Change Crucial to VF's Success & Growth?

This consolidated supply chain management system proved vital to VF's business in three main ways. First, it reduced a lot of costs throughout the entire supply chain. VF reinvests part of the saved money in marketing. Second, the change eliminated duplication. Now, the corporation has only six supply chains for all of VF, instead of the approximately 20 that VF previously had; this produced huge economies of scale.

Third, the vastly improved supply chain takes a more consumer-oriented approach to business. In fact Robert K. Shearer, VF's vice president of finance and chief financial officer, referred to this as *"Consumerizing" the Corporation – Restructuring Business around Customer & Consumer Needs.*

Steps Used to Implement This Organizational Change

Over a number of years, the total cost of VF's supply chain makeover is about $200-million. It is proving to be worth every penny. The change consisted of four main steps.

Step 1. Reengineered 4 key processes used throughout VF

These processes were

◆ Supply chain process

◆ Sales chain process (sales, order processing, etc.)

◆ Product and service development chain

◆ Financial infrastructure chain

Step 2. Installed new information technology (IT) hardware and software systems

This IT enhancement supported the reengineered processes done in Step 1, above.

Step 3. Implemented Corporate "Shared Services Concept"

This marked the beginning of using "world-class" best practice processes across all six business units. These shared services include key transaction processing business functions, in areas such as

◆ Accounts Payable

◆ Accounts Receivable

◆ Finance/General Ledger

◆ Global Outsourcing

◆ Human Resources

◆ IT

◆ Payroll

Step 4. Training

VF provided training to support the best practices and shared systems throughout the corporation.

Measurable Improvements Produced by the Organizational Change

The company will reap four huge improvements from consolidating and vastly upgrading its supply chain management system. These improvements are summarized in Diagram 1.

Measurable Improvement 1: Reduce supply chain costs about $200-million/year

Here is a very important point: The total cost for VF's supply chain reengineering totals about $200-million. Yet, VF plans to reap $200-million each year – *year after year* – from its $200-million investment. That provides a fabulous return-on-investment from this huge undertaking.

Measurable Improvement 2: Grow sales 10%/year

Measurable Improvement 3: Reduce inventory 40%

Much of this improvement will result from doing more just-in-time manufacturing based on specific customer demands for VF apparel.

Measurable Improvement 4: Decrease cycle time 40%

This 40% reduction in cycle time was produced in three key chains: Sales chain, supply chain, and product and service development chain.

Diagram 1. **Results of VF Corporation's Absolutely Fabulous Organizational Change**

Category	Improvement
Supply chain costs	$200-million/year less
Sales	10% increase
Inventory	40% reduction
Cycle time	40% decrease

Unmeasurable Improvements

Payne found the vastly improved supply chain management system also produced three valuable, although unmeasurable, results.

Qualitative Improvement 1: "Teamwork on a monstrous scale"

This major organizational change transformed VF from an "Every tub on its own bottom" culture to a *"Shared Services"* culture, according to Payne.

Qualitative Improvement 2: "Best Practices Mentality"

Payne observed the change catalyzed a search for excellence mentality in all employees from the top of the organization to the lowest level of employees.

Qualitative Improvement 3: Huge benefits from training

The training supported the best practices and shared systems used throughout the corporation. The training made sure VF employees obtained the knowledge and skills needed to do their jobs more efficiently and productively.

Organizational Change Ingredient 1:
Successfully Leading the Organizational Change

As a management consultant and business psychologist, when I advise executives about how to lead organizational change, my advice always includes this insight: The only organizational change that produces the desired results is change that provides a logical advancement of the company's culture and vision. Also, leaders insure their organizational change plans get turned into reality through well-organized goal-setting carried out using enthusiastic teamwork. With this in mind, let's examine how Payne and his team led major organizational change at VF Corporation.

VF Corporation's Corporate Culture

I continually find the best way to determine a company's culture is to uncover the story the company's employees know – and retell. This story invariably contains, in a nutshell, the essence of the company's culture.

Since VF Corporation previously acted somewhat like a conglomerate or holding company, with about 20 separate companies, each company within VF had its own story.

However, Payne told me the following story that many VF employees know:

Creating the World's Best Western-Style Jeans

VF decided it would manufacture the best Western-style jeans in the entire world. To do this, VF did in-depth research. It tore apart and analyzed jeans made by other manufacturers to find out what they did well – and what the other apparel companies did poorly.

Also, VF interviewed real cowboys. After all, who would know better than actual cowboys about what really is needed in "Western-style" jeans?

The cowboys gave VF first-hand insight into which features prove absolutely crucial in Western style jeans. This included (A) more room in the seat and thighs – to make it more comfortable to ride horses, (B) raised pockets – so they would not sit in the saddle on their billfolds and cans of chewing tobacco, plus (C) flare to fit over cowboy boots.

The bottom line result: VF jeans became the best-selling jeans among members of the Professional Rodeo Cowboy Association (PRCA). Importantly, by the way, PRCA has a huge membership – which translates into potential buyers of VF jeans. Also, PRCA is influential in how customers decide which jeans to buy. After all, who would be better for prospective customers to observe to see which Western-style jean to wear than actual cowboys?

Culture – or Main Focus – of VF

Payne explained the story illustrates three vital elements of VF's corporate culture:

Focus 1: Extremely consumer-oriented
Focus 2: Dominate sales to VF's target audience (consumers)
Focus 3: Be-the-best quality focus

Big, Exciting Vision of VF Corporation

Outstanding companies always live by a *vision* that the company will accomplish extraordinary goals on a grand scale. Since people and companies tend to achieve only what they aim for, having a big, exciting vision focuses a company on creating huge business success. Also, importantly, I repeatedly notice effective organizational change helps a company move closer to achieving its big, exciting vision.

Payne mentioned VF's vision is the following:

Our key goal is to be the
world's largest supplier of fashionable apparel for consumers.

This vision certainly is big and exciting – *"world's largest."* Also, Payne pointed out VF's vision sheds light on the company's approach to *"Consumerization."* This entails VF being *right* in three ways, specifically, having the *right*

 ◆ *products* — apparel customers deeply want to buy
 ◆ *place* – 	apparel in retail stores that appeal to consumers of VF clothes
 ◆ *time* – 	delivering the right products to the right retail stores at the time customers want to buy VF apparel

Ways the Organizational Change Fits into VF's Vision

The major organizational change makes it possible – and extremely likely – that VF will advance toward its vision in four ways. First, the change makes VF vastly more efficient by consolidating through multiple *sharing* approaches, namely, sharing (A) services, (B) capabilities, (C) supply chains, and (D) IT hardware and software. Second, the change drove out redundant costs. Third, this major organizational change enables VF to be the low-cost producer. Fourth, it saved the company money which now can be put into VF understanding and supplying consumer needs.

Goal-Setting to Accomplish the Company's Major Organizational Change

VF established corporate-wide *"Process Leaders"* for the three main shared chains, specifically, (A) supply chain, (B) sales chain, and (C) product and service development chain.

These Process Leaders assure the company as a whole puts into action best practices across the entire company. In contrast, Payne remarked, previously each of VF's 20 or so business units would "do its own thing."

Payne set two key goals for himself as the executive in charge of this major organizational change.

Goal 1: Reduce supply chain costs by $200-million/year within 3 years.
Goal 2: Reduce inventories 40% within 2 years.

Teamwork to Accomplish Goals

To implement its major organizational change – development of a sophisticated, very successful supply chain management system – VF used huge amounts of teamwork and interdepartmental collaboration. Four methods proved highly effective:

Teamwork Method 1: Common location

VF moved all 60 employees who worked on the supply chain reengineering team into one building at its corporate headquarters.

Teamwork Method 2: Full-time participation

All 60 employees worked full-time on this massive project.

Teamwork Method 3: Organized all reengineering employees into teams

The 60 reengineering employees were divided into five main teams:

- Forecasting & Planning Team
- Product Development Team
- Retail Sales Team
- Distribution Team
- Manufacturing Team

Teamwork Method 4: Special financial incentives

All 60 employees earned financial incentives based on achieving objectives by predetermined deadlines.

Organizational Change Ingredient 2:
Successfully Handling Employee Problems during the Organizational Change

One of the biggest roadblocks to successfully implementing organizational change is resistance and objections from employees. As such, organizational change endeavors always need to include handling employee problems. Payne paid special attention to handling employee resistance at VF Corporation so the major organizational change would proceed as planned.

Actions of Employees Who Resisted – or Undermined – VF's Major Organizational Change

The resistance took two forms: (A) body language from some employees and also (B) people, as Payne put it, "giving 1,000 reasons why something would not work – but not one reason about how to make it work."

Resistance arose in two groups. First, some IT managers disagreed with the notion of shared, common systems. To handle such resistance, VF

- reassigned certain people
- changed priorities for IT projects to put the reengineering on the front burner

Second, some executives mouthed public commitment – but expressed private reservation about the proceedings. Payne said they felt threatened with VF moving from a fairly hands-off holding company to a coordinated operating company.

Importantly, Payne spent 10 - 20% of his time handing the resistance. This is a large time and energy commitment by a high-level executive. However, if he did not effectively address and overcome the resistance, it would have posed serious consequences for the development of VF's new, highly sophisticated supply chain management system.

Effective Methods to Handle Employees Who Resisted the Organizational Change

Payne found four methods particularly useful in handling employees' resistance and roadblocks.

Method 1: Continuous Message from the Chief Executive Officer
The CEO repeatedly conveyed the high-level importance of the new supply chain management system. He continually talked about how it was crucial to VF's growth to change from a hands-off holding company to a consolidated operating company. The CEO also stressed how VF must succeed in the major supply chain project to boost the company's prospects and profits.

Method 2: Consensus Building
"That's the CEOs style" – to ask everyone for input, rather than act in a highly directive manner, according to Payne.

Method 3: "War of Attrition"
"We wore everyone down until they accepted that we would make these changes," explained Payne.

Method 4: Re-Directed IS
Payne got VF's approximately 500 IT employees responsible for corporate-wide IT. This contrasts sharply with what VF did before, when each IT employee was responsible only to one of VF Corporation's 20 or so business units.

Comparing VF's "Old-Style" Employees with Its Needed "New-Style" Employees

Employees who did fine on-the-job before a major organizational change sometimes do not do well after the change is implemented. I refer to these as "old-style" and "new-style" employees, respectively. The ability of a leader to identify traits needed in "new-style" employees – and help transform "old-style" employees into "new-style" employees – proves crucial for successful organizational change. The following table shows Payne's comparisons of the two types of employees at VF.

Old-Style Employees	New-Style Employees
Works in 1 department	Interdepartmental
Solo work	Teamwork
Likes receiving direction	Likes independence
Prefers to be told what to do	Prefers shared leadership
Focus: Seniority & experience	Focus: Updating & expanding skills
Loyal to 1 business unit	Loyal to entire corporation

Transforming "Old-Style" Employees into "New-Style" Employees

VF Corporation found three methods worked quite well in transforming the company's "old-style" employees into its needed "new-style" employees.

Transformation Method 1: Training

Payne emphasized that training played "a big part in the project's ultimate success."

Transformation Method 2: Redesigned jobs

In the white-collar workforce, VF redesigned jobs to focus employees on start-to-finish processes. This entailed developing jobs that are

◆ more process-oriented for the entire company

◆ less oriented toward only one department's work

Transformation Method 3: Skill-based compensation

White-collar employees' skill-based pay rewarded employees for skills they bring to the corporate-wide processes they work on.

Recommendations to Employees Working in Companies Undergoing Organizational Change

With numerous companies making major changes, a question on many employees' minds is the following: "How do I succeed and come out ahead during and after the organizational change?" I cannot imagine anyone better to ask than an executive who led major organizational change, such as Tom Payne at VF Corporation. Here are Payne's recommendations to employees:

Tip 1: "Recognize there is a burning business need to change"

Tip 2: Figure out specifically what you need to do to serve customers

Tip 3: List skills you can develop to better serve the company's customers

Doing so helps fulfill the company's vision. For example, at VF, developing certain skills can help the company in its vision: *Our key goal is to be the world's largest supplier of fashionable apparel for consumers.* Also, such skills could avail the employee to earn skill-based pay for possessing crucial skills.

Tip 4: "If you don't like this, get off the train."

I believe this recommendation proves quite important. If all an employee wants to do is bellyache or complain, then the employee truly is better off getting a job elsewhere. Importantly, in my seminars and book on *Hire the Best – & Avoid the Rest™*, I always point out, "Past behavior is the best predictor of future behavior."*

If a company hears an applicant complaining about his or her previous employer or boss, then that company should keep this in mind: That applicant, if hired, very likely will find reasons to complain and moan on his or her new job. As such, it is wise to avoid putting complainers on the payroll. *

Organizational Change Ingredient 3:
Successfully Managing Yourself during the Organizational Change

From my consulting to companies, I repeatedly observe that the leader in charge of implementing change sets the tone for all the employees involved in the change endeavors. Traits of highly successful leaders include the following:

♦ optimism in actions, attitudes, and words
♦ history of developing powerful career talents starting at an early age

As such, it proves instructive to see how Payne's optimism and history helped him succeed in implementing a major, highly profitable organizational change at VF Corporation.

Optimism Helped This Executive Succeed in Implementing Major Organizational Change

My research on highly successful people led to the conclusion that they almost invariably are highly optimistic people.*

They display a confident, "Can-Do" approach to their work. They focus on solutions, not problems – and get employees on-board by providing a great role model for them.

"Readers can find out more about Dr. Mercer's pre-employment tests, seminars and book on *Hire the Best – & Avoid the Rest™* by referring to the Materials You Can Order section in the back of this book

Payne certainly is an optimist. Indeed, he stated,

Optimism is essential. You can't do major change without it. You've got to focus on solutions and opportunities – and not focus on rocks in the road. It's valuable to have people who can identify every rock – problem – in the road. But, you can't let them make decisions about whether to go down that road.

After all, a rock-pointer never will see the reward for taking the risk.

Attitudes That Greatly Help This Executive

Payne holds four key attitudes near and dear. They help him in his leadership role.

Attitude 1: Optimism

Attitude 2: Trustful of people

He shows this attitude by delegating and coaching on-the-job. "Doing this means you have to trust people. You can't be a control freak."

Attitude 3: "Networking gets things done"

Payne finds networking across the organization incredibly valuable and essential. As he put it, "Networking gets things done. You can't be an island."

Attitude 4: Evaluate risks and rewards

He combines facts and his gut feelings to determine if a project or method is worth pursuing.

Phrase This Executive Says to Keep Focused & Optimistic

He particularly likes using the phrase "So what?" Here is how Payne does it:

When someone points out a potential problem, I ask, "So what? So what if that happens?"

In a lot of cases, it's no big deal, so you just pick yourself up – and get yourself going. Saying "So what?" keeps things in perspective.

---

*You may benefit from Dr. Mercer's tool kits, books, speeches and seminars on (1) *How Winners Do it: High Impact People Skills for Your Career Success* and also (2) *Spontaneous Optimism*[TM]: *Proven Strategies for Health, Prosperity & Happiness.* For details, you can look in the Materials You Can Order section in the back of this book.

How This Executive Gets Employees to Focus on Solutions – Not Problems

Optimists overwhelmingly focus on solutions. Pessimists love focusing on problems and complaining. As a leader, Payne needs to make sure employees focus on solutions. He uses three methods.

Method 1: "Stay upbeat. Don't let people see you sweat."
Method 2: "Absolutely refuse to be taken aback by anything."
Method 3: Don't let people dwell on a problem

When a person points out a problem to Payne, he does not dwell on the problem. Instead, Payne asks,

♦ "What would you need to solve this problem?"
♦ "What would you need to do to remove those problems?"

This Executive's Favorite Story

One research method I used to devise pre-employment tests is to do the following: (A) create a list of questions, (B) use the questions to interview successful and unsuccessful employees in specific jobs, (C) type interview transcripts, and then (D) identify how successful employees answered differently than unsuccessful employees. From this, I chose good test questions, and developed a scoring method. Then, I did many other test-development and "validation" research steps. Companies use my tests to help them hire successful employees – and avoid hiring underachievers.*

I found one powerful question is to ask for a person's favorite story. High-achievers always cherish stories conveying themes of success and accomplishment.

Payne's favorite stories are in two books by Ayn Rand. She was a great novelist and libertarian philosopher. Her two books Payne found most influential were (A) *Atlas Shrugged* and (B) *The Fountainhead*. What theme or message from Ayn Rand's books influenced Payne the most?

He found it most powerfully significant that both books "tell stories about heroes." Payne explained these heroes

♦ *"are very self-reliant"*
♦ *"develop competency and skill in their endeavors"*

---

*Information on how you can use Dr. Mercer's pre-employment tests, workshops, book, and *Hire the Best – & Avoid the Rest*™ methods is available in the Materials You Can Order section in the back of this book.

◆ *"believe in the power of the individual to control his or her own destiny"*

◆ *"overcome all obstacles thrown in their paths"*

This Executive's Role Models – & Lesson Learned from Each One

Every person learns useful lessons as he or she goes through life. As a business psychologist who consults to many companies, I discovered that highly successful people go through life finding superb role models. The role models' words and actions impart lessons. These lessons help the person in personal and career endeavors. Payne considers three people as his chief role models.

Role Model 1: Ayn Rand, novelist and philosopher. *Lesson Learned:* Self-reliance.

Role Model 2: Retired president of Jeanswear Company (part of VF Corporation). *Lesson Learned:* "Always appear optimistic and cheerful. He was the best cheerleader possible. Through his cheerful personality, he got everyone to work together – even when they may not have wanted to."

Role Model 3: Payne's boss at Blue Bell (a company bought by VF). *Lesson Learned:* "He taught people to define problems in such a way that the problem could be solved."

Reflections on What This Executive Accomplished

In looking back on the major organizational change he led – development of a sophisticated, highly successful supply chain management system – Payne feels justly proud. He commented his primary objective now is the following:

> *Take all the work we've done in best practices to make VF Corporation the best, predominant supply chain in the entire apparel industry. Now, VF ought to be able to dominate all the businesses we're in. The best practices we've put into place will give our entire company a huge competitive advantage.*

11

INTUIT

Creating A Business
on the Internet

Intuit's *Vision*:
*Our key goal is to
revolutionize the way people do financial work.*

When millions of people think about computerized methods to handle their financial life, they immediately think of one company: Intuit.

Intuit is famous for electronic finance, especially its *Quicken* software – such as *QuickBooks* and *TurboTax* – that makes finance and accounting easy for people to do.

Importantly, Intuit decided to jump into a potentially huge market by opening up a consumer finance business on the Internet. Thus was born the business unit headed by Brooks Fisher, vice president and general manager of Intuit's Consumer Internet business. Click onto this, and you enter the world of consumer finance in three main arenas: personal finance, mortgages, and insurance.

Extremely notable is that Fisher and his team created Intuit's Internet business using hyper-speed. It used the method Fisher excitedly described as *"Just run and keep running."* This rapid implementation played a huge and decisive role in Intuit successfully launching its Internet business.

Intuit's Major Organizational Change

The major organizational change for Intuit was starting a new business, distribution and service mode to consumers over the

Internet. In an incredibly short time, Intuit assembled – both from scratch and acquisitions – three consumer finance businesses over the Internet:
1. *Personal finance via Quicken.com*
   This includes a wealth of financial market data, portfolio tools, business news, plus retirement planning services.
2. *Mortgages via QuickenMortgage*
   Here, a person can study mortgage rates and apply over the Internet.
3. *Insurance via QuickenInsuremarket*
   With this, a consumer can find the right insurance and sign-up on the Internet.

Creating this online business is a major shift for Intuit as a company. Previously, Intuit based its success on its superb software that people bought in traditional ways, such as stores, mail, and "800" order-taking numbers.

But, the company saw a gigantic opportunity to offer an array of consumer finance services over the Internet. It also saw that early entrants into an Internet business inherently developed an advantage in terms of hooking in customers and building the business rather quickly. This is the opportunity Intuit rushed after by creating its consumer Internet business unit. Intuit brought in Brooks Fisher to lead the charge into finding treasures for Intuit in the online business world.

How Was This Change Crucial to Intuit's Success & Survival?

Fisher explained Intuit's running start into doing business on the Internet was
quite critical, because if we didn't accomplish this, the company could die. The reason is the possibly stalled prospects for the future of the desktop software industry. If the company couldn't figure out a way to embrace the Internet, then it would miss the most important business platform trend ever.

Steps Intuit Used to Implement This Crucial Organizational Change

Fisher and his team used five main steps to get Intuit's Internet business up and running.

Step 1: "Skin in the Game"
This is Fisher's phrase meaning "you bet your own money." Intuit invested heavily and placed dates on what it needed to accomplish.
Fisher started by telling the CEO that Intuit had "90 days to invest in the new distribution strategy." For example, Intuit invested $40 million into Excite! – an Internet portal – for a 20% interest. In doing this, Intuit became the finance channel for Excite! Intuit then set a very difficult deadline to establish the channel. This forced Intuit to launch a personal finance channel in the amazingly short timeframe of only three-and-a-half months. Without this incredible time crunch, Intuit probably would have taken a year!

Step 2: Make a Big & Clear Organizational Decision
Intuit closed down a company in Pittsburgh that it acquired. Then, Intuit moved that company's key 17-person engineering team west to Intuit headquarters. This engineering team became the backbone of Intuit's Internet business.

Step 3: Separateness
The third step involved setting up a personal finance team separate from Intuit's Quicken team. This included separate profit-&-loss statements, as well as a separate Internet business
♦   engineering team
♦   product management team
Fisher emphasized, "The reason for this separateness was so we could have flexibility to go after *new* models of business and *new* customers." Also, Intuit's Internet business had very different work to do than Intuit's desktop software business, so separateness made even more sense.

Step 4: Senior Management Support
Intuit's top executives publicly showed their powerful support for the new Internet business. They did this through
♦   Management meetings
♦   Company meetings
♦   Communication meetings of all Intuit employees
♦   Budget
Communication meetings at Intuit, typically held monthly, include all employees. These meetings provided a forum for the top executives to discuss and show enthusiasm for the new Internet business.

As for the budget, this required hard decisions the top brass needed to make – and make quickly. These included decisions to
- invest in the new Internet business
- fund Internet acquisitions and investments

Importantly, all the executives' expressions of support would not have really meant anything tangible, unless the top executives budgeted money to kick-start the new Internet business.

Step 5: "Lead by Example"

Fisher highlighted the following:

I was just looking for momentum. Just run and keep running. I thought it was very important to win a little bit very quickly. When you do fundamentally new stuff, it's crucial to show progress right away. We definitely couldn't afford much time to get anything done.

And what did the Internet business accomplish at hyper-speed? Here are four examples:

1. Launched a competitive personal finance channel in only about three months, although everyone else said it would take one full year
2. Did a major deal fast – in just three months
3. Landed a new ad contract – immediately upon starting the Internet business
4. Made a distribution deal ultra-fast with Excite!

Fisher's speed and momentum approach — his *"Just run and keep running"* – sharply differed from the usual business method of careful analysis and perfection before executing a new product. Employees in the Internet business thrived on such challenges. In retrospect, Fisher summarized the employees' accomplishments by stating, "The employees did an awesome job."

Measurable Improvements Produced by the Organizational Change

Intuit did an amazing business feat extremely well. Just look at these incredible results (also, see Diagram 1):
- Stock in Intuit soared from $20 to $100 in only two years
- Grew the Internet business from zero to over $50 million in only 18 months; importantly, all this money came from sources Intuit never had before
- Flew from zero to #1 or #2 in "reach" (audience numbers) for a personal finance Internet channel in only 6 months

- Dashed from zero to #1 in online mortgage origination in just 15 months
- Rushed from zero to absolute technology and product leadership in online auto insurance sales
- Surge in page views of Quicken.com from 15 million to 160 million in just 2 years

Diagram 1. **Results of Intuit's Absolutely Fabulous Organizational Change**

Category	Improvement	Before	After
Stock price	500% in 2 years	$20	$100
Intuit's Internet business	$50-million	Zero	$50-million
Audience numbers ("reach") for personnel finance Internet channel	#1 or #2 in 6 months	N/A	#1 or #2
Page views of Quicken.com	1,067% increase in 2 years	15-million	160-million

Unmeasurable or Qualitative Improvements

Fisher stated the start-up and quick development of Intuit's Internet business resulted in three key qualitative improvements.

Qualitative Improvement 1: Whole Company Change

Fisher went from being the only executive talking about what Intuit was doing on the Internet to one of 20 executives talking – and enthused – about the Internet business.

Qualitative Improvement 2: New Power from Older Assets

Intuit's Internet business injected power into Intuit's previous assets in two ways. First, the company discovered connectivity can reinvigorate Intuit's older software business. Example: *QuickBooks* connected to some service delivery providers became a new service, for instance, linking accounting to payroll. Second, Intuit now can sell new services to its old customer base. For instance, (A) postage can be sold over the Internet to *QuickBooks* users and (B) 401-K and other retirement planning advice could be marketed to *Quicken* users.

Qualitative Improvement 3: Morale Improved

Fisher explained the phenomenon of Intuit's Internet business success boosted morale for all Intuit employees:

When you have a successful company like Intuit, with a history of success – and then you make a huge change – it can feel like everything you did feels like a failure. With the success of the Internet business – including dollars-and-cents measures – everyone in the company felt better. The company felt exciting again in a new way.

Organizational Change Ingredient 1: Successfully Leading the Organizational Change

When I consult to organizations, I continually emphasize that organizational changes which produce the desired results always fit in with the company's

◆ culture
◆ vision

This is necessary but not sufficient. Also, the plans for the organizational change only turn into reality through very organized goal-setting and exciting teamwork. As such, it proves quite instructive to see how Fisher and his team led Intuit's major organizational change.

Intuit's Corporate Culture

I devised a way to uncover an organization's culture: Discover the story employees all know and tell to other employees. In fact, hearing the company's signature story is a sort of right-of-passage for new employees. Hearing the story implicitly tells a new employee the actions, values and priorities the organization expects. Fisher told me Intuit's signature story is the following:

"Follow Me Home"

Scott Cook, founder of Intuit, was so focused on understanding and fulfilling the customers' needs that he invented "Follow Me Home." He would go to a store where Intuit's software was being sold. Then, while a customer was buying Intuit software, he would ask if he could follow the customer home. At the home, he would watch how the customer installed and used the software.

Given Intuit's story, what is the company's culture – or main focus? Fisher says the story conveys the company's culture which is *"The customer always is first."* And, as Fisher puts it, *"That's how you win."*

Links between Intuit's Culture & Its Major Organizational Change

Fisher noted Intuit's culture and the major change of launching its Internet business flow together quite well in two ways. First, "The Internet is the best medium ever invented for *Follow Me Home.* The great thing about the Internet is it gives Intuit instant feedback about what and how customers use our services."

Second, Fisher found the Internet business assured Intuit "retained consumer finance leadership by providing customers with the best experience available for online buying of insurance, mortgages, and personal finance services."

Big, Exciting Vision of Intuit

I keep finding that amazingly successful companies have a vision of a big, exciting future. I attribute much of Intuit's success to having an extremely compelling vision, which Fisher summed up as the following:

Our key goal is to
revolutionize the way people do financial work.

Note: After telling me Intuit's vision, Fisher added, "And I do mean *revolutionize!*"

This certainly is a big, exciting vision. And, importantly, Intuit's major organizational change of starting an Internet business rapidly advances Intuit's vision to *"revolutionize the way people do financial work."*

Goal-Setting to Accomplish Intuit's Major Organizational Change

Fisher insisted all goals (A) be measurable – especially in terms of revenue – and (B) have deadlines. This way people *"own revenue,"* he explained, because they must meet or exceed specific dollars-and-cents targets. For example, when Fisher started Intuit's Internet business he set four goals.

Goal 1: Lead personal finance online, measured by "reach" (audience numbers) and page views in 12 months. *Status of Goal 1:* Accomplished! Note: Fisher considered this goal crucial in a number of respects. He said, "We will have failed if we're not in the top 20 Internet sites in "reach" and page-views within one year."

Goal 2: Launch online mortgage business so we have live

transactions within 6 months. *Status of Goal 2:* Accomplished!

Goal 3: Launch online auto insurance business to have live transactions within 1 year. *Status of Goal 3:* Accomplished!

Goal 4: Sell advertising to the tune of $15 million during the first year. *Status of Goal 4:* Accomplished!

Teamwork to Accomplish Goals

Fisher found three teamwork methods worked particularly well.

Teamwork Method 1: "The buck stopped here at the beginning of our Internet business."

When Intuit started the business, Fisher himself made decisions quickly when people did not know what to do or if there was disagreement. This assured progress in the critical start-up phase of the new business.

Teamwork Method 2: Changed organization frequently

This enabled Fisher to find better decision paths and cooperation.

Teamwork Method 3: Management training & a lot of coaching

For instance, it proved very useful for Fisher to give talks about "how this business could and should work." His talks and coaching made sure everyone knew what direction to go in and stayed on course.

Organizational Change Ingredient 2:
Successfully Handling Employee Problems during the Organizational Change

Every organizational change prompts some employees to feel uncomfortable and queasy. All-of-a-sudden, their normal way to do work can become a thing of the past. They quickly must adopt new ways to do work. This makes some people feel uneasy. They then express their uneasiness through an array of resistance to the change. The speed and effectiveness with which leaders handle such employee problems quite often determines the (A) success – or failure – of the change effort and also (B) leader's career success – or failure. As such, the manner in which Fisher and his team handled employee problems proves enlightening.

Emotional Reactions of Employees Who Slowed Down Intuit's Major Organizational Change

Fisher used one word to sum up the emotional reactions of employees who put a damper on Intuit starting its Internet business: *"Discomfort."* He needed to handle employees' discomfort with

◆ ambiguity
◆ unknown future
◆ chaos
◆ lack of structure
◆ huge amount of stamina required
◆ hyperactive pace

In fact, Fisher colorfully described the hyperactive pace as *"like trying to sip water from a fire hose."*

Methods Used to Handle Employees who Resisted – or Undermined – Intuit's Organizational Change

Fisher found the best way to handle resistance was through him directly talking with employees. He did this in two main ways. First, he spent a lot of time talking one-to-one with key people. In these discussions, he found it most helpful to discuss their

◆ career goals
◆ feelings about their work, especially what they felt happy or unhappy about
◆ suggestions to improve the work environment

Second, with some resisting employees, Fisher would say, "I can't order you to be happy. And if you're not happy here, I can't order you to stay here."

Comparing Intuit's *"Old-Style"* Employees with Its Needed *"New-Style"* Employees

Employees who did well before a major organizational change – "old-style" employees – may not possess talents or attitudes needed to do well after the change is implemented. So, *"new-style"* employees usually are needed after implementing change. At Intuit's Internet business, Fisher found the following differences between the "old-style" employees and "new-style" employees:

Old-Style Employees	New-Style Employees
Focus on product (software) revenue business	Focus on service model business
Focus on 1-time retail customer purchase	Focus on multiple customer purchases
Likes lengthy timeframes to research, develop & market product	Likes fast product launches
Prefers consistent decision-making process	Invent decision-making processes from scratch as you create a new business
Process-oriented & highly focused on processes to do work	Flexible & experimental

Transforming *"Old-Style"* Employees into *"New-Style"* Employees

Fisher found three methods particularly effective to help *old-style* employees transition into *new-style* employees.

Transformation Method 1: Early Successes

"It's hard to buy into all that chaos if you don't see successes," explained Fisher.

Transformation Method 2: Leading by Example

"I'd actually go out and do a deal, and then come back and tell everyone." These deals included distribution deals, ad sales, or forming partnerships with a financial institution.

Transformation Method 3: Be Open about Your Failures

"We openly told employees about problems we encountered." Such openness greatly boosts the level of trust employees feel with executives leading the organizational change.

Recommendations to Employees Who Work in Companies Undergoing Organizational Change

Since Fisher possesses expertise in leading change, he holds insights into how employees in any organization can thrive, grow, and "come out ahead" during organizational change.

Tip 1: "Get with the Program"

"Decide if you're in or out – don't be halfway," Fisher advises

Tip 2: "Look for the Joy"

"If you don't believe in the change in a compelling way, don't stay. If you do believe in the change, figure out how you can improve your career skills and level of excitement."

Tip 3: Be a Team Player

Fisher strongly recommends an employee

◆ avoid in-fighting
◆ act strongly cooperative
◆ is profoundly helpful

Hiring Methods to Help Achieve Intuit's Major Organizational Change

Through my extensive work on my pre-employment tests, hiring-related workshops and book *Hire the Best – & Avoid the Rest*™, I repeatedly find successful organizations do whatever is needed to hire people who show a high likelihood of success on-the-job.*

When implementing organizational change, it becomes even more crucial to hire high-achievers and avoid underachievers. Toward this end, Fisher focuses on hiring people who

◆ are "really sharp" – bright
◆ communicate clearly
◆ have high energy
◆ "show great passion for the revolution we are part of and what we are creating"
◆ excel at teamwork

Organizational Change Ingredient 3: Successfully Managing Yourself during the Organizational Change

Leaders of successful organizational change exhibit certain characteristics. They tend to be strongly optimistic. In fact, I tested highly successful managers and executives – using my *Abilities & Behavior Forecaster*™ tests – and they scored high on the Optimism scale. As optimists, they look for solutions, rather than problems.

*For more information on Dr. Mercer's pre-employment tests, workshops and books, you can look in the Materials You Can Order section in the back of this book.

Plus, these outstanding leaders have focused for years on living a highly achievement-oriented lifestyle, often starting in childhood.

Optimism Helped This Executive Succeed in Implementing Major Organizational Change

In a book I co-authored – *Spontaneous Optimism™: Proven Strategies for Health, Prosperity & Health* – my co-author and I described how highly successful people almost invariably are optimists. These are people who go through life with a confident, "Can-Do" attitude. They figure out how to get things done – and then persist in doing it.*

Fisher impressed me as a very optimistic person. He remarked:

I feel like a very optimistic person. It keeps me sane. Optimism helps me see through many difficulties.

I tell managers who report to me that if they can't come to work upbeat and positive, they should just go home.

Optimism is central to my personal life, also. I changed careers several times which comes from my optimism that I can learn, stretch, and do something different.

Attitudes of This Executive That Help Him Succeed

Fisher attributes much of his success to firmly holding four key attitudes:

Attitude 1: "Belief in what I'm doing and that I can succeed."
Attitude 2: "Treat people with respect."
Attitude 3: "Expect people to be responsible for their own actions."
Attitude 4: "Expect people to treat others with respect and compassion."

Expressions This Executive Says to Keep Focused & Optimistic

Two of Fisher's favorite phrases convey his enthusiasm and optimism. Also, by using these phrases with employees, he communicates his enthusiasm. Since enthusiasm is contagious, this helps propel the motivation of Intuit's Internet business employees. Fisher likes to say:

 ◆ *"It sure is exciting!"*

Fisher remarks, "I say that all the time."

---

*For information on the *Spontaneous Optimism™* book, audio-book and presentations, please see the Materials You Can Order section in the back of this book.

◆ *"This is a special moment in time – and it won't last very long. Being part of this is tremendously fulfilling."*
His phrase "This is a special moment in time – and it won't last very long" feels especially compelling. It clearly conveys to everyone around him that their work is ultra-special, will help millions of people, and features an excitement that will never be replicated. So, enjoy the experience now while it still exists.

How This Executive Gets Employees to Focus on Solutions — Not Problems

Optimists focus on solutions, while pessimists focus on problems or complaining. As such, a key duty of a leader is to teach – though personal example – the importance of zooming in on solutions, rather than wallowing in problems.

How does Fisher do this? He gets people to shift the metaphor from "problem" to "issues" or "conflict." For example, Fisher might say, "Explain to me why you have a *conflict* with that person? We then immediately go into how to resolve the conflict, instead of just feeling irritated about it."

Importantly, Fisher provides employees with an excellent role model in this regard. For instance, he summed up his solution-focused approach by saying, *"We talk about problems with the specific focus of coming up with resolution or solutions. I don't allow sessions of unfettered complaining."* This is incredibly astute advice every leader can use to greatly benefit his or her employees, company, and career.

Formative Childhood Events that Help in His Career

Everyone has profound childhood experiences that affect him or her for a lifetime. High-achievers, such as Fisher, use their good and bad experiences to help form a better life for themselves. Fisher described major childhood events that helped shape him as a person with the following comments:

My parents split up when I was five years-old, and my mother never re-married. Although we never were poor, we never did have much money.

I got a wonderful break when I earned a scholarship to a very fine private boarding school, The Hotchkiss School in Connecticut, based on need. At Hotchkiss, I learned a sense of social consciousness from being one of only 30 scholarship kids out of 500 students. At the end of my senior year, while many of my boarding school classmates got sports cars as graduation presents, I received an electric typewriter to use at college.

I earned a scholarship to college based on need. While there, I greatly enjoyed writing fiction, often using the typewriter I received as a high school graduation gift.

Two elements of Fisher's most formative childhood experience strike me as crucial. First, he and his mother did not allow lack of money to stand in the way of Fisher obtaining an opportunity to vastly improve his life: They found a way for him to attend an acclaimed boarding school. In that setting, he certainly spent a great deal of time with many high-achieving students who came from families with high-achieving parents. Such experiences can prove very influential in a person's life. Indeed, he has progressed through his career in a very high-achieving fashion.

Second, Fisher expressed how he "greatly enjoyed writing fiction." If you think about it, fiction writing is the ability to create something where nothing existed before. It requires *organized creativity*. Fiction writing sharpened certain mental muscles, so to speak. Now, at Intuit, he has a magnificent arena in which to put his organized creativity into action in real-world, high-stakes business endeavors. Indeed, he led the creation of something big – Intuit's Internet business – where no such business previously existed at Intuit. That definitely shows Fisher's keen ability in large-scale organized creativity.

This Executive's Role Models – & Lesson Learned from Each One
Fisher named three people as his most important role models. It appears evident he used the lessons he learned from each role model to significantly enhance his personal and career success.

Role Model 1: High school hockey coach. *Lesson Learned:* "Character is the most important asset anyone can build. This includes integrity, compassion, respect, and effectiveness in whatever you do."

Role Model 2: Bill Campbell, former CEO of Intuit. *Lesson Learned:* "How to work with and coach people in business."

Role Model 3: Richard Ford, a writer who taught Fisher's writing class in college. *Lesson Learned:* "He taught me how to develop my own talent: Work real hard, listen to myself, and express my own ideas, rather than say only what other people expect me to say."

12

EXCELL GLOBAL SERVICES

Turning Your Human Resources Department into a Profit Center™

Excell Global Services' *Vision*:

Our key goal is to be the
world's leader in providing world-class wholesale agent
and data-related customer interaction centers.

When you place a call to obtain a phone number in a distant city, state or province, you probably think the person giving you the phone number you want is a phone company employee. But, you may well be speaking to an "agent" working for Excell Global Services, Inc.

Or, when you call the customer service department of a utility company to sign-up for service or to investigate a problem with your service, you most likely figure you will talk with an employee of the company you are calling. However, you actually might receive customer service from a well-trained employee of Excell Global Services.

Turning Your Human Resources Department into a Profit Center™ is

♦ Trademark of The Mercer Group, Inc.
♦ Book by Michael W. Mercer, Ph.D.
♦ Speech and workshop delivered by Dr. Mercer

For information on Dr. Mercer's *books, speeches* and *workshops,* you can refer to the Materials You Can Order section in the back of this book.

In fact, a key reason many companies outsource their customer service-type work is because of the magnificent job done by Excell Global Services. The company operates call centers in the United States, Canada, Europe, and Asia Pacific. These call centers handle two types of transactions:

♦ Short transactions, such as long-distance directory assistance

♦ Long transactions, for instance, customer service for companies in several industries

As you can imagine, all these transactions take thousands of Excell employees who are carefully trained, supervised, and managed. The executive in charge of Excell's monumental human resources and training operation is Lori F. Ulichnie, Vice President of Human Resources.

Excell Global Services' Major Organizational Change

Under Ulichnie's leadership, Excell's human resources (HR) department took a variety of actions to boost the company's bottom line through

♦ Decreasing costs

♦ Improving profits

All actions were based on thoroughly researching key measures of productivity and efficiency in how Excell operates.

I must admit to feeling very proud of how superbly Excell's HR department has done. Why? First, Excell has used my pre-employment tests – the *Abilities & Behavior Forecaster*™ tests – to predict applicants' interpersonal skills, personality, motivations and mental abilities.

Second, Ulichnie had me serve as the featured speaker at her annual HR team meeting. At the meeting, I conducted two half-day *workshops* for all of Excell's HR team members:

♦ *Turning Your Human Resources Department into a Profit Center*™ workshop

♦ *Absolutely Fabulous Organizational Change*™ workshop

Only HR employees attended my morning session on *Turning Your Human Resources Department into a Profit Center*™. Then, in the afternoon, managers from many departments – HR, finance, operations, marketing, sales and other departments – participated in my *Absolutely Fabulous Organizational Change*™ workshop.*

Importantly, Ulichnie then directed all the HR managers to actually put into action what I taught them in my workshops. One of the results is that under Ulichnie's leadership Excell's HR managers truly have become part of the profit-generating team that runs the company. This is all the more impressive, since most HR departments are cost centers. But, *Excell's HR department certainly is a profit center – measurably contributing to the company's bottom line.*

Ulichnie and the HR managers took many actions to turn Excell's HR department into a profit center. Here are five of the key actions.

Organizational Change 1: 50% Turnover Reduction from Improving Pay Structure

Excell improved the pay for the "agents," employees who handle calls coming into its call centers. Previously, Excell paid agents with (A) base pay plus (B) a monthly financial incentive. The monthly financial incentive was based on the three factors of individual, team, and call center-wide performance. Initially, this seemed like a good idea. Unfortunately, it diluted the ability of each individual agent to determine how much – or how little – his or her actions impacted their incentive pay.

Now, Excell uses a *New & Improved Pay-Per Call* program composed of both (A) base pay and (B) pay-per-call incentive pay. Specifically, if an agent in any day handles over a certain number of calls per hour, then the agent gets paid several cents/call above that threshold. And there is even more: If the agent had perfect attendance that week, then the agent earns an additional amount per call above the threshold. Note: To earn incentive pay, Excell also requires agents to handle calls with certain high quality standards. Any agent who does not live up to the quality standards does not earn pay-per-call incentive pay.

What did the new pay plan accomplish? It compensates agents for one of the most important parts of Excell's business, which is the cost per call. As a result, agents now possess a vested financial interest in helping Excell boost its bottom line. The *New & Improved*

---

*For information on Dr. Mercer's *Abilities & Behavior Forecaster*™ tests – or his speeches, workshops and books – you can refer to the Materials You Can Order section in the back of this book.

Pay-Per-Call program also reduced agent turnover by more than 50%.

Turnover proves expensive in two ways. First, a company has costs associated with recruiting, hiring, training, and supervising employees. When productive employees leave the company, this costs money and lowers productivity until a productive replacement is in the job and trained. Second, in a company like Excell, much of what Excell provides its customers is its employees' services. As such, turnover of Excell's productive employees impacts the company's ability to provide the services its customers require and its prospects seek. This could put a crimp in Excell's profitability. So, Excell's 50% turnover reduction produced many business benefits for the company.

Organizational Change 2: $2.3-Million/Year Decrease in Benefits Costs

Excell's self-funded medical benefits expenses were sky-rocketing. To provide employees with a comprehensive benefits package with a level of cost controls, Excell carefully examined each item in its benefits program. Resulting from this study, Excell went from a self-insured plan to a creative dual option of (A) a health maintenance organization with a large physician network and (B) a point-of-service plan with expanded services and flexibility. Ulichnie explained, "Although our final solution was not the lowest cost option, it was the one that met our goals of both cost savings – over $2.3-million – and employee satisfaction."

Organizational Change 3: $141,000/Year Savings by Not Re-hiring Former Excell Employees

As author of the book *Hire the Best – & Avoid the Rest*™, I always recommend companies look into the biodata – that is, biographical data – of its successful and unsuccessful employees.* Excell conducted a superb biodata study from a variety of angles. It came up with an interesting – and profitable – finding.

Specifically, it is common practice for companies to re-hire former employees who left on good terms. However, in examining data on its former employees that Excell re-hired, the company found over 50% of those re-hired did not stay over 60 days! This data definitely ran quite contrary to the common practice used by many companies!! The result is Excell stopped re-hiring former

---

*You can find out more about Dr. Mercer's *Hire the Best – & Avoid the Rest*™ materials, pre-employment tests and presentations by referring to the Materials You Can Order section in the back of this book.

employees, even those who left the company on good terms. Excell used the 6-step cost-benefit analysis formula I taught its staff during a workshop partly based on my second book, *Turning Your Human Resources Department into a Profit Center*™. My formula involves laying out six steps: (1) Business Problem, (2) Cost of Business Problem, (3) Solution to Business Problem, (4) Cost of Solution, (5) $ Improvement Benefit, and (6) Cost-Benefit Ratio. Using my cost-benefit formula, Excell showed its solution produced a magnificent 39:1 cost-benefit ratio. See Diagram 1.

Diagram 1. **Cost-Benefit Analysis of Changing Re-hire Process at Excell Global Services**

Business Problem
High turnover among re-hired employees –
plus a large number of them are not meeting performance expectations.

Cost of Business Problem
$144,510

Costs include:
A. Application/Interview Process = $1,320
B. Retraining Process = $88,730
C. Rehire Base Wages = $54,460
Cost of Problem: A + B + C = $144,510

Solution to Business Problem
1. Partner with Operations to ensure accurate re-hire status reports
2. Provide training to Service Managers on re-hire status documentation
3. Implement a 6-month waiting period for re-hires

Cost of Solution
$3,600

Costs include:
A. HR staff time to train = $600
B. Manager training time = $3,000
Cost of solution: A + B = $3,600

$ Improvement Benefit
$140,910

Cost-Benefit Ratio
39 : 1
$140,910 : $3,600

Sources:
A. This 6-step cost-benefit analysis formula is from the book *Turning Your Human Resources Department into a Profit Center*™ by Michael Mercer.
B. Numbers shown in this diagram were provided by Lori Ulichnie, Vice president of HR, Excell Global Services.

Organizational Change 4: 20% Reduction in Workers'
Compensation Claims

On-the-job injuries cost the company money and also impacted productivity and employee morale. Again, using its data-based decision-making process, Excell researched the data on its workers' compensation claims. The company came up with a combination of three actions to reduce possible on-the-job injuries: (A) ergonomic changes, (B) equipment changes, and (C) involving supervisors to improve agents' awareness of how to sit, hold their hands, and use equipment.

Organizational Change 5: 66% Decrease in Drug Testing Costs

Excell used to give drug-detection tests – tests to see if a person is abusing drugs or alcohol – to all final applicants. Upon examining its data, Excell changed its drug testing approach. Rather than testing all job *applicants*, Excell now does random drug testing of 30% of its *employees*. This produced two key results. First, Excell saved a lot of money by giving less drug tests. Second, although somewhat harder to measure, Excell noted an increase in employee morale. This increased, because the random drug testing of *employees* reduced employees' worry that drug activities might be going on around them at work.

Using my 6-part HR Profit Center formula, Ulichnie showed this improvement in how Excell uses drug testing produced a *13:1 cost-benefit ratio*. That provided a very fine pay-back for a highly useful solution.

Steps Used to Implement the Crucial Organizational Changes

Ulichnie led an 8-step approach to turning Excell's HR department into a profit center.

Step 1: Put Together Interdepartmental Team to Do Research

This team included employees from all four departments affected by the organizational changes: HR, Operations, Training, and Finance.

Step 2: Input from Excell's Top Brass

All Excell's officers and department directors offered their ideas. Ulichnie found out this not only provides tremendous input, doing this also decreased resistance to the organizational changes, specifically because every high-level manager had the opportunity to provide input.

Step 3: Analysis of Research Results & Brainstorming of Process
        Improvements
Step 4: Implement the Changes on Trial Basis
Step 5: Review Results
Step 6: Broad Communication to All Employees Affected by the
        Changes
Step 7: Implement the Actual Changes
Step 8: Review to See If Implementation Proceeded as Planned &
        Achieved Desired Results

Improvements Resulting from the Organizational Change

As described earlier, the changes produced wonderful, measurable results. These measurable results are summarized in Diagram 2.

Diagram 2. **Results of Excell Global Services' Absolutely Fabulous Organizational Change**

Category	Improvement
Turnover reduction	50%
Medical benefits cost decrease	$2.3-million
Not re-hiring former Excell employees	$141,000/year
Workers' compensation claims reductions	20%
Drug-detection cost decrease	66%

Turning their HR department into a profit center also produced two fine unmeasurable or qualitative improvements, according to Ulichnie. First, HR team members saw the need to (A) do research and (B) make decisions based on facts – not intuition. Second, by doing research and fact-based decision-making, Excell's HR managers learned that when they implement changes, they can

◆ provide quantitative reasons for the organizational
  changes
◆ earn more support for the changes

Organizational Change Ingredient 1:
Successfully Leading the Organizational Change

My consulting and research repeatedly show that the only organizational changes that take hold and produce the desired

improvements are those that
+ fit in with the company's unique culture
+ propel the company toward its big, exciting vision
+ use structured goal-setting with measurable goals and deadlines
+ provide an arena in which teamwork and collaboration make a huge difference

All these factors played key roles in Excell's successful organizational changes.

Excell's Corporate Culture

I find the finest method to discover a company's culture is to unearth the story every employee knows and also passes on to other employees. Usually the story revolves around actions taken by the company's founders near the time the company was born. The story's central idea lays out an image of how employees in the company are expected to act, react and handle situations while working in the company. In short, the story conveys the corporate culture.

Here is Excell's story.

The Kitchen Table

The folklore of many technology-related companies involves the company's founding in a garage. But, Excell's story is quite different: The company was founded by two people at a kitchen table, Dan Evanoff and Dan Pearce. Those two people became Excell Global Services' President & CEO and the Chairman/CEO of Excell's International Operations.

The two founders boldly planned to start a brand new company to provide call center services, such as directory assistance, to a major telecommunications company within three years. To put it mildly, achieving this bold goal in three years seemed highly unrealistic. Any knowledgeable businessperson would tell them they needed much more than three years to accomplish such a huge feat!

Well, how did the founders do?

The fact is the two founders landed Excell's first major contract only one year later!

Amazingly, that was before Excell's service even was operational!!

And there is even more to the story: Excell started at the top. Its first contract was with one of the world's largest companies!!!

Culture – or Main Focus – of Excell Global Services

The Kitchen Table story perfectly communicates Excell's corporate culture which Ulichnie sums up as the following: *Exceed Expectations – and stretch beyond all limits of what we can do.*

Excell certainly has lived up to its *Exceed Expectations* culture. While other companies failed miserably in the call center business, Excell Global Services has succeeded, thrived, and grown at a rapid pace.

Link between Excell's Corporate Culture & Its Major Organizational Change

Excell's *Exceed Expectations* corporate culture definitely permeates its HR department. As someone who addresses a lot of HR groups on my *Turning Your Human Resources Department into a Profit Center*™ methods, I typically find most HR staffers possess limited interest and knowledge of how their HR work impacts the bottom line. In delightfully sharp contrast, I always feel very impressed that all Excell's HR employees are fully aware and enthusiastic to use HR to boost profits. Ulichnie explained,

> *Our corporate culture of going above and beyond, stretching the limits and exceeding expectations is practiced by the HR department. We are a non-traditional HR department. We play an integral role in the business itself – a true business partner, fully aware of our impact on the company's financial success. Each HR team member is trained to perform the [call center] agent's job – and also understands our business and financial measures.*
>
> *Our daily HR management and projects show we don't accept the typical HR approach or answers. Instead, we always strive to be an HR department that plays a significant role in positively impacting the bottom line.*

Big, Exciting Vision of Excell Global Services

Every successful company has a really big, ultra-exciting vision of what it aims to accomplish. It is the sort of vision that employees feel enthused about participating in achieving. Importantly, effective organizational change must provide a way for the company to escalate its march toward the company's vision.

Ulichnie described Excell's vision as the following:
Our key goal is to be the
world's leader in providing world-class
wholesale agent and data-related customer interaction centers.

Notice how Excell's vision contains the two decisive factors that go into creating a fabulous organization's vision: It is (1) very big and (2) extremely exciting. For instance, the company does not aim to be one of the leaders – it seeks to be the *"world's leader."* Excell does not just want to provide good services — its stated intention is to provide *"world-class"* services. It would prove hard to get a bigger or more exciting corporate vision.

Ways the Organizational Change Fits into Excell's Vision

Importantly, Excell measures its effectiveness in achieving its vision in three ways: employee satisfaction, customer satisfaction, and long-term investor value. Given these three measures, the methods Excell used to turn its HR department into a profit center certainly helps the company progress toward its big, exciting vision. All five organizational changes noted by Ulichnie accomplish the following:

1. *Promote employee satisfaction*

Examples: (A) Incentive pay based on employee productivity, (B) reducing job-related injuries, and (C) creating a drug-free workplace

2. *Boost customer satisfaction*

Examples: (A) Handling calls faster – propelled by Excell's *New & Improved Pay-Per-Call* program and (B) high quality call handling done by low turnover employees – resulting in more experienced employees tackling call center duties of helping customers

3. *Increase long-term investor value*

Since all the HR organizational changes boost the bottom line, all the changes directly link to improving long-term investor value.

Goal-Setting to Accomplish the Major Organizational Changes

All goal-setting by Excell's HR employees focuses on helping achieve the company's #1 goal each year: Increase revenues by a certain percent annually. Sample goals the HR staff aim to achieve to help Excell meet its revenue growth goal include the following ("X" is used in place of the exact number used at Excell):

◆ Reduce (or maintain) cost per call by X%/year.
◆ Increase call volume by X%/year.
◆ Reduce turnover at each call center by X%/year.

Teamwork to Accomplish Goals

Ulichnie uses six powerful methods to make sure employees use teamwork and interdepartmental collaboration.

Teamwork Method 1: Actively support interdepartmental teams

In fact, all projects include employees from a variety of departments.

Teamwork Method 2: Support interdepartmental job transfers

If an employee feels interested in obtaining a job in another department, Ulichnie's HR team helps the employee get on project teams involving that department. Such exposure to the other departments helps the employee meet key players in that department. It also gives the department an opportunity to work with and evaluate the employee.

Teamwork Method 3: Meetings with all levels of employees

Ulichnie and other executives "skip levels" by having meetings with all levels of employees, not just employees who report directly to them.

Teamwork Method 4: Fun get-togethers

I personally can attest to this. When I delivered workshops at Excell's annual HR meeting, I *immediately* observed the buoyant, upbeat, and high-energy atmosphere. It was a delightful, fun event.

Many people say "communication" is important for people to work together. Few comments miss the mark more. Actually, I continually notice in my consulting work that highly effective teamwork and work relationships are marked by lots of *fun* communication. The Excell employees I met – in HR and many other departments – definitely appear to have *fun* working hard with each other.

Teamwork Method 5: Spread-the-wisdom presentations

Employees make presentations every three months to show what they did during the previous quarter. In fact, HR people from each call center can attend other call centers' quarterly meetings. This spreads the wealth of information about fabulous HR endeavors done in one call center that can be implemented in Excell's other call centers.

Teamwork Method 6: Everyone pitches in during disasters

When disasters strike – for example, when a hurricane affected Excell's call center in Florida – Excell offered all employees the opportunity to help handle calls at another call center. At the conclusion of this disaster-handling, Excell gave everyone who helped a tongue-in-cheek *Hurricane Survival Kit*. The kit contained "basic survival necessities," such as small bandages, crackers, and chocolate!

In fact, this demonstrates a key principle of social psychology: When people collaborate to effectively handle an extreme situation – such as a disaster – the result is people *emotionally bond* together. They tend to (A) like each other more, (B) enjoy working together more, plus (C) work more productively together. The extreme situation brings people together. It nurtures teamwork that results in high productivity. Excell's experiences certainly give a tremendous example of this exciting way to boost productive teamwork.

Organizational Change Ingredient 2:
Successfully Handling Employee Problems during the Organizational Change

Every organizational change in every company meets resistance or roadblocks from some employees. Also, the *old-style* employees who did fine on-the-job *before* the change may need to transform, if possible, into the *new-style* employees the company needs *after* the organizational change. How well the executives handle the employee problems often correlates with how well the organizational change gets implemented and produces the desired results. As such, it always proves useful to find out how a company that successfully implemented major organizational changes – such as Excell Global Services – handled employee problems.

Actions of Employees Who Resisted – or Undermined – Excell's Organizational Change

Ulichnie found resistance is overcome by communicating relevant research data on what in fact does – or does not – work at Excell. As an example, some agents or call center employees objected to the new incentive pay structure. However, when they were taught about the improved pay structure, they found out they could earn 50% more money. With this knowledge, they quickly dropped their opposition.

In fact, one of the phrases often used by Gil Mauk, President of Excell Agent Services, is the following:

What gets measured gets done.
What gets paid for gets done more!
We pay for exceeding expectations.

Comparison of Excell's "Old-Style" Employees with Its Needed "New-Style" Employees

After an organizational change, the employees who performed fine before the change – *old-style* employees – may not possess the talents or attitudes required. Instead, the change requires *new-style* employees. The following table compares differences between these two groups.

Old-Style Employees	New-Style Employees
Works in 1 department	Interdepartmental
Solo work	Teamwork
Likes receiving direction	Likes independence
Prefers to be told what to do	Prefers shared leadership
Focus: Seniority & experience	Focus: Updating & expanding skills
Rote compliance	Creative thinking
Non-owner perspective	Business owner perspective

Ulichnie explained *"business owner perspective"* means Excell employees often ponder a question like this: "If this was my money, would I spend it that way?"

Methods Excell Used to Transform Its "Old-Style" Employees into "New-Style" Employees

Ulichnie and Excell's HR staff found four methods work particularly well to help transform *old-style* employees into the *new-style* employees the company needs after the organizational changes.

Transformation Method 1: Incentive pay

Excell's *New & Improved Pay-Per-Call* program rapidly converted employees to Excell's slogan of "What gets measured gets done. What gets paid for gets done more! We pay for

exceeding expectations."
Transformation Method 2: Thrill of receiving upper management atten-
tion when your project succeeds
By basing HR projects on research and facts, HR employees possess data to prove what they did really works in bottom line reality.
Transformation Method 3: Determine strategy, be clear about it, & live
by it
Why? If employees know what the rules of the game are, they can play by the rules – and succeed by the rules.
Transformation Method 4: "Communicate 500 Times"
The intriguing phrase "Communicate 500 Times" proves popular and highly useful at Excell. Ulichnie emphasized, "Managers must reiterate time and time again what the company's strategy is."

Organizational Change Ingredient 3:
Successfully Managing Yourself during the Organizational Change

Employees learn how to act and react during organizational change by observing the behavior of their leader. As such, a leader who exudes optimism, confidence and a "Can-Do" attitude proves crucial. Reason: Employees "catch" these emotions and ways to handle situations from the executive leading the change.

Optimism Helped This Executive Succeed in Implementing Major Organizational Change

Ulichnie credits her *"confidence in people"* with proving incredibly valuable in leading Excell's organizational change. For instance, her optimism came out in confidence she showed to employees working on the various organizational changes. Her confidence included her deeply held belief that they could

♦   see beyond the typical answers
♦   conjure up creative solutions

Lo and behold, her confidence proved warranted: The employees did collect data, analyzed the data, planned highly useful changes, and successfully implemented them.

Attitudes of This Executive that Most Help Her Succeed

This vice president holds two attitudes near and dear. They tremendously help her in her executive role.

Attitude 1: Believe each individual wants, needs, and deserves respect
Attitude 2: Not being limited by other people's experience or expectations
Ulichnie gave these two examples. First, she stated, "Some people say HR should be limited to only certain activities – and I don't believe that." Second, "For Excell Global Services, the company does not feel it should see any ceilings that would prevent success." As such, Ulichnie's attitude perfectly fits with Excell's corporate culture, as described earlier, which Ulichnie sums up as the following: *Exceed Expectations – and stretch beyond all limits on what we can do.*

How This Executive Focuses on Solutions – Not Problems

Optimists invariably concentrate on finding solutions, while pessimists burn up their energy looking for problems. Given this situation, how does Ulichnie focus on solutions – and how does she convey her solution-focus to Excell employees. She uses two main methods.

Method 1: Not looking at short-term impacts of an issue
She finds, "The immediate hurdles often seem so large that we have to focus on our long-term goals."
Method 2: Performing at a high level is our norm
Since high performance is the "norm" at Excell, Ulichnie makes sure "we should not let short-term obstacles slow us down."

This Executive's Favorite Story

Years ago, when I was doing research to develop a pre-employment test, I experimented with various ways to find out what makes a person tick. One of my findings is that a person's favorite story inherently communicates a great deal about the person's personality and view of their world. Ulichnie's favorite story is the following:

The Starfish Story

A person is walking along the beach, throwing back individual starfish that had washed up onto the sand.

Another individual approaches, and asks, "There are so many starfish here, how can you make a difference by throwing them back and saving them?"

And the person replies, "I might not be able to throw all the starfish back into the ocean, but I'm making a difference to each individual starfish I do throw back in."

Choosing this story reflects on a few aspects of Ulichnie's personality and work behavior. As the story's theme conveys, she is a person who values (A) initiating action, (B) helping people, and (C) not letting others' possible doubts impede her progress. Indeed, these are some of the reasons she has been very successful in her career.

This Executive's Role Models — & Lessons Learned from Each One

A role model gives a person vital life lessons that can positively impact the person's career and personal life. Ulichnie says she learned especially important lessons from two role models.

Role Model 1: Father

Ulichnie feels her most powerful childhood experiences involved watching how her father developed multiple areas of expertise. Her father is an anesthetist, however he has many interests outside of medicine. Ulichnie explained, "He dabbles in many activities, and seems to become an expert in all of them. He travels to the hospitals where he works. Then, he comes home and achieves in all sorts of other arenas." For example, in addition to his medical expertise, he also developed expertise in activities, such as

◆ doing excellent carpentry
◆ running a farm
◆ winning horse shows

She summed up what she saw her father doing: "He is a master of many disciplines, and truly enjoys doing all of them very well."

Lesson Learned: "His approach is to learn something, practice it, and excel and be a success in it."

Role Model 2: CEO of Excell Global Services

The CEO showed Ulichnie the importance of balancing personal life and work.

Lesson Learned: "You can have an excellent personal life, while still accomplishing incredible success at work."

13

WASHINGTON MUTUAL

Profiting from Acquisitions

Washington Mutual's *Vision*:
*Our key goal is to be one of the
nation's premier financial services companies.*

Washington Mutual is one of the largest financial institutions in the United States focusing on retail consumers. The company offers customers a full array of financial products and services, including

◆ savings accounts
◆ checking accounts
◆ loans, such as mortgages and consumer loans
◆ investments in stocks, bonds, and mutual funds

The company grows by offering spectacular service with an incentive-compensated workforce.

Importantly, the company also has grown by acquiring leading financial institutions. Washington Mutual instills its dynamic, growth-oriented culture into each institution it takes over.

Leading the acquisition integration is senior vice president Dyan Beito.

Washington Mutual's Major Organizational Change

The major organizational change Washington Mutual has done is acquisitions of many financial institutions. These are not just small local banks. Instead, Washington Mutual has taken over very

large financial institutions, including
- Great Western Savings
- American Savings
- Home Savings

Readers may well think these acquisitions sound familiar. Reason: All Washington Mutual acquisitions attract major press coverage due to their size and scope. As such, it is likely readers found out about these takeovers in publications such as *The Wall Street Journal, Forbes, Fortune, Financial Times, Investors Business Daily*, and many other sources.

In fact, Beito was an executive at Great Western, a huge California savings bank that Washington Mutual bought. As a company that recognizes talented individuals, Washington Mutual placed Beito in a key senior management role of making sure acquired companies are integrated into the very special, very profitable way Washington Mutual does business.

How Was This Change Crucial to Washington Mutual's Success & Growth?

These acquisitions proved absolutely crucial for Washington Mutual. This organization prides itself with being a growth company. And to continue growing, Washington Mutual needed to buy thrifts, especially in the fast growing California market, and in other states. As such, the acquisitions fit in beautifully with Washington Mutual's vision of growth for the future.

Steps Used to Implement This Crucial Organizational Change

How did Beito successfully integrate the acquired companies into the Washington Mutual fold? This proves especially crucial, because many companies do takeovers, but a large percentage of acquisitions fail to meet the desired financial results. Yet, Beito and her team at Washington Mutual certainly devised a winning formula for integrating acquired companies – and making them even more profitable as a result of their new Washington Mutual affiliation. She uses five key steps to produce profitable acquisition integration.

Step 1: Clear understanding of Washington Mutual's Mission

This includes an examination of Washington Mutual's (A) values and (B) mission. The company's values and mission are clearly laid out for all to see on both 6-inch X 8-inch laminated cards and also wallet-sized cards an employee easily can carry in a wallet, purse, or pocket. Diagram 1 shows the company's mission and values statements. Such visual aids serve as a constant reminder to executives and employees of what the company is all about. They also clearly communicate that Washington Mutual expects all employees' actions to advance the company's "Mission" which aims to benefit the 4C's:

1. Customers
2. Co-Workers
3. Communities served by the company
4. Capital Markets

Diagram 1. **Washington Mutual's Mission & Values Statements**

OUR MISSION

To be one of the nation's premier financial services companies by:

✓ providing exceptional service to customers

✓ making our communities better places to live and work

✓ recognizing outstanding efforts of employees

✓ delivering a superior long-term return to shareholders

OUR VALUES

ETHICS   All actions are guided by absolute honesty, integrity and fairness.

RESPECT   People are valued and appreciated for their contributions.

TEAMWORK   Cooperation, trust and shared objectives are vital to success.

INNOVATION   New ideas are encouraged and sound strategies implemented with enthusiasm.

EXCELLENCE   High standards for service and performance are expected and rewarded.

Step 2: Acquisition Integration Team Creates "Tactical Plan"

This plan incorporates input from people throughout the company. Once the acquisition integration team creates the "Tactical Plan," the team meets once each week to make sure the "Tactical Plan" is carried out.

Step 3: CEO Speaks to All Employees at the Acquired Company

CEO Kerry Killinger speaks at meetings in nearly every facility of the institution Washington Mutual is acquiring. His exciting theme is the following: "*1 Company – Endless Possibilities.*" In his speech, the CEO emphasizes how Washington Mutual

◆ creates *one* corporate culture in all of its many branches and business units

◆ does business

Importantly, he stresses how the Washington Mutual culture and way of doing business continually produce tremendous returns for customers, communities, co-workers, and capital markets. By adopting the Washington Mutual way, employees of acquired companies discover how they can contribute and share in a remarkably successful financial institution.

Step 4: Reinforce CEO's Message with Communications & Supporting Materials

Washington Mutual's CEO has said that a *company's mission, vision and goals need to be repeated seven times to sink in.* The point: Employees need to hear the same, consistent message over and over again. Once is not enough.

How does the company accomplish this? First, executives keep repeating the CEO's message in their many dealings with employees. Second, all employees receive the company's *Mission and Values* on laminated cards and wallet-sized cards, as explained earlier. The more reminders acquired employees receive concerning what Washington Mutual is about and how it does business, the better.

Step 5: Everyone Is Constantly & Systematically Told "What The Next Steps Are"

One key "next step" is computer conversions so all information systems and technology meld into a seamless system. Another major "next step" always entails consolidation of branches. This includes publicizing factors employees think about, including possible redeployment, attrition, and layoffs. A third "next step" is getting the acquired employees into the exciting

Incentive-Based Compensation plan that enables them to earn more money based on their productivity.

Measurable Improvements Produced by the Organizational Change

The way Washington Mutual integrates its acquisitions certainly produces winning results. Beito credits a number of quantitative improvements to Washington Mutual's successful acquisitions:

- ◆ Great boosts in market share in growing markets, especially California and Florida
- ◆ Washington Mutual continues to grow
- ◆ Huge numbers of existing and new customers sign-up for free checking

The free checking – which Beito calls Washington Mutual's "entry product" – is a monstrous draw. After the usual flood of customers sign up for free checking, Washington Mutual sets in motion its well-oiled *cross-selling* of an array of other financial products to the same customers. These products include savings accounts, consumer loans, mortgage loans, and investments like mutual funds, stocks, and bonds. The end-result is a sizeable surge in customers placing more and more of their financial assets in the hands of Washington Mutual.

Qualitative or Unmeasurable Improvements

The way Washington Mutual goes about acquiring companies and merging them into its operation provides a number of intangible improvements, according to Beito. First, employees at the acquired companies tend to feel they were treated with tremendous dignity and respect.

Second, the fact that the CEO of the huge Washington Mutual addresses every employee instills much loyalty and trust in the Washington Mutual way of doing business. Importantly, Beito points out that when employees feel they are treated with dignity and respect, they – in turn – act respectful to customers. This enhances customer relations.

Third, people enjoy their jobs more. This stems partly from Washington Mutual clearly and repeatedly showing employees how they fit into its exciting, highly successful organization. This makes acquired employees feel good. And when employees feel good about where they work, Washington Mutual finds they also tend to increase productivity.

Organizational Change Ingredient 1:
Successfully Leading the Organizational Change

My many years of consulting to companies – and previous experience as a manager in major companies – showed me first-hand that organizational change produces the desired improvements when certain elements work together. First, the change must logically and smoothly flow from the organization's culture and vision. Second, the organization must carry out the change using structured goal-setting and tremendous amounts of well-coordinated teamwork. These are the same ingredients Beito and her team use especially well in integrating acquired financial institutions into Washington Mutual.

Washington Mutual's Corporate Culture

I created a method to uncover an organization's culture: Find out what story the company's employees (A) all know and (B) tell to every new employee. The anecdote usually focuses on the company's founders. The tale conveys the legend about the behaviors, attitudes and convictions that form the core of how the company expects employees to act on-the-job. Here is the legend on which Washington Mutual's culture is based:

Fire Destroys – & Creates

On June 6, 1889, a glue pot boiling in a Seattle wood shop started a huge fire. Seattle was completely destroyed and devastated by the fire.

In fact, a young English journalist – Rudyard Kipling – soon thereafter visited Seattle. Kipling wrote the devastation was so total that Seattle looked like "a horrible black smudge, as though a hand had come down and rubbed the place smooth."

After this monstrous catastrophe, six citizens met to figure out how to re-build Seattle. Their solution was to found a loan business, initially called Washington National Building Loan & Investment Association – later renamed Washington Mutual. This financial institution started expressly to lend money to help people re-build their lives.

And – very importantly – Washington Mutual continued to grow specifically by helping people build and re-build their lives.

Culture – or Main Focus – of Washington Mutual

Beito explained this story conveys Washington Mutual's culture of *community involvement*. She said the company always stays very focused on helping people in each community in which it does business.

This community involvement comes in many forms. Of course, the financial services and products Washington Mutual offers help people build or re-build their lives, just like the company's founders helped people create better lives for themselves. Also, Washington Mutual has a *Community Involvement Kit*. Branch managers visit schools in their communities. The branch managers use the kit when they deliver classroom presentations to teach students how to save and reach certain financial milestones.

And the company's commitment and involvement in its communities does not stop there. For every checking account opened, the company donates $1 to that community's schools. Plus, employees are given time off to work in community events. All these activities help community residents while, simultaneously, helping make Washington Mutual a highly preferred provider of personal financial services.

Links between the Corporate Culture & the Major Organizational Change

One of the best parts of each acquisition, emphasized Beito, was bringing Washington Mutual's corporate culture – *community involvement* – to each community in which it acquired a financial institution. For example, the company held meetings in every community in California and Florida in which it acquired branches. Washington Mutual's CEO, other executives and the local branch manager all attended. The company invited all city officials, local and statewide politicians, and local school superin-tendents, principals, and teachers. At these community meetings, Washington Mutual officials spoke about the company's

- ◆ business mission and values
- ◆ educational programs
- ◆ foundation
- ◆ lending for low income housing
- ◆ core products (checking, savings, loans, and investments)

The company also used a rather dramatic follow-up that showcased its *community involvement* culture. A year later,

Washington Mutual officials returned to each community. In a local ceremony, the company publicly gave a $1 check for each checking account opened in that community's branch.

Big, Exciting Vision of Washington Mutual

Every company I ever advised found a great deal of its success rested in the fact that the company had a clear, concise, very big, and quite exciting vision. Its compelling vision pointed the direction in which the company and its employees were heading. There never was any question that the company would make a big mark on the world it served. Beito explained Washington Mutual's big, exciting vision is the following:

Our key goal is to be one of the nation's premier financial services companies.

Ways the Organizational Change Fits into the Company's Vision

Beito pointed out the company's way of acquiring and integrating financial institutions directly flows out of Washington Mutual's vision *"to be one of the nation's premier financial services companies."* The company accomplishes this by getting employees behind Washington Mutual's vision. How? By focusing employees on benefiting the company's lifeblood 4C's:

1. *Customers: Provide exceptional customer service* – improved from the service level the acquired company previously provided
2. *Co-Workers: Recognize employees' productivity*
3. *Community: Focus employees on helping the community* be a great place to live and work
4. *Capital Markets: Produce long-term return-on-investment,* ROI, so people will invest in Washington Mutual

Goal-Setting to Accomplish the Major Organizational Change

Washington Mutual uses a clear-cut goal-setting method to assure its acquisitions advance in the direction the company deems important: Each manager takes responsibility for *measurable* goals with firm *deadlines*. They have production goals – for example, open a specific number of checking accounts by a certain date – plus training goals and other relevant types of goals.

Beito told me of four recent goals she set to successfully merge acquired companies into the Washington Mutual family. These goals give insight into how the executive in charge of merger integration breaks down the zillion details of a successful acquisition into the key, measurable parts. The key parts focus on (A) selecting branch managers, (B) training employees, (C) remodeling to expand business, and (D) computer-related conversions. For example, four recent goals Beito set were the following:

Goal #1: *Select all 42 branch co-managers (out of a pool of 85) by [specific date].*

Goal #2: *Train all employees about work they need to do to contribute to the "Tactical Plan" by [specific date].*

Goal #3: *Remodel branches to handle increased business volume by [specific date].*

Goal #4: *Convert to a single computer and information system – hardware and software – by [specific date].*

Teamwork to Accomplish Goals

Beito emphasized the importance of actively promoting teamwork and interdepartmental collaboration to make acquisitions work. She does this in three ways.

Teamwork Method 1: Consistent Language

For example, after three recent acquisitions, Beito made sure acquired employees referred to the company as "Washington Mutual" or "WaMu." She discouraged employees from referring to where they worked by the names of the companies Washington Mutual acquired. This helped employees get on with joining Washington Mutual, rather than carrying on traditions of the acquired companies.

Teamwork Method 2: Get Acquired Employees Involved in Decision-Making

Beito consistently encouraged teams to help make decisions about how to operate the business. These teams are composed of employees from Washington Mutual and each acquired company.

Teamwork Method 3: Lots & Lots & Lots of Communications

For this, Beito said *over*-communication proves vastly preferable. Two great benefits of *over*-communicating is it (A) makes employees feel more comfortable with each step in the acquisition and integration into Washington Mutual's way of doing business and (B) decreases rumors and gossip.

She *over*-communicates via e-mail and voice-mail to all branch managers and assistant branch managers of every acquired branch. These methods provide Beito with ready access to the far-flung facilities for which she is responsible. By doing this, she makes sure each of these many managers all forge ahead in the same direction.

Organizational Change Ingredient 2:
Successfully Handling Employee Problems during Organizational Change

One of the chief reasons Washington Mutual succeeds in the high-stakes acquisition game is that its executives appropriately tackle resistance and roadblocks erected by employees. By skillfully handling employee problems, Washington Mutual has been able to meet and exceed the financial targets for which it made each acquisition.

Actions of Employees Who Resisted Washington Mutual's Organizational Change

Beito discovered an interesting way to determine which employees in an acquired company resist the organizational changes. Specifically, during meetings she opens up discussion by asking for questions from employees. During these question-&-answer sessions, Beito detects which employees are resisting. She discovered the resisting employees

- ◆ act withdrawn
- ◆ do not participate
- ◆ always try to find fault with Washington Mutual
- ◆ attempt to get other employees to resist the changes

Effective Methods to Handle Employees Who Resist the Organizational Change

If an employee continues to resist the organizational changes, Beito puts two solutions into action. First, she encourages regional and branch managers to tell each resisting employee, "If you don't believe in Washington Mutual's philosophy, then maybe this isn't the place for you to work."

Second, Beito discourages managers from trying to talk employees out of leaving when employees submit resignations.

From her vast experience with employees who resign, she finds, "It's not worthwhile bending over backwards to retain them."

Comparing Washington Mutual's "Old-Style" Employees with Its Needed "New-Style" Employees

Employees who perform well before a major organizational change – "old-style" employees – may not be the type of employees who perform well after the change – "new-style"employees. This certainly proved true at Washington Mutual as it acquired other financial institutions. Beito sums up the differences between the two types of employees in the table below:

Old-Style Employees	New-Style Employees
Works in 1 department	Interdepartmental
Solo work	Teamwork
Likes receiving direction	Likes independence
Prefers to be told what to do	Prefers shared leadership
Focus: Seniority & experience	Focus: Updating & expanding skills
Very structured sales approach	Entrepreneurial sales approach
Told how to manage	"It's up to you!"

Of all these differences, Beito claimed two differences stand out above the rest. First, she continually finds the successful "new-style" employee likes independence, whereas the "old-style" employee likes receiving direction.

Second, "old-style" employees typically used a very structured sales approach. In sharp contrast, Washington Mutual cultivates an exciting, entrepreneurial sales approach. The company even reinforces this through its innovative, powerful Incentive-Based Compensation program. In general, here is how the program works: Each branch is measured on net income per full-time equivalent employee. To grow net income, each branch manager is given freedom to focus on products that are "hot" in his or her market. For example, checking might be "hot" in one market, while loans are "hot" in another market.

Actions to Transform "Old-Style" Employees into "New-Style" Employees

From her vast experience leading merger integration, Beito said it takes about three years to get everyone on board and accepting Washington Mutual's philosophy. How does she promote this transformation or "buy-in" by acquired employees? She focuses on communicating the benefits of Washington Mutual for each employee using two methods.

Transformation Method 1: Explanatory Workshops

First, she and branch managers reporting to her conduct workshops. In these workshops, they talk to employees who are having trouble understanding or accepting the changes accompanying the acquisition.

Transformation Method 2: Profit Model Clinic

Second, she uses a *Profit Model Clinic*. Practically every branch employee can earn incentive pay or bonuses for productivity in selling or promoting Washington Mutual products and services. To start, each employee pinpoints exactly how much money he or she wants to earn. Then, each employee is told precisely what he or she needs to do to make that amount of money. Every method of earning incentive pay is laid out so all employees know exactly how they can earn their desired income at Washington Mutual.

After the explanatory workshops and the *Profit Model Clinic*, Beito observed, "It's real clear after awhile who is going to make it and who won't. I can tell by their actions and facial expressions during our meetings."

Recommendations to Employees Who Work in Companies Making Major Organizational Change

When you want pragmatic advice, ask an expert! With this in mind, I asked Beito for tips she would give to employees who want to grow and come out ahead as their employers undertake major organizational change. She offered these wise tips:

Tip 1: Find out everything about the acquiring company.

For example, who are the executives and how do they do business?

Tip 2: Find a mentor.

Hook up with a *successful* employee who worked for the acquiring company a long time.

Tip 3: Find out the acquiring company's vision and goals.

Tip 4: Get on-board by putting the acquiring company's vision and goals into action on-the-job.

Tip 5: Ask lots of questions.

Tip 6: Keep an open mind. Be fluid and flexible.

Hiring Methods to Advance the Organizational Change

Beito involves herself in hiring branch managers. To do this, she uses a variety of methods to evaluate candidates. Importantly, when she finds a candidate whom she would seriously consider hiring, she does a realistic job preview. A realistic job preview, as I explain in workshops I deliver and my third book – *Hire the Best – & Avoid the Rest*™ – entails telling and showing the candidate precisely what doing the job will be like.*

In Beito's case, her realistic job preview entails speaking in a very forthright manner about how Washington Mutual does business. She especially talks a lot about the company's

◆ Incentive-based compensation method
◆ Mission
◆ Goals

Importantly, the discussion of Washington Mutual's superb incentive-based compensation method takes pressure off of salary negotiations. That is because the company has a base salary for just six grades of branch manager – plus the potential to make a good amount of incentive pay. This weeds out applicants who just want a simple paycheck.

Organizational Change Ingredient 3:
Successfully Managing Yourself during the Organizational Change

Admit it: Executives who lead organizational change are role models to all the employees. They look at how the executive acts, reacts, thinks, and handles situations. From my experience as a business psychologist who consults to many companies, I continually find effective leaders exude optimism in their thoughts, words, and deeds.**

---

*For information on Dr. Mercer's pre-employment tests, hiring tool kits, workshops and book on *Hire the Best – & Avoid the Rest*™, you can refer to the Materials You Can Order section in the back of this book.

**To find out about Dr. Mercer's materials on career success and optimism, you can look at the Materials You Can Order section in the back of this book. These materials include (A) *How Winners Do It: High Impact People Skills for Your Career Success* and also (B) *Spontaneous Optimism*™: *Proven Strategies for Health, Prosperity & Happiness.*

Also, on a very personal basis, they extract valuable lessons from their experiences and people they admire.

Given the highly effective job Beito does in leading Washington Mutual's acquisition integration, let's look at how she manages herself.

Optimism Helped This Executive Succeed in Implementing Major Organizational Change

Beito's strong focus on *written* goals – a characteristic of optimists – extends from her personal life to her business life. She mentioned that when she and her family *write* a goal, they accomplish it. In a similar vein, Beito transfers the importance of *written* goals to her team. She observed, "We write our goals as a team on a flipchart. Once we *write* it, we always accomplish it."

Along the same lines, Beito also finds three *attitudes* contribute immensely to her success.

Attitude 1: "It can be done"

In fact, she says her *can-do* approach is her "most important" attitude.

Attitude 2: Act upbeat and positive all the time

Attitude 3: View challenges that pop up as "not so monstrous"

Phrases This Executive Says to Keep Focused & Optimistic

In many ways, a person creates her life by the phrases she says to herself – self-talk – and repeatedly says in interactions with others. Beito holds five phrases particularly near and dear.

Phrase 1: "Nothing's impossible."

Phrase 2: "What can we do to solve it?"

Phrase 3: "What can we do to get it done?"

She especially uses this question when people tell her she or her team cannot accomplish something.

Phrase 4: When something doesn't work, she never says, "I told you so."

She says she would not want someone to say that to her. So, instead, she asks, "Well, what did you learn from that – and what would you do differently next time?"

Phrase 5: "Attitude" poster on her wall

Beito hung an "absolutely huge" poster on her wall entitled,

Attitude. It contains a quote from Charles Swindoll that goes like this:

The longer I live, the more I realize the impact of attitude on life. Attitude, to me, is more important than facts. It is more important than the past, than education, than money, than circumstances, than failures, than successes, than what other people think or say or do. It is more important than appearance, giftedness or skill. It will make or break a company [or] a home. The remarkable thing is we have a choice every day regarding the attitude we will embrace for that day. We cannot change our past . . . we cannot change the fact that people will act in a certain way. We cannot change the inevitable. The only thing we can do is play on the one thing we have, and that is our attitude . . . I am convinced that life is 10% what happens to me and 90% how I react to it. And so it is with you . . . we are in charge of our attitudes.

She explained that the quote on her poster means a great deal to her, because it conveys her philosophy: *"It's not what happens, it's how you react to it – your attitude – that matters most."*

How This Executive Focuses Employees on Solutions – Not Problems

A key characteristic of optimists is that *optimists focus on solutions,* but pessimists focus on problems, complaining, moaning, and blaming. As a leader, Beito needs to make sure employees continually see her use a problem-solving mode, rather than just a problem-finding manner. When a red flag or sticky issue comes up, she always asks:

◆ "How can we handle that?"
◆ "How can we go around the problem?"
◆ "Give me some options. Let's talk about our options."

All in all, Beito explains, "I always tell my folks if there's an issue, tell me about it – *but always come up with a solution,* also."

This Executive's Favorite Story

A person's favorite story unlocks her most heartfelt motivations. Beito's favorite story involves one of her biggest successes. She reports:

After two of Washington Mutual's large acquisitions, I was responsible for consolidating over 100 branches – to reduce overhead – of Home Savings and Great Western. We had 1,600 employees involved. I successfully re-deployed all 1,600 employees, except one who got severance pay. And we still hit our profit per FTE [full-time equivalent employee] target.

Picking this as her favorite story is revealing. It shows Beito's strong enthusiasm for

◆   her executive duties of leading acquisition integration
◆   measurably improving profits
◆   helping employees succeed

Formative Event in This Executive's Childhood That Helps Her Career

Beito says one childhood experience that helped shape her life was being the oldest of nine children. She explained,

From the time I was four years-old, I was responsible for helping my parents with the other children.

I always was the leader and first to do everything.

My mother would say, "You're the oldest, so you have to be responsible." I learned responsibility at a very young age.

Lo and behold, her formative experience tremendously helps Beito succeed in her career. For instance, at Washington Mutual, she – in effect – continues to use three skills she developed as a child, namely, being

◆   a leader
◆   first
◆   responsible

At the company, she is (A) a *leader* of acquisition integration, (B) one of the *first* at the company to lead the major organizational changes and, ultimately, (C) one of the executives *responsible* for each acquisition achieving its desired financial goals.

This Executive's Role Models – & Lessons Learned from Each One

Highly successful leaders, such as Beito, are excellent role models for their employees. Importantly, these leaders themselves benefited from role models from whom they learned deeply important lessons. Beito says two of her role models provided her with lessons that she carries into her work and personal life.

Role Model 1: Father. *Lessons Learned:* "Optimism and moral values. My father was the most optimistic person in the world. I also learned lots of moral values from him. He would say, "If you're going to do a job, do it right the first time – or don't do it at all.'"

Role Model 2: Regional manager at Beito's third banking job. *Lessons Learned:* "Time management and discipline in doing the activities she needed to do to succeed each day. She stuck to each task until she completed it."

It seems apparent that a major reason for Beito's career achievements and success as a leader stems from her applying lessons she learned from her two role models:

- optimism
- moral values
- "do it right the first time"
- time management discipline

14

CITY OF INDIANAPOLIS

Cutting Taxes, Reducing Regulations, & Improving Government Services

City of Indianapolis' *Vision*:
Our key goal is to be America's most competitive city, specifically, the best city in the United States in terms of
- ◆ *safe streets*
- ◆ *strong neighborhoods*
- ◆ *thriving economy*

It seems like most government organizations do horribly well at raising taxes, providing below-average to lousy services, and squandering taxpayers' hard-earned money. This is perpetuated through the legalized confiscation of taxpayers' money, commonly called taxes. After all, if someone does not pay taxes, that person could go to jail! This seems like a never ending cycle of many government organizations.

Fortunately, there has been a huge, glorious exception: The City of Indianapolis government under the forward-thinking leadership Mayor Stephen Goldsmith, a Republican. The mayor was assisted for his first six years in office by Skip Stitt who, most recently, served as senior deputy mayor, similar to a company's chief operating officer.

Under Goldsmith's leadership, the City of Indianapolis has become a markedly better place to live, work, and conduct business. Importantly, his leadership produced (1) lower taxes, (2) reduced regulations, and (3) outstandingly improved government services. In many ways, he impressively turned around a city that previously was falling into a downward spin.

Indeed, the city government led by Goldsmith has put Indianapolis on the map as an often-visited place by government officials from across the United States and other nations. Why? Because many government officials want to learn how Goldsmith and his hard-charging staff rescued a large city and made it a shining example of how government can help citizens and businesses while reducing taxes and regulations.

City of Indianapolis' Major Organizational Change

When Mayor Goldsmith was elected, he spent the 90 days prior to taking office outlining his plans to make Indianapolis a competitive city in terms of

◆ Jobs
◆ Companies wanting to operate and expand facilities in Indianapolis
◆ Economic activity

To accomplish his admirable plans, he initiated four major organizational changes: (1) managed competition, (2) regulatory reform, (3) labor-management partnerships, and (4) business process reengineering.

Organizational Change 1: Managed Competition

Mayor Goldsmith broke up the city government's monopoly on many city services. He asked city government (public) employees to compete with private firms for the right to deliver city services. Since many services provided by government bodies had been untouchable by private firms, this truly was a revolutionary change. These services included

◆ managing airports
◆ waste water treatment
◆ city's administrative services
◆ park facilities management
◆ maintenance of city vehicles

Organizational Change 2: Regulatory Reform

Skip Stitt – who served as senior deputy mayor for Mayor Goldsmith during part of his term, and now is President of Competitive Government Strategies consulting firm in Indianapolis – described the situation at the start of Goldsmith's first term as mayor: "We were totally bound in red tape. We *de-*

layered, eliminated unneeded regulations, and streamlined cumbersome rules. There were scores of activities that required a city permit that no longer require permits."

The results of reducing regulations are significant. The city eliminated 68,000 permits/year. For example, it eliminated or streamlined many business and occupational licenses for small businesses. This included reducing regulation in the taxi industry in Indianapolis. Previously, only a limited number of people could obtain taxi licenses. Now, it is easier to get a taxi license if an applicant meets all health and safety requirements. This brought with it the usual benefits of increased competition: Lower taxi costs and better service.

I experienced this improvement first-hand. On a recent business trip to deliver a speech in Indianapolis, I took limousines that cost the same or less than taxis. Usually, limos cost more than taxis. But, in Indianapolis, I enjoyed the elegance and comfort of a luxury limo – along with a very courteous driver – for slightly less than cab fare for the same rides! This only proved possible because the mayor pushed through a wonderful amount of deregulation.

Organizational Change 3: Labor-Management Partnerships

Mayor Goldsmith inherited the city's bad relationship with labor. That was not all: Since he wanted to privatize some services, labor was upset.

His solution was the creation of a team-based incentive system which employees considered exciting. In fact, Stitt commented, "Some employees even suggested eliminating their jobs. If employees suggested eliminating or privatizing their jobs, they were given an opportunity to take another job with the city government."

In many governments, employees get paid based on three factors: (A) span of control, (B) number of employees, and (C) budget they have control over spending. Goldsmith turned this around by saying he no longer cared about these three factors. Instead, he said each employee is appraised by the value that employee brings to citizens of Indianapolis. First, to do this, the mayor eliminated hundreds of traditional job descriptions and classifications.

Second, he led the charge to break employees out of a typical *"silo"* management system in which an employee works only in one area or department. In its place, Goldsmith instituted putting employees to work on projects that could include government employees from multiple departments and even non-government people. For example – before the major organizational change – when redeveloping a neighborhood, employees from the streets department, parks department and planning department only would work on their own department's piece of the project. To improve on such situations, the mayor had relevant people form a team from all affected groups: (A) government, (B) neighborhood, social and business organizations, plus (C) companies working on the project.

Organizational Change 4: Business Process Reengineering

Doing business process reengineering brings marketplace reality to work done by the city government. The Indianapolis government worked with employees and consultants to "every day work a little better," explained Stitt. For example, Indianapolis developed an operational measure for fixing streets. Instead of just doing repair work, as before, now road crews measure themselves on factors of filling a pothole, including

 ◆ quality
 ◆ quantity
 ◆ financial measures

Now, employees know they can fill a pothole for $305/ton, which is better than most private companies. When the Indianapolis government's road crews could not beat private firms' costs, the government farmed out the work to private companies.

How Was This Change Crucial to City of Indianapolis' Survival & Growth

When Mayor Goldsmith assumed office, Indianapolis was like many – if not most – major cities. It was losing (A) residents, (B) jobs, and (C) economic opportunities. Goldsmith took as his charge the need to turnaround the city to make it not just survive – but also to evolve quickly into a metropolis that proves mighty attractive to both businesses and residents. Stitt put it this way:

> *As taxpayers leave, costs on those who remain go up. A city has market share, somewhat like a corporation has market share. For the city, market share is the number of people who want to live and work in the city.*
>
> *To be a vibrant and successful city, we had to make people*

want to live, work, and open businesses here. So, the city government needed to greatly improve its quality and cost structure to influence people to stay in Indianapolis or move here.

Within two weeks after his election, Mayor Goldsmith got his staff to think 20 years into the future – to imagine what sort of city would prove desirable for residents and businesses.

And then Mayor Goldsmith said, "Let's go create it!"

Steps Used to Implement This Major Organizational Change

Mayor Goldsmith quickly set in motion a series of eight steps designed to transform the City of Indianapolis government.

Step 1: Eliminated the bureaucratic rules that did not add value

Step 2: Set crystal clear goals

Step 3: Attracted really bright, high-energy staff who shared the mayor's vision for the city

Step 4: Put talented people in place – and then turned them loose by giving them tremendous authority

Step 5: Created an atmosphere of "If It Isn't Broke, Then Break It!!"

This atmosphere among the mayor's team created a *"relentless idea factory,"* observed former Senior Deputy Mayor Stitt. Mayor Goldsmith even gave his staff massive reading lists on many management topics. And that was not all. In an extremely bold, far-sighted way, the mayor also strongly encouraged his staff members to deliver presentations to audiences where the audience would challenge them. This helped Goldsmith's staff develop and further refine their ideas, strategies, and tactics.

Step 6: Instituted philosophy of "Thoughtful Risk-Taking"

The mayor did not mind if one of his staff members made a mistake. But he encouraged them not to make the same mistake twice, often saying, "Make a new mistake next time!"

Step 7: Set really high standards for everybody on the Mayor's staff

Step 8: Gave city employees an emotional and financial ownership in their departments

For example, the mayor worked to get city employees to view their departments like a "business unit" over which they exerted a great deal of control. This mindset extended into all city functions, whether it was managing the city's vehicle fleet or managing outside vendors.

Measurable Improvements Produced by the Organizational Change

The business-like changes in how the City of Indianapolis government operated under Mayor Goldsmith produced spectacular results. Unfortunately, few other government organizations could match Indianapolis' absolutely fabulous track record. Indianapolis' government improvements – in eight years of Goldsmith's tenure as mayor – included the following (see also Diagram 1):

◆ 4 property tax cuts
◆ Quadrupled city's savings account
   How? *Not* by raising taxes!! Instead Indianapolis grew its tax base from people opening businesses. Reason: The city became a highly desirable place to do business.
◆ Reduced unfunded liabilities from $1.5-billion down to zero – without raising taxes!
◆ 45% fewer government employees in 8 years
   (not including police and fire department employees) If police and fire employees are included, Indianapolis now has 25% fewer employees.
◆ Decreased city budget
◆ 90% less labor grievances
◆ 27% decrease in percentage of tax rate used for debt service (from 11.5% down to 8.4%)
◆ Only large U.S. city with AAA (triple A) rating – highest possible – from all three bond rating firms, namely, Moody's, Standard & Poor's, and Fitch.

Diagram 1. **Results of City of Indianapolis' 8 Years of Absolutely Fabulous Organizational Change**

Category	Improvement
Property tax rate	4 tax cuts
Savings account of city	4 times more (quadrupled) – without raising taxes
Unfunded liabilities	Decreased from $1.5-billion down to zero
Government employees	45% fewer in 8 years (not including police & fire)
	25% less (including police & fire)
Budget for city	Decreased
Labor grievances	90% less
Percent of tax rate used to pay debt	27% decrease (from 11.5% down to 8.4%)
Bond rating	AAA rating at all 3 rating services
	(only big U.S. city with AAA bond rating)

Unmeasurable or Qualitative Improvements

The organizational changes produced an *esprit de corps* and higher enthusiasm level among employees that did not exist before Goldsmith was elected mayor. Stitt observed the city's employees

♦ work harder
♦ work smarter
♦ must compete for their work with private firms

For example, now Indianapolis' government employees compete against private waste pick-up companies for trash collection jobs. Result: If they keep their jobs, the city's employees possess irrefutable proof they are the best at doing their jobs in a cost-efficient manner.

Organizational Change Ingredient 1:
Successfully Leading the Organizational Change

Consulting I provide to many organizations gives me great opportunities to observe how highly effective executives lead successful organizational change. My experiences brought me to this conclusion: The only organizational changes that produce the desired results are those that smoothly fit in with the organization's culture and vision. Changes that do not fit in with the culture and vision tend not to work well.

Since city governments are composed of both elected officials and on-going employees, it is fascinating to see how Mayor Goldsmith and his staff forged an exciting, strongly achievement-oriented organizational culture and vision.

City of Indianapolis' Organizational Culture under Mayor Goldsmith

I discovered, during my consulting to organizations, an amazingly on-target way to discern an organization's culture: Uncover the story almost every employee knows and repeatedly tells. The story's theme gives a clear picture of the organizational culture. The story in the Indianapolis city government – as recounted by Stitt – is the following:

"THE POTHOLE STORY"

All Indianapolis employees probably know "The Pothole Story." It goes like this: The mayor came into a cabinet meeting one morning. He sat at the head of the table, looked at his cabinet

members, and he asked, "What does it cost to fill a pothole?"

Everyone looked quite uncomfortable – since no one had the wildest idea what the cost was. Each cabinet member hoped the mayor would not call on him or her for the answer.

Finally, a department head gave the entire Streets Department budget – but not the cost to fill a pothole.

The mayor said, "Filling potholes is one of our core services. And if we're going to be the best at providing our core services, we better find out how much money it costs to do each of our core services – and then see if anyone in private industry can do it better or if we can do it better."

Stitt – who participated in that intense cabinet meeting – reflected that the cabinet's experience with *The Pothole Story* "launched our entire process of becoming a truly competitive city."

Culture – or Main Focus – of City of Indianapolis

The Pothole Story illustrates how Mayor Goldsmith turned the city government's culture into the *"relentless pursuit of providing citizens with the very best value for their hard-earned tax dollars,"* explained Stitt. Everyone focused on that issue.

To keep everyone focused on the culture he was creating, Stitt noticed Mayor Goldsmith *frequently* pointed out to every employee within earshot, *"If we don't provide a dollar of services for a dollar of value, we're stealing from taxpayers."* As such, each organizational change was part of Goldsmith's plan to (A) become the most competitive city and (B) provide full value for every dollar Indianapolis takes from taxpayers.

Big, Exciting Vision of the City of Indianapolis

I always find that successful organizational change grows out of a clearly defined, hugely compelling vision of what the organization aims to achieve. It is the sort of vision that leaves employees excited about coming to work to help the organization move toward its big, exciting vision. Mayor Goldsmith and Stitt framed the city government's vision as follows:

Our key goal is to be America's most competitive city, specifically, the best city in the United States in terms of

- ◆ *safe streets*
- ◆ *strong neighborhoods*
- ◆ *thriving economy*

To achieve the city's vision, the Indianapolis government needed to get its cost and service structures under control plus greatly improve them. Each major organizational change clearly advanced Indianapolis from where it was before Mayor Goldsmith to where his vision said it ought to be.

Goal-Setting to Achieve the City of Indianapolis' Major Organizational Change

Stitt described the exciting tone and manner in which the mayor went about goal-setting:

Mayor Goldsmith insisted his staff set completely unrealistic goals with completely unrealistic timelines – and then he told us we could achieve them. The mayor was perpetually calm – regardless of storms his administration faced. And he kept telling us, "We can do it."

He gave us the expectation we could hit a home run every single time. And if we didn't, we just went right back up to the plate and hit again

This reminds me of a comment by hockey superstar Wayne Gretzky. He once pointed out, "I miss every shot I don't take!" Mayor Goldsmith definitely made sure his staff never hesitated to take action on matters that could advance the vision of making Indianapolis a magnificent city to live and work.

For example, when Goldsmith first took office, Stitt was in charge of enterprise development. One of Stitt's first big, "completely unrealistic goals with completely unrealistic timelines" was the following: *Save $1-million/month without reducing services.*

Notice: This goal required making the Indianapolis government vastly more cost efficient and competitive – just like almost all private companies strive to do. This marvelous goal contrasts sharply from the "typical" government agency – outside of Indianapolis, of course! – that predictably insists any cost reduction automatically requires reductions in services provided to citizens and businesses. Fortunately, under Mayor Goldsmith, Indianapolis learned the lesson of providing *more services with less money*, just like tens of thousands of companies learn – and succeed in doing – every year.

Organizational Change Ingredient 2:
Successfully Handling Employee Problems during the Organizational Change

One of the chief hurdles of organizational change is employees' resistance and roadblocks. Angry employees channel their energy into directly and indirectly making sure the organizational change fails. Some employees feel incredibly threatened, some fear losing their jobs, and some simply do not want to make any changes, even strongly needed improvements in how they work.

Actions of Employees Who Resisted – or Undermined – City of Indianapolis' Organizational Change

In Indianapolis, according to Stitt, some city employees very early in the administration resisted by doing the following actions:
- sabotaged equipment
- reduced productivity
- resigned
- instigated rumors and gossip
- acted like fear mongers

As such, the mayor and his staff faced some rather strong opposition among the city employees they inherited when they took office. Some resistance, very early on, even took a strange tone. For instance, Stitt remembered, "For the first year Mayor Goldsmith was in office, when I got on an elevator in the morning, many city employees would get off."

Compare City of Indianapolis' *"Old-Style"* Employees with Its Needed *"New-Style"* Employees

In every organization, some employees who performed fine *before* major organizational change – *old-style* employees – may perform poorly in the dramatically changed landscape. For this reason, after major organizational change, an organization may need so-called *new-style* employees who exhibit the skills, talents and attitudes the changed organization needs. According to Stitt, the following two columns compare what City of Indianapolis needed both before and after its major changes under Mayor Goldsmith:

Old-Style Employee	New-Style Employee
Works in 1 department	Works on interdepartmental projects
Solo work	Teamwork
Likes receiving direction	Likes independence
Prefers to be told what to do	Prefers to be self-led by working on self-managed work teams
Focus: Seniority & experience	Focus: Updating & expanding skills
Checks brains at door	Uses brains everyday
Risk-averse	Thoughtful risk-takers
Civil service mentality	Entrepreneurial mentality
Feels like "Employee" only	Feels like "Owner"

In terms of the last comparison – Feels like "Employee" only versus Feels like "Owner" – the difference is conceptual, not literal; the employees, after all, did not own the city government. What Stitt saw is after the major changes, increasing numbers of employees used the word *"our"* when talking about their work. For example, when referring to their work, employees used terms like *"our* shop" and "our contract to do city work."

I find this last phrase – *"our* contract to do city work" – particularly revealing and significant. Specifically, usually government employees automatically get work that *supposedly* only government agencies should do. However, the spectacular Indianapolis change required government departments to compete for contracts with private firms. This meant that when a city department landed a contract to do certain work, the city's employees really did win the contract by being the best available. They earned the right to feel proud. And their increasing use of the word "our" shows a boost in the number of employees feeling they emotionally "owned" the work they did, rather than just being employees who are cogs in a wheel.

Actions to Transform *"Old-Style"* Employees into *"New-Style"* Employees

The major organizational change under Mayor Goldsmith was an exciting and exhilarating time for the city's employees. This rather electrical atmosphere helped many city employees makeover themselves into needed *new-style* employees. Goldsmith's unique leadership – never before seen in the City of Indianapolis government – included four actions that helped employees transform to meet their new challenges.

Action 1: Demanded employees show strong financial value for their work

Action 2: Measured performance of each employee and each city department

Action 3: Provided incentives

Action 4: Gave freedom to fail in this new, dramatically more business-like environment

Recommendations to Employees Who Work in Organizations Undergoing Major Changes

Upon reflection of his role in the City of Indianapolis, Stitt offered these words of wisdom to employees in any organization implementing major changes:

Recommendation 1: Embrace the Change

"If the train's going down the track, you may as well be in the locomotive," enthused Stitt.

Recommendation 2: Make Sure You Understand Your Organization's Exact Vision & Goals

"Ask leaders to tell you exactly where the organization and you are going," Stitt said.

Recommendation 3: Understand This Is the Wave of the Future

Stitt suggested, "Use the organizational change as an opportunity to learn new skills, because this is how it's done now. It's impossible to return to the old way the organization did work. So, this is your big chance to learn how to ride the wave of the future."

"De-Employment" to Make City of Indianapolis' Organizational Change Succeed

Indianapolis used three types of de-employment or other employment changes to institute the changes Goldsmith brought to the city:

- ◆ Small number of layoffs, almost exclusively among mid-level and senior mid-level managers who did not share the new vision
- ◆ Some voluntary and a few involuntary reassignments
- ◆ Limited employee-suggested early retirements

Improvements in Hiring Methods to Sustain the City of Indianapolis' Organizational Change

As a business psychologist, I have done a lot of work with companies to help them improve their hiring methods. This resulted in my third book, *Hire the Best – & Avoid the Rest™*, customized interviewing methods, plus the *Abilities & Behavior Forecaster™* pre-employment tests I developed*

Indianapolis introduced great hiring improvements to help bring employees on board who would help the city's organizational changes succeed in a big way. First, the mayor relentlessly pursued new talent among people he met. Second, the mayor required each cabinet member to find, attract, and develop new people. Third, the head of the human resources department became a member of the mayor's cabinet, which previously was not the case. Fourth, in hiring employees, Goldsmith's team focused less on job skills listed in job descriptions and more on personal work traits. The traits included (A) energy, (B) passion for providing people with great value, (C) enthusiasm, (D) leadership, (E) intellectual capacity, and (F) shared vision – specifically, enthusiasm for Indianapolis' vision that the city needs to be competitive.

Organizational Change Ingredient 3:
Successfully Managing Yourself during the Organizational Change

No organizational change succeeds in a big way, unless the executives leading it exhibit certain personal qualities. The qualities include

◆ optimism
◆ upbeat attitudes
◆ using phrases that promote enthusiasm for change
◆ personal background that includes a track record of overcoming obstacles and succeeding in important life and work goals

I wrote about these vital attributes in two of my books: (A) *Spontaneous Optimism™: Proven Strategies for Health, Prosperity &*

---

*For information on Dr. Mercer's *Customized Hire the Best Tool Kit™*, seminars, speeches, and *Forecaster™* tests, you can turn to the Materials You Can Order section at the end of this book.

Happiness and also (B) *How Winners Do It: High Impact People Skills for Your Career Success** Mayor Goldsmith is an incredibly exciting, inspiring person to be around. And he possesses the traits that enabled him to lead the instrumental organizational changes in the Indianapolis city government.

Optimism Helped This Executive Succeed in Implementing Major Organizational Change

Mayor Goldsmith certainly exudes optimism. He said, "We set out to change government so it would serve people. To do this, optimism was very important. I have a problem-solving philosophy, continually encouraging city employees to solve problems." Indeed, my research and writings on the vital role of optimism in career success discovered *"a problem-solving philosophy"* exists at the core of optimism. And, since success is based on problem-solving and taking action, Goldsmith's philosophy appears aligned with the optimism of great achievers.

Attitudes of This Executive that Most Helped Him Succeed

Goldsmith attributes much of his success to three of his firmly entrenched attitudes. These certainly are the attitudes of someone who can lead dramatic organizational changes – and make them succeed on a large scale:

Attitude 1: Strongly Dislike Process & Admire Chaos

He pointed out, "My goal was to reduce city bureaucracy, and focus people on problems with a fixed timetable. To accomplish this, I needed to establish a clear vision and encourage employees to think beyond the process as it had been."

Attitude 2: Be Clear about Goals & Loose about the Process to Achieve Goals

Attitude 3: Industry – Hard Work & Concentration

---

*More information on *Spontaneous Optimism*[TM] and also *How Winners Do It* is available by referring to the Materials You Can Order section in the back of this book.

Phrases This Executive Says to Keep Focused & Upbeat

Excellent leaders and other accomplished people repeat phrases to themselves and those around them to maintain focus on what counts the most. Goldsmith takes great delight in using three of his favorite phrases:

Phrase 1: "We have only so many days to change the world. So we need intensity and results."

Phrase 2: "Every moment counts."

Phrase 3: "Every day we don't have a solution to a problem, a person's life is directly affected."

It is fascinating to note that each of the mayor's favorite phrases include a sense that time is limited, so it is important to take action rapidly. The phrases convey his strongly held view on the importance of *taking action* now.

How This Executive Got His Staff to Focus on Solutions – Not Problems

Optimists focus on solutions, while pessimists focus on problems. As the executive in charge of organizing and leading the Indianapolis government's changes, Goldsmith automatically undertook the task of serving as the role model for those around him. How did he make sure that staff were problem-solvers, rather than just problem-finders? He used three main methods, which are quoted below in the mayor's own words.

Method 1: "I encouraged results, not committees and studies."

Method 2: "The reason problems exist is because people are scared to take risks. So, I told my staff to take risks. I encouraged them not to worry about making mistakes. I offered to step between my staff and risk."

Method 3: "When staff came to me with problems without resolve, we worked together to find a solution. Sometimes they needed resources that were unavailable; or sometimes it was a lawyer to advise them legally."

As a business psychologist who consults to executives, I noticed two factors emerging in Mayor Goldsmith's methods. First, he strongly encouraged his staff to get things done, regardless of any and all obstacles – emphasizing results. Second, he conveyed trust to his staff. His actions and demeanor consistently communicated his belief that these talented people would find ways to go over, under, around or through almost any roadblock to achieving the organization's vision:

> *Our key goal is to be America's most competitive city, specifically, the best city in the United States in terms of*
> ◆ *safe streets*
> ◆ *strong neighborhoods*
> ◆ *thriving economy*

Favorite Story of This Executive

When I ask a person to tell me his or her favorite story, I always gain a tremendous wealth of insight into that person's personality. I learn about what makes that person tick, both personally and professionally. Goldsmith's favorite story likewise proves wonderfully revealing about what he considers truly important:

> *After forcing enormous change through the city government system, I went to work with a street repair crew laying asphalt and fixing streets. This was being filmed by a television station that was doing a report on how we improved Indianapolis.*
>
> *When the TV film crew turned off its cameras, I asked a street repair worker, "What do you think about having to compete to keep your job?"*
>
> *He looked at me, and he answered with a great look of confidence and optimism, "Mayor, if we have to compete, we'll compete with the best companies. I don't care if you force us to bid on every job, because we'll win every time."*

This story conveys Goldsmith's commitment to helping people feel a strong sense of pride and high self-esteem from accomplishing important goals. It showed the organizational changes he undertook were meant not just to improve government operations and the city, but also to show people they could accomplish more than they realized. It is his simultaneous linking of personal, executive and organizational achievements that make Goldsmith an inspiring leader.

Formative Events in This Executive's Childhood That Help Him in His Career

The most striking elements of Goldsmith's most formative childhood events are twofold:

◆ speed – he accomplished goals fast and either on-time or ahead of schedule
◆ being a leader in *multiple* ways

Formative Event 1: Earned Eagle Scout badge in record time. To accomplish this, Goldsmith said he learned two important lessons. First, he learned that when he stays focused, he can achieve speedy – and effective – results. He decided he wanted to be an Eagle Scout "as quickly as possible." In fact, when Goldsmith earned his Eagle Scout badge, he was the youngest – or one of the youngest – Eagle Scouts in the U.S. at that time! Second, Goldsmith learned confidence. He felt tremendous satisfaction in accomplishing this feat.

Formative Event 2: Student leadership positions in school. For example, he was elected student council president.

Formative Event 3: Newspaper editor in high school & college. This powerful experience helped Goldsmith's quest to be a leader. As he put it, "I had to get the newspaper published on-time every week, often through the work of unmotivated writers."

15

ROBERT MONDAVI CORPORATION

The Thrills, Spills & Chills of a Successful Restructuring

Robert Mondavi Corporation's *Vision:*
Our key goal is to be the
world's preeminent fine wine producer.

The name Mondavi – officially Robert Mondavi Corporation – is indelibly linked to fine wine. The company is, explains Dr. Alan Schnur, senior vice president of human resources, in the "luxury goods business."

Specifically, Robert Mondavi grows grapes, makes wine, plus markets and sells the wine. Its highly respected brands include

◆ Robert Mondavi Winery
◆ Woodbridge Winery
◆ Robert Mondavi Coastal
◆ Byron Vineyards & Winery
◆ Vichon Mediterranean

The company also carries out an array of joint ventures, including wineries in Chile and Italy. Its one thousand employees produce annual sales approaching one-half billion dollars.

Robert Mondavi's Major Organizational Change

Robert Mondavi's organizational change was its major restructuring to increase the company's ability to compete. The company's executives planned the restructuring for six months.

Then, the company moved quickly and decisively implemented much of the reorganization in only one week.

The restructuring affected everything in the company, except the sales department. Specifically, the company

◆ eliminated redundancies

◆ centralized all staff functions

◆ eliminated jobs the company no longer could afford

◆ streamlined processes and procedures

◆ reduced layers of management to increase accountability and decrease costs

◆ made every employee more accountable for business performance, and subsequently revamped its compensation and performance management programs to drive desired behavior change

How Was This Change Crucial to Robert Mondavi's Success, Survival, & Growth?

The major reorganization was essential to the company's success – and even its business survival. By restructuring, the company realized it broke an *un*written contract it had with employees to insulate them from changes.

But, market forces made the restructuring necessary. Specifically, the wine business has turned into an extraordinarily competitive industry. This fact illustrates the competition: When Robert Mondavi started, Napa Valley, California – one of the world's premier wine growing regions – contained only 29 wineries. Now, more than 250 wineries reside there. This is about a nine-fold increase in the number of wineries Robert Mondavi competes against just in Napa Valley.

And that is not all. Schnur explained that roughly 12% of the U.S. population drinks 88% of the wine. So, the more market penetration Robert Mondavi can get into that 12% of the population, the more it can capture market share to increase sales. Also, as any wine consumer sees, hundreds of wines are available on store shelves everywhere. As competition increases in the wine business, there will be an industry consolidation, predicted Schnur. So, Robert Mondavi's reorganization proved crucial to its

◆ current profitability

◆ future growth

Steps Used to Implement This Crucial Organizational Change

Robert Mondavi carried out its major restructuring using seven main steps.

Step 1: Gain consensus at the executive and family level that change was mandatory

Step 2: Involve Robert Mondavi family in the organizational change planning

The company is publicly traded, and the family owns a very large percentage. So, the family's support for the restructuring was absolutely essential.

Step 3: Thorough planning

This included two main arenas. First was thorough planning of how to implement the reorganization. Second was planning how to communicate the restructuring to all the company's constituencies, including

◆ Wall Street
◆ vendors
◆ employees
◆ distributors
◆ consumer groups, such as retail chains

Step 4: Training for managers who would implement the restructuring

A key component of this training entailed teaching managers how to lay-off employees with "compassion, elegance, respect, and dignity," emphasized Schnur. "We didn't want laid-off employees to think that this was personal or, worse, that they were flawed people. We wanted them to know the company could no longer afford their jobs."

Step 5: Implement reorganization "flawlessly"

Step 6: Very effective open, honest communications

These communications aimed to impart to employees and other constituencies accurate information about the restructuring and, importantly, the rationale and data behind all decisions.

Step 7: Frequent follow-up & tracking

To assure the effectiveness of the reorganization, the company often checked to see if all went well. This also enabled managers to take needed actions for any changes that did not proceed as planned.

Measurable Improvements Produced by Robert Mondavi's Restructuring

The restructuring produced three key results that went right to the bottom line, as shown in Diagram 1:

◆ 1 - 2% improved return on assets

◆ 5% lower payroll

◆ 6 - 7% reduced cost structure

Robert Mondavi's cost structure decreased in large part due to the company needing less staff, which eliminated many expenses.

Diagram 1. **Results of Robert Mondavi's Absolutely Fabulous Organizational Change**

Category	Improvement
Return on assets	1 - 2% increase
Payroll	5% less
Cost structure	6 - 7% lower

Unmeasurable Improvements

Importantly, Schnur mentioned the quality of the Robert Mondavi wines stayed high, despite all the major organizational change at the company. Plus, the reorganization resulted in two magnificent qualitative changes.

First, Schnur found, not surprisingly, the reorganization resulted in "big time culture changes." Now, importantly, most employees strongly understand they need to directly contribute in *measurable*, bottom line ways to the profitability of (A) their business unit and (B) the company as a whole. This profound shift should translate into long-term measurable boosts in quality and profits.

Second, the reorganization required employees to improve efficiency. Schnur explained, "This occurred because we had fewer people to do the work. As a result, unnecessary work previously done by laid-off employees was eliminated and work tasks considered unimportant fell by the wayside."

Organizational Change Ingredient 1: Successfully Leading the Organizational Change

Consulting I provide to companies, plus my research, repeatedly point to this reality of organizational change: The only change that produces the desired results is change that logically and directly bolsters the company's culture and vision. Then, the organizational change only gets implemented properly through structured goal-setting and enthusiastic teamwork to accomplish the goals. Given these realities of how companies make dramatic improvements, it is enlightening to see how Robert Mondavi Corporation put these insights into action in its major restructuring.

Robert Mondavi's Corporate Culture

I discovered the best way to uncover an organization's culture is to find out what story about the company each employee hears within the first week on-the-job and automatically tells to new employees. The story usually centers on the company's founder. The gist of the story encapsulates the way of thinking and behaving the company expects employees to put into action on-the-job.

Schnur explained the story conveying the company's culture is Robert Mondavi's life and his passion for producing fine wine and a magnificent lifestyle:

Robert Mondavi's Life

Robert Mondavi's life is winemaking. He recognized early in his career – and long before it was recognized as a leading wine region – that the Napa Valley had the soil and climate to grow high quality wine grapes. He risked absolutely everything he had to pursue his extreme passion for making fine wine. He borrowed heavily to build his own winery – a winery built in the then unorthodox California mission architecture. With the borrowed money, he built the Robert Mondavi Winery.

Indeed, Robert is so passionate about producing fine wine in the Napa Valley that he is known to use phrases like these:

→ *"There is no such thing as too much fine wine."*
→ *"Do everything with all your heart and all your soul!"*
The second phrase "Do everything with all your heart and all your soul!" – is very meaningful to employees who, in turn, will do everything it takes to ensure our success.

Culture – or Main Focus – of the Robert Mondavi Corporation

Founder Robert Mondavi's extreme passion for making fine wine, according to Schnur, conveys the company's culture. He says the culture has an overwhelmingly *"quality-driven focus.* For people at Robert Mondavi, wine-making never is finished until a very high quality level is achieved."

In fact, Robert Mondavi himself remarked, "Our wines belong among the *world's* greatest." Such a statement by the company's founder and visionary leader gives clear direction to employees. They do not make just any wine. Instead, the mission – the only purpose for anyone to work at Robert Mondavi – is to produce wine of *world-class quality and stature.* This provides an exciting place where employees know they play a role in something incredibly special not just at their work site – but also globally.

Link between Robert Mondavi's Culture & Its Major Organizational Change

Despite the business necessity to dramatically reorganize Robert Mondavi, this entire major organizational change was carried out with the company's quality-driven culture clearly in mind. Schnur pointed out, "Quality still is the #1 single most important thing we're about. We wanted people to know that our quality would not fall as a result of cost-cutting." That explains why – when he discusses the major restructuring – Schnur always makes sure to reiterate Robert Mondavi's quality remained high throughout the change, and quality continues to increase (as recent wine ratings attest).

Vision of the Robert Mondavi Corporation

From my experience of consulting to many companies, I always find every amazingly successful company does everything based on its vision of achieving a big, exciting status. Generally, this vision entails being the best and/or biggest in its industry, often with worldwide ambitions.

What is Robert Mondavi's big, exciting vision? Schnur summarizes the vision as follows:

Our key goal is to be the
world's preeminent fine wine producer.

Ways the Organizational Change Fits into Robert Mondavi's Vision

Robert Mondavi executives conjured up the restructuring to advance the company toward its vision. As Schnur explained,

We restructured to progress toward our vision of becoming the world's preeminent wine producer. It often takes five years to get a positive return-on-investment in the wine business. So, we had to streamline if we truly wanted to become the world's best.

Highly successful executives excel at forward thinking. All too often, underachieving companies have executives who focus on how to operate better now or in the near future. In sharp contrast, executives leading highly successful companies simultaneously juggle (A) getting work done on a short-term basis and (B) improving the company to prepare it to excel many years ahead.

Goal-Setting to Accomplish the Company's Major Organizational Change

Robert Mondavi Corporation used a well-organized two-part method to set goals. First, executives pledged to the company's board of directors that they would achieve a set of three broad goals, as follows:

1. *Financial Goals*

These included detailed financial targets. The targets included reducing headcount by a certain percentage and decreasing overhead by a designated amount.

2. *Quality Goals*

Such goals focused on Robert Mondavi's high quality of wine, especially harvesting practices, vineyard developing practices, and winemaking.

3. *Efficiency Goals*

The efficiency goals delved into support staff, such as HR and Finance, assisting the growing, winemaking and sales operations. Efficiency goals also zoomed in on productivity levels, including how the number of cases bottled on each particular line could be maintained or increased despite having fewer employees.

Second, executives translated the company's three broad goals into specific goals their departments would accomplish within a promised timeframe. For example, Schnur set these five goals in his role of senior vice president of human resources.

Goal #1: Assure restructuring took place flawlessly by [a specific date].

Goal #2: Keep layoff-related budget within 5% of plan by [a specific date].

Goal #3: Complete layoff with no legal actions by [a specific date].

Goal #4: Insure clear understanding by all employees of the rationale and planning associated with the restructuring.

Goal #5: Develop programs and activities to accelerate the healing process.

Teamwork to Accomplish Goals

Three main ingredients went into promoting teamwork and widespread collaboration throughout the company.

Teamwork Method 1: Brought Executive Team On-Board

Importantly, most of Robert Mondavi is operated by senior managers. As such, getting all members of this executive team going in the same direction proved crucial. How did the company do this? Schnur led an off-site session of the senior managers. He later looked back and remarked, "That session led to the startling realization that a significant change was unavoidable and absolutely necessary."

Teamwork Method 2: "Broaden the Circle"

The senior managers brought the vice presidents into the restructuring process in a careful and logical way. This reaped more support for what the company needed to do.

Teamwork Method 3: Teambuilding Sessions After the Restructuring

As needed, the company conducted teambuilding sessions after restructuring. These sessions, designed to accelerate the healing process, helped employees

◆ discuss the restructuring openly
◆ understand the restructuring
◆ work together to set new goals to improve business performance

Organizational Change Ingredient 2:
Successfully Handling Employee Problems during the Organizational Change

Each time a company implements organizational change, some employees are bound to throw up roadblocks. Such resistance can

derail even the best-planned change. That explains why successful
organizational change requires executives who firmly, yet tactfully,
handle the employee problems that are bound to pop up.

**Actions of Employees Who Resisted – or Undermined – Robert
Mondavi's Organizational Change**

At Robert Mondavi, Schnur observed resistance among a
portion of the workforce. This was to be expected, given the
significant restructuring. He noticed some employees

♦ unable to cope with the changes, including the loss of
   respected co-workers
♦ openly resisted the changes, either vocally and/or
   behaviorally
♦ wondered "what was next?"

On the positive side, many employees welcomed the
restructuring with open arms. Schnur found some employees
made comments like, "This is great! It's about time the company
made changes like these."

**Emotional Reactions of Employees that Slowed Down the
Organizational Change**

Behind the actions of employees who resist the organizational
change is an array of uncomfortable emotions. For instance,
Schnur observed some employees felt

♦ shock
♦ fear
♦ betrayal
♦ anger

The anger especially was directed at the company's
management, including much anger directed at Schnur. Some
comments employees made to managers included (A) "You
betrayed us!", (B) "I can't believe you'd do this!", plus (C) other
emotional comments that cannot be repeated in this book!

Based on consulting I provide to organizations undergoing
major organizational changes, I know these are uncomfortable –
yet very typical – emotional reactions. It is noteworthy that some
employees felt betrayed. This is an incredibly typical feeling
among employees.

Once I delivered a speech at a major conference where
reporters were in attendance. From my presentation, business

magazines, newspapers and even a few TV shows widely quoted this comment I made in my speech: *"A typical emotional reaction of employees during organizational change and reorganizations is betrayal. In fact, it feels like a spouse or lover just walked out on you!"*

Similarly, in organizations, employees often fall into the habit of *expecting* their work environment to remain the same. When this status quo is broken – by a company restructuring or a significant person walking out – a person feels *betrayed.*

Effective Methods to Handle Employees Who Resisted the Organizational Change

Robert Mondavi Corporation used three main methods to deal with employee resistance and discomfort. First, Schnur prepared the executive team for the emotional reactions employees would throw in their faces. He especially taught executives to allow employees to "vent" their emotions – voice their feelings while the executive expressed understanding.

Second, managers were told to allow employees a lot of time to be emotional. This was not always easy. After all, work needed to get done. Yet, at the same time, if employees could not voice their uncomfortable emotions, they probably would have shown more work resistance. Such resistance might have been work slowdowns or badmouthing the company rather than being productive on-the-job.

Third, and very importantly, about two months after the restructuring, managers quietly met one-to-one with employees who still felt bitter. In these meetings, Schnur explained, managers basically said something like this to each resistant, bitter, or negative employee: "We know you're still very angry – but since we're not going back, you either need to accept the changes and get on-board or find another place to work."

This third tactic the company used proves crucial in carrying out restructuring of any type. The phrasing shows an excellent method used by expert negotiators and persuaders.

In my book, speeches and workshops entitled, *How Winners Do It: High Impact People Skills for Your Career Success,* I show how expert negotiators use a two-step method to persuade another person*:

---

*You can find out more about Dr. Mercer's materials, book, audio-book and presentations on *How Winners Do It: High Impact People Skills for Your Career Success* by referring to the Materials You Can Order section at the back of this book.

Step 1 is the negotiator helping the person feel comfortable by showing understanding of his or her concerns. For example, "We know you're still very angry."

Step 2 involves the negotiator leading the person to making a choice. For instance, "you either need to accept the changes and get on- board or find another place to work."

By Robert Mondavi Corporation using this two-step method, the company used empathy, expert negotiating, and – as needed – gave highly resistant employees a reasonable ultimatum. This is crucial. At some point, each employee needs to accept that the company's way of doing things is the company's way of doing things. No amount of bellyaching or complaining or badmouthing or resisting will change that. Employees who cannot accept that truly are better off moving on to an employer whom they like more.

However, based on my experience, employees who cannot accept changes at one company simply take their personalities with them to their next job. So, if you interview an applicant who badmouths his or her employer, do not expect that applicant to behave any differently if you hire that person. The person would find reasons to badmouth you and your company, also.

In my hiring tool kit, workshops, speeches and book on *Hire the Best – & Avoid the Rest*™, I point out, "*Past behavior is the best predictor of future behavior.*" I also inform people that "Whatever behavior you see from an applicant during the screening process [testing, interviews, etc.] is likely to be the *best* behavior you ever will see from that person." *

So, if a job applicant complains about his or her previous employer, boss or work situation, you can expect that applicant will act the same if you put hire him or her. So, make sure you pay close attention to how job applicants talk about their prior work experiences.

---

*For information on Dr. Mercer's pre-employment tests, hiring tool kits, presentations and book on *Hire the Best – & Avoid the Rest*™, you can refer to the Materials You Can Order section in the back of this book.

Comparing Robert Mondavi's "Old-Style" Employees to Its Needed "New-Style" Employees

At every company implementing organizational change, some employees who do well on-the-job before the change – I call them "old-style" employees – do not perform well after the change. At that point, the company needs "new-style" employees with skills, attitudes or talents that differ from the company's "old-style" employees. The table below summarizes Schnur's comparison of Robert Mondavi's employees using my dichotomy:

Old-Style Employees	New-Style Employees
Focus: Seniority & experience	Focus: Updating & expanding skills
Resists change	Embraces or accepts change
Adheres to tradition	Seeks new traditions
"We've always done it this way!"	Seeks way to improve productivity & profits
Avoids conflict	Deals directly with matters affecting job performance, employees & business

Transforming "Old-Style" Employees into "New-Style" Employees

Robert Mondavi used three key methods to create the *"new-style"* workforce it needed.

Transformation Method 1: "Let some people go"

In certain instances, the company terminated some employees.

Transformation Method 2: "Brought in new blood – like Moses in the desert"

Schnur explained his colorful phrase:

> *Moses wandered the desert for decades, because the people were not ready for freedom. By wandering the desert for decades, the people who were used to the old system – slavery – died and the people left were those who only knew freedom.*

By analogy, as Robert Mondavi has brought in "new blood" in the months since the restructuring – hired employees from outside of the company – it acquired talented people who had no personal history with Robert Mondavi's pre-restructuring business operations. These new employees hired from outside only knew the new, improved post-restructuring company. So, they were much more likely to dive into their work as the *"new-style"*

employees Robert Mondavi needed after its reorganization. For instance, they were more likely to be employees who
- focus on updating and expanding skills
- embrace change
- seek new traditions
- deal directly with matters affecting work, employees, and business

Transformations Method 3: Tell employees actual behaviors expected from them

Robert Mondavi managers focused on consistently communicating *specific behaviors* employees needed to succeed. Managers clearly informed everyone how to be the *"new-style"* employees the company needed post-restructuring. Schnur emphasized, "We told everyone what the right answer is: We told employees *this* is what you need to do to succeed here."

Recommendations for Employees of Companies Undergoing Organizational Change

Employees whose employers are implementing major change often wonder what they can do to make sure they come out ahead during and after the change. Who could be better to ask than an executive who led major organizational change? So, I asked Schnur what he recommends to employees. He offered five wise tips:

Tip 1: Do your job extremely well.
Tip 2: Know how your job contributes to the company's bottom line.
Tip 3: Speak your mind, looking for ways to add greater value.
Tip 4: If you don't make it there, then go and do something else.

"There are plenty of other places to work," Schnur remarked.

Tip 5: Have a life.

"Make sure you have both a work life and a personal life," Schnur recommended. "People who handle change well tend to have a strong personal life. These people don't live or die for work."

"De-Employment" to Implement Robert Mondavi's Major Organizational Change

Robert Mondavi laid-off four percent of its employees. The company identified jobs it could not continue to afford. If the affected employees could not be offered reassignments, the company offered both

- generous severance packages
- compassionate outplacement programs

Importantly, Robert Mondavi worked hard to help de-employed individuals leave with their egos intact. This is exceedingly difficult for any company. And the company handled it in an exemplary manner. Managers explained to each laid-off employee that the lay-off was due to the company changing – and was not a reflection of the individual employee's productivity. As Schnur put it, "We worked to avoid employees thinking their lay-off was personal or a reflection of their work."

Hiring Improvements to Reinforce the Organizational Change

When I help companies implement my *Hire the Best – & Avoid the Rest*™ methods, I always emphasize that a company needs to decide what characteristics its successful employees possess – and then evaluate each applicant to find out if he or she possesses those key traits. By evaluating applicants using tests, interviews, and other prediction methods, a company increases its likelihood of hiring a productive, dependable workforce.

Given the major changes at Robert Mondavi, it is interesting to see how the company altered its hiring method post-restructuring. In hiring, the company continues its previous careful hiring process – with one significant addition. Now, the company also prefers job candidates who worked in companies that instituted major organizational change. By doing this, new employees are more likely to accept and not feel alarmed by changes Robert Mondavi undertakes.

Organizational Change Ingredient 3:
Successfully Managing Yourself during the Organizational Change

Every manager implementing organizational change brings two vital personal ingredients to how he or she leads the change endeavors. These ingredients are the leader's personal

- optimism, confidence, and "Can-Do" approach
- history that prepared the person to succeed as a leader

Let's look at these factors in Dr. Alan Schnur, Robert Mondavi Corporation's senior vice president of human resources.

Optimism Helped This Executive Succeed in Implementing Major Organizational Change

Schnur found his optimism played a "huge role" in planning and implementing Robert Mondavi's restructuring. He commented that an executive "needs to have vision, conviction and believe in the longer-term value of the process" to make a major organizational change succeed.

Along these lines, Schnur mentioned four "beliefs" he holds near and dear:

Belief 1: A company must continually reinvent itself.

Belief 2: On-going change is required; it builds strength the company needs to survive and prosper.

Belief 3: Every organizational change must be right for the company long-term.

Belief 4: People are resilient; it may be hard to make changes, but most can get through it.

Reinforcing his optimism and beliefs, Schnur also has a few phrases he likes using:

Phrase 1: "Relentlessly focus on our goal."

Phrase 2: "This will work – hang in there."

Phrase 3: "Don't let the difficult people get you down."

How This Executive Gets Employees to Focus on Solutions – Not Problems

Schnur impressed me as a strong role model – for Robert Mondavi employees – of an optimistic, solution-focused leader. For instance, he remarked, *"I hardly ever complain. Instead, I listen to a problem, and then make sure we come up with four or five solutions to the problem."*

Importantly, he firmly takes for granted that "people who find the solutions are far more valuable" than people who just pose problems or complain. That is, he strongly assumes optimistic people (who are *solution*-focused) will achieve greater heights in their careers than pessimists (who are *problem*-focused).

How does Schnur cultivate this solution orientation among Robert Mondavi employees? He does it by (A) listening to problems, and then (B) immediately asking the person for solutions. Here are two examples. First, when someone puts forward a problem or complaint, he is likely to make this request to that person: *"Give me a solution."* Second, when he hears someone complaining, Schnur looks at the person and says, *"You're digging a hole for yourself. Show me the ladder."* The "ladder" he asks for is the solution.

This Executive's Favorite Story

Being an avid reader and student of the stage and films, Schnur has many stories he enjoys and appreciates. One that stands out to him is the following:

The Princess Bride

This is a story of true love – through barriers thick and thin. This story relates to business. After all, it is a story of romance, passion, belief that there is such a thing as true love, and the adventures encountered in the pursuit of true love and happiness.

And – as in business success – in the end the person achieves goals he feels passionate about and, in doing so, experiences the joys of winning.

Actually, it seems quite fitting that Schnur's favorite story outwardly concerns "romance, passion . . . and . . . adventures," yet he links it to success in his career. What makes this so fitting is that Schnur is an executive at Robert Mondavi Corporation, the famous fine wine company. Part of the mystique of making fine wine is a sense of romance and a passion for creating something wonderful for many people to enjoy. In fact, Schnur mentioned that founder Robert Mondavi has been fond of saying, *"Do everything with all your heart and all your soul!"* As such, Schnur's favorite story certainly appears well suited for his leadership role at Robert Mondavi Corporation.

Formative Events in This Executive's Early Life That Help in His Career

Schnur considers three childhood and young adult events as extremely influential in shaping his career successes. The first event was growing up in a large, vocal family. He found this helps him deal with large numbers of people with skills he learned in his big family, especially

- ◆ self-confidence
- ◆ sense of humor
- ◆ strong communications skills

His second very formative event was, at age nine years old,

moving from a small Ohio town to Berkeley, California, which he describes as "a very exciting urban environment." From this, he "learned a new way of life fast. That builds strength. You quickly have to figure out who you are."

Finally, his third most formative event was going to the University of California at Berkeley during the Vietnam War. During that time, Berkeley was a hotbed political environment. In this setting, Schnur says he developed inquisitiveness. He reflected,

> *I was taught to question everything. I also learned the answer is rarely in the book! In fact, some answers may at first appear like low hanging fruit – easy to reach – but the best, most elegant solutions are hard to reach. And you have to create new rules and new ways to do things.*

These three formative childhood and young adult events certainly helped in his career. He learned to get along and stand out in the crowd – key skills needed to reach his executive rank. He also learned to use his reasoning skills to see beyond the tried-and-true to new, creative, better ways to make companies successful. This ability serves him well in his leadership role, as well as in helping plan and implement Robert Mondavi's major organizational change. Executing the change certainly required him to look far past the "low hanging fruit – easy to reach" way the company did business before the restructuring to "create new rules and new ways to do things."

This Executive's Role Models – & Lesson Learned from Each One

Everyone has role models. As a business psychologist who consults to companies, I repeatedly observe that high-achievers find role models who impart powerful guidance which helps in their careers and personal lives. Schnur is reluctant to name any specific role models, but he outlined attributes he finds motivating:.

Role Model 1: Those who take high risks in the pursuit of passionately held goals or dreams. *Lesson Learned:* "Too few of us follow our heart. Be passionate about what you hold most dear. Do not compromise on those things you know to be true."

Role Model 2: Those who develop breakthrough ideas. *Lesson Learned:* "Thinking *differently* takes strength and courage. Thinking differently, which requires knowledge and passion, is essential to creativity and success."

Role Model 3: Those who lead others to successes few would have anticipated. *Lesson Learned:* "Visionary leadership is an all too rare commodity. It's a lonely job, not for the weak. For those of us who have known true leaders, our lives have been changed forever. And for those of us who have assumed leadership roles, our lives, too, have been forever changed."

16

Harley-Davidson

From Survival To Growth

Harley-Davidson's Company Mission:
We fulfill dreams through the experiences of motorcycling.

Harley-Davidson is a name synonymous with the most exciting motorcycles created on the planet. It is the stuff of lore. The company's fame is firmly entrenched in the images millions of people hold about its big, powerful motorcycles. This image includes Hells Angels who will ride nothing else, movies featuring the big machines and, increasingly, corporate executives and professionals spending weekends motorcycling on their machine of choice, namely, a Harley-Davidson.

The company is doing well now. However, not that long ago, the company was teetering on the brink. Its very survival as a corporation – despite its fame – was in jeopardy. In fact, it could have gone under. If that happened, then Harley-Davidson would have been reduced to a name in the dustbin of motorcycle history.

Fortunately, in 1981 a group of executives took the helm of the revered Harley-Davidson Motor Company – and steered the company away from the brink of disaster to new heights of prosperity. The 1980s were all about survival. The 1990s were about growth while maintaining high quality.

Jim McCaslin started with the company in 1992 as head of Harley-Davidson's only assembly plant, located in York, Pennsylvania. Every plant in a manufacturing company is important – or else it would be closed down. However, can you imagine the supreme importance of a plant that is the *only* assembly plant of a company? In 1992, the York facility was the bottleneck hindering future growth. It was the task of McCaslin and his team to turn this situation around.

The Major Organizational Change

McCaslin and his team planned and implemented a major plant turnaround. The Harley-Davidson plant in York is a vertically integrated facility with processes including machining, forming, welding, plating, painting and assembly. McCaslin's philosophy is: "I want it all. In the assembly plant, this meant breaking loose bottleneck issues in order to grow, while at the same time improving safety, improving quality, and reducing per unit costs."

How Was This Change Crucial To Harley-Davidson's Growth?

The York Assembly Plant was Harley's only assembly plant at that time. So, it played a crucial role in Harley's ultimate success – or failure – in the marketplace. Other Harley plants made components, such as engines and plastic parts. But only the York Assembly plant put them all together into the motorcycles Harley is famous for.

So, as McCaslin put it, "When you're the bottleneck, anything you build additional goes straight to the bottom line." This presented a huge opportunity to improve on Harley-Davidson's success.

Steps Used to Implement This Crucial Organizational Change

McCaslin realized major changes were needed to effectively turnaround this assembly plant. He approached this in the spirit of a phrase he likes a lot: *"If you always do what you've always done, you'll always get what you always got."*

Step 1: Made Safety the #1 Concern

McCaslin believes that a plant's safety record is a leading indicator of the plant's performance. Invariably a plant with a worsening safety record is headed for increased cost and quality problems, not to mention deteriorated employee attitudes. In 1992, York's safety record had deteriorated from the previous year. So, McCaslin started talking safety "all the time" to impress on everyone the importance of improving the plant's safety record.

Step 2: Met Every Employee

McCaslin spent a month walking around the plant with

supervisors, introducing himself to, and shaking the hand of, each of the plant's 2,100 employees. Some of these employees would freely talk about the plant's problems. After talking to 2,100 people, certain themes around plant issues became apparent. These formed the basis for which problems needed to be attacked first.

Step 3: Made List of Issues & Problems

Importantly, McCaslin learned that sometimes what seemed like a problem was not *the* real problem. For example, people complained about an "absenteeism problem." However, upon closer investigation, McCaslin discovered this actually was a "poor planning problem." This occurred when managers allowed employees to take vacation days, especially Fridays and Mondays, but then would not plan how to make sure enough production employees were available for assembly.

Step 4: "Make Sure Your Staff Is for You"

McCaslin said this is especially important for him, since he was new to the organization. His staff needed to quickly realize that they needed to improve operations. And if they could not, someone else would. McCaslin believes that the "new" guy has to protect against the "old" guys waiting you out, expecting or hoping that you will not make it.

Step 5: Created Daily 1-Page Operating Report

McCaslin established a one-page daily operating report around the critical operating parameters of the plant and its departments which included: quality, volume produced, productivity levels, flow of critical parts, and safety statistics. There is a tremendous desire by people to put more and more information in operation reports so that they get too big to read and, therefore, do not get read on a regular basis. As McCaslin explained, the daily one-page operating report "focused everyone on priorities of what was most important."

McCaslin managed the plant with the one-page operating report and attendance at the 8:10 a.m. daily line-up meeting. At this meeting, 50 - 60 people representing all plant functions would attend. In 10 minutes if the plant was running great and in 20 minutes if the plant was having problems, the group reviewed yesterday's results and today's issues. This was also the time McCaslin could give messages on his philosophy and on his concerns around plant performance. His message would fan out to the rest of the plant from this meeting.

Step 6: Walk the Floor Everyday

Keeping close to the floor is essential to running a complex operation. "You not only find out what is going on, you become very sensitive to the mood of the plant," explained McCaslin. It helped personalize the major changes going on in the plant, since employees had access to ask and receive answers on current problems and future opportunities. McCaslin also stated, "There is another benefit to walking the floor, especially when things aren't going well. Employees need to know that the boss knows. If you're on the floor, they know you know."

Improvements Produced by the Organizational Change

Over a five-year period, McCaslin and the employees succeeded in turning around this absolutely vital Harley-Davidson plant (see Diagram 1). The metrics prove it, including 1992 - 1997 results like these:

◆ 75% increase in production volume – from 75,000 motorcycles/year up to 132,000/year
◆ 90% improvement in safety lost time accidents
◆ 100% first run quality improvement
◆ $200/motorcycle labor cost decrease

Also, McCaslin credits the turnaround with transforming the organization from a "you can have quality or quantity, but not both" attitude to a "we can have it all" attitude.

Diagram 1. **Results of Harley-Davidson's Absolutely Fabulous Organizational Change from 1992 - 1997**

Category	Measure
Production volume	75% increase
Safety	90% improvement
First run quality	100% improvement
Labor cost per motorcycle	$200 decrease

Organizational Change Ingredient 1: Successfully Leading Harley-Davidson's Major Organizational Change

In consulting I provide to many companies, I continually notice organizational changes that work and produce a positive return-on-investment are those that "fit in" with the company's culture and vision. So, let's look at those two vital factors, as well as how McCaslin used goal-setting and teamwork.

Harley-Davidson's Corporate Culture

I found from experience that the best and quickest way to discover a company's culture is to find out what *story everyone in the company knows and retells.* McCaslin referred to his company's story as *The Turnaround of Harley-Davidson Motor Company in the 1980s.* Thirteen Harley executives bought Harley-Davidson from AMF Corporation in a leveraged buy-out (LBO) in 1981. But, this was a horrible time for business in general and Harley-Davidson in particular, as made clear by these horrifying facts:

- Inflation was 18 - 20%
- Japanese motorcycle companies owned the U.S. market
- Harley's sales dropped by half
- Harley-Davidson had a terrible quality reputation
- Harley was leveraged to the hilt from the LBO
- Dealers had excessive inventory
- Harley-Davidson's core buyers were working-class or blue collar – and blue collar workers were being laid-off in record numbers

The solution to these woes was staging a major turnaround of Harley-Davidson on four fronts: quality improvement, new products, niche marketing, and strong financial controls. The company's impressive turnaround included these company-wide improvements from 1981 - 1986:

- 49% increase in productivity
- 68% reduction in scrap (i.e., wasted materials) and the need to rework
- 175% increase in inventory turns

After succeeding in its incredible turnaround, Harley went public with its initial public offering (IPO) in 1986.

Apparently, the company staged an extremely magnificent turnaround. For instance, its earnings and stock price continue to rise. Since its 1986 IPO, the company's stock has split four times. A $1,000 investment in 1986 was worth about $100,000 14 years later.

In many ways, this story is a real-life example of the *Phoenix Rising from the Ashes* tale told in mythology. Or, to put it in Harley-Davidson's words, as printed in one of its colorful ads:

We survived four wars, a depression, a few recessions, 16 U.S. presidents, foreign and domestic competition, racetrack competition, and one Marlon Brando movie.
Sounds like party time to us.

Culture of Harley-Davidson

McCaslin explained the story of Harley-Davidson's spectacular turnaround embodies the company's culture. This corporate culture, McCaslin emphasized, "focuses on *cultivating and balancing mutually beneficial relationships with all stakeholders.*" For example, Harley-Davidson needed to improve relationships with its stakeholders in the 1980s to accomplish its survival. The stakeholders included:

◆ Customers – "had to convince end users and dealers that we were building quality again"
◆ Employees – after reducing the workforce (hourly and salaried) by 50% in 1981-2, had to win back their hearts and minds
◆ Suppliers – needed their support in extended terms and also in the quality improvement initiative
◆ Investors – needed their support for cash and patience in paying off the loans (loan covenants were being violated)
◆ Government – provided a tariff on Japanese heavyweights

In the 1990s, Harley-Davidson continued and expanded its emphasis on the mutually beneficial relationships with its stakeholders.

Links between Harley-Davidson's Culture & the Major Organizational Change

McCaslin explained the links between Harley-Davidson's corporate culture and his plant turnaround are threefold. They relate to carrying out Harley's values and business issues to serve the company's stakeholders. McCaslin outlined three factors.

Factor 1: Values

The values are (A) Tell the Truth, (B) Be Fair, (C) Keep Your Promises, (D) Respect the Individual, and (E) Encourage Intellectual Curiosity.

Factor 2: Business Issues

Business issues include (A) quality, (B) participation, (C) productivity, (D) flexibility, and (E) cash flow.

Factor 3: Stakeholders
This factor encompasses (A) customers, (B) suppliers, (C) employees, (D) investors, (E) society, and (F) government.

Harley-Davidson's Big, Exciting Company Mission

I continually find that only organizational changes that fit in with a company's vision/mission ultimately succeed. A vision/ mission is a big, exciting overarching goal the company as a whole seeks to accomplish. It is so big and exciting that employees feel enthused to come to work so they can play their role in helping the organization move toward its ambitious, very special vision/ mission. McCaslin summarized Harley-Davidson's mission as follows:

We fulfill dreams through the experiences of motorcycling.

He emphasized the two key words in the company's mission are *"fulfill dreams."* This makes a lot of sense. After all, no one *really* needs a motorcycle. And, if someone gets a motorcycle, it does not need to be a prestigious Harley-Davidson motorcycle. The reason many people crave Harley-Davidson motorcycles is because their motorcycle craving includes the exciting *dream* to ride the best, namely, a Harley-Davidson. As such, Harley-Davidson truly is a company whose ultimate success is realized only through its ability to *"fulfill dreams."*

Ways Harley-Davidson's Major Organizational Change Fit into the Company's Mission

McCaslin explained his assembly plant's turnaround readily fit into the company's vision/mission in two ways. First, to *"fulfill dreams"* requires the company to assemble motorcycles the company can sell so customers can fulfill their dreams. Turning around Harley-Davidson's only assembly plant certainly moved the company toward that monumental task.

Second, the health of Harley-Davidson requires high-quality products. A key component of turning around the company's assembly plant was improving quality. After all, even a company with Harley-Davidson's mystique cannot survive if it does not offer world-class quality products.

And the assembly plant turnaround McCaslin led certainly fulfilled this need. Among the many measurable improvements the turnaround produced, quality came out way ahead. Specifically, the organizational change helped produce a 100% first run quality improvement! Such spectacular quality keeps customers coming back for more. In fact, a whopping 96% of Harley-Davidson customers plan to buy more Harley products in the future. Such customer loyalty plays a central role in the company's survival, growth, and prosperity.

Goal-setting to Achieve Harley-Davidson's Major Organizational Change

Harley-Davidson uses a system akin to management-by-objectives (MBO). The company calls it the PEP Process. At the York Assembly Plant, McCaslin and his staff announced the plant's overall goals. These goals focused on producing measurable improvements in four main arenas:
1. Productivity
2. Quality
3. Safety
4. Volume

Then, McCaslin's staff made sure everyone reporting to them made – and accomplished – goals that helped achieve the plant's goals. Importantly, all employees were put on an incentive system. The system linked incentive pay to achieving measurable goals and overall company profitability.

Teamwork to Achieve Goals

Goals are not achieved alone. And goals needed to pull off a major organizational change definitely require huge amounts of teamwork and interdepartmental collaboration. Hourly and salaried teams were regularly used at York to improve safety, quality and productivity. Hourly teams redesigned work areas for one piece flow, set time standards and balanced the work on the assembly lines. In certain areas, hourly and salaried teams moved and redesigned whole departments. Here are McCaslin's learnings while working at Harley-Davidson and York.

Learning 1: Develop trust

McCaslin emphasizes, "Trust is the huge, #1 issue among all employees. Of particular concern is trust between the plant management and the union leadership. It's critical that you can agree to disagree without damaging the trust relationship."

Learning 2: Consensus management in the company
Since 1993, the Harley-Davidson organizational structure at the leadership level is based upon self-managed teams. The position of executive vice president was eliminated and replaced by the self-managed team. There are three teams or circles: *Produce Products* (plant managers, engineering, purchasing and quality), *Create Demand* (international and domestic sales and service, marketing, styling, parts and accessories and general merchandise), and *Provide Support* (finance, human resources, information systems, legal, planning and communication).

Each team operates with consensus decision making around operating and capital budgets, policy, long- and short-range planning, and high-level hiring, promotions, evaluations and pay. Consensus is not voting; it is getting all members of the team to support the direction. That means the decision may not be your favorite, but it is one that you can support. Once agreed, it is expected that all members will support and assist when necessary the implementation of the decision. As with all teams, the establishment of trust among the members is paramount.

Learning 3: Consensus management in the plant
McCaslin is a proponent of the High Performance Work Organization (HPWO). In an HPWO, decisions around the work are made by those closest to the work: the workers. A key component of an HPWO is self-managed teams on the factory floor. Decision-making is through team consensus. The York employees and management committed to an HPWO backed by contract language. HPWOs are difficult to implement and, in McCaslin's opinion, even more difficult to manage. But the payoff is a 30 - 40% productivity improvement over normal plant operations. York has been in the implementation stage for several years and is ahead of the expected productivity improvement timeline.

All the Harley-Davidson facilities are enacting partnering agreements between management and labor. Some, like the Kansas City operation, are on the cutting edge of self-managed teams and employee involvement. Others are not as far along, but the journey continues. It is worth it.

Organizational Change Ingredient 2: Successfully Managing Yourself during the Organizational Change

I notice executives who plan and implement successful organizational changes tend to use optimistic, upbeat actions and expressions. Indeed, research using my *Abilities & Behavior Forecaster*™ tests showed that highly successful leaders score high on the test's Optimism scale.

At Harley-Davidson, McCaslin said a vital ingredient of the organizational change he engineered was helping employees progress to an optimistic *"We Can Have It All"* philosophy. Of paramount importance is the fact that employees tend to "catch" the emotions conveyed by their leaders. In this case, McCaslin's optimistic, buoyant approach to work and dealing with people trickled down – over a period of time – to employees throughout the Harley-Davidson assembly plant.

How Optimism Helped This Executive Succeed in Implementing Harley-Davidson's Major Organizational Change

McCaslin told me, "I don't think you can underestimate the importance of being optimistic." He found if employees think the boss is having trouble with the organizational changes, then the employees will exhibit trouble with the changes, also. McCaslin found, in his daily walking the floor, "people always looked for a smile on my face. On those days that I wasn't smiling, I would quickly have someone ask, `What's wrong?'"

McCaslin explained, "If the boss gets down, then the troops are authorized to get down, too." This insight gives all the more reason for the leader to feel and outwardly *show an optimistic, can-do, confident outlook all the time.*

Attitudes of This Executive that Help Him Succeed

McCaslin credits much of his success to using five attitudes each day.

Attitude 1. Hard work pays off
Attitude 2. Smile
Attitude 3. Can-Do attitude
Attitude 4. Desire to listen – and follow-up
Attitude 5. Have fun

Phrases This Executive Says to Keep Feeling Optimistic

He mentioned a few phrases that keep his mood positive:

◆ "The difference between being good and great is a little extra effort."

McCaslin learned this phrase from his father who said it daily.

◆ McCaslin kept little signs on his office wall to remind him to do two things all the time:

✓ "Walk the floor"

✓ "Listen"

◆ "Set the goal and then you'll see."

He explained, "You don't need to know how you'll accomplish a goal before you see it. If you truly believe in the goal and let your subconscious mind work on it, solutions and action plans will 'pop up' out of the blue."

This Executive's Focus on Solutions – Not Problems

Optimists focus on solutions. Pessimists focus on problems. Given this situation, how did McCaslin serve as a role model to his staff by modeling the need to focus on solutions?

McCaslin explained, "Perhaps it's my engineering background. I focus on the problem, and talk about it. Then, I come up with a method to measure it. I find that by keeping the measure in front of the people, they eventually come up with solutions."

Favorite Story of This Executive

As a business psychologist, I often test, interview, and coach managers to help them improve their level of success. I find it helpful to ask what his or her favorite story is. The theme of the story reveals a great deal about the person.

McCaslin's favorite story was one he read in an Aikedo book. It goes like this:

A Japanese warrior fell off a cliff, and he caught himself by holding onto a branch growing out of the cliff wall.

He realized he could drop down to the ground, but then a lion on the ground below would kill him and eat him. And, if he climbed up, there was a bear waiting at the top of the cliff, which would kill and eat him.

Then, all of a sudden, he saw a beautiful, luscious strawberry growing out of the side of the cliff.

He eats the strawberry, smiles, and exclaims, "Exquisite!"

When I asked McCaslin what his favorite story meant to him, he explained, "This is like an executive's life. You've got all sorts of problems and pressures all around you, above you and below you. So, you have to be sure to always take the time to enjoy your life and your job." Indeed, in implementing a spectacularly successful turnaround of a vital part of Harley-Davidson, McCaslin certainly had problems and pressure all around him all the time. Nevertheless, he persevered. And, importantly, he found enjoyment along the way.

Formative Events in This Executive's Childhood That Help Him in His Career

If you want to uncover a person's habits that lead to his or her current level of success, ask the person to list a few formative events from childhood, ages 1 - 21 years old. As you get to know the person, you will see these formative events play out in the person's work each day.

For McCaslin, his father — who also was named Jim – played a very formative role in his life and, ultimately, his current career success in two ways. First, as McCaslin explained,

My dad took a very active role in our early years. He made us recite our lessons to him. It caused us to work hard, because he didn't let you get away with anything. Everyday of his life, he would say this phrase: "The difference between being good and great is a little extra effort."

The second way McCaslin's father profoundly influenced him had to do with interpersonal skills. He explained,

My father owned gas stations, and I worked in them. In this, I learned how to deal with customers. He taught me how to deal with people at gas stations – and that helped me a lot in working with people in manufacturing plants. My dad's nickname in the gas station was "Smiling Jim." So, I learned the power of a smile from him.

Another momentous formative event for McCaslin was working in the cooperative education program when he majored in engineering at a General Motors-owned college. McCaslin said that working while going to college taught him valuable lessons on how to survive in the business world.

Role Models of This Executive – & Lessons Learned from Each One

Everybody has known people they consider role models. These are people who helped us by the lessons they directly or indirectly taught us. McCaslin considers three people to be his biggest role models.

Role Model 1: Vice President of Manufacturing at Volkswagen of America where McCaslin worked. *Lessons Learned:* McCaslin considers this person his "primary mentor." He learned his management style from this VP. Notably, McCaslin's mentor demanded excellence. Phrases his mentor drummed into McCaslin's head are the following:

♦ "TMT & TME – Tell me the truth and tell me early."
♦ "Plan for the worst – and hope for the best."
♦ "The 4M's: Manning, Method, Machine & Material"
♦ "The speed of the team is the speed of the leader."

Here is a fact definitely worth mentioning: This wonderful mentor – Richard Dauch – wrote the book entitled, *Excellence in Manufacturing.*

Role Model 2: A manager at Chevrolet's corporate office, John Bachochin, who dealt a lot with assembly plants. *Lessons Learned:* This manager taught McCaslin a lot about politics in the workplace. From him, McCaslin learned that workplace politics boils down to getting people to do what you need them to do. This manager made his methods of influencing others transparent, and easy for McCaslin to see. Importantly, this person always landed on his feet.

Role Model 3: An assembly plant manager at Chrysler, Durward Roller. *Lessons Learned:* This manager taught McCaslin how to handle pressure. In addition, his collaborative style in working with union leadership taught McCaslin that working with unions is not a matter of who is strongest and who can force what. Working with unions (and with anyone else for that matter) is finding areas of mutual need and working together on solutions that help both.

17

Secrets
of
Absolutely Fabulous
Leaders

*The credit belongs to the person who is actually in the arena,
who strives valiantly; who knows the great enthusiasms, the
great devotions, and spends himself in a worthy cause; who at the
best, knows the triumph of high achievement; and who, at the
worst, if he fails, at least fails while daring greatly, so that his
place shall never be with those cold and timid souls who know
neither victory nor defeat.*

— THEODORE ROOSEVELT

Based on consulting I provide to companies, plus my in-depth
research, I wrote the book *Absolutely Fabulous Organizational
Change*™: *Strategies for Success from America's Best-Run Companies*. I
even had many magnificently successful leaders take my *Abilities
& Behavior Forecaster*™ tests to pinpoint how they score on this
widely used pre-employment test.

The result is my book that includes detailed examples from
some of America's best-run companies using *my three-ingredient
model of organizational change.* The three ingredients are successfully

1. leading the organizational change
2. handling employee problems that pop up during
   organizational change
3. managing yourself – as a leader – during organizational
   change

These organizations are IBM, Harley-Davidson, The Ritz-Carlton Hotel Company, Intuit, Robert Mondavi Corporation, VF Corporation, Egghead.com, Washington Mutual, Outback Steakhouse, Inc., City of Indianapolis, and Excell Global Services.

I described exactly how these companies' highly profitable organizational changes used my three-ingredient model. The changes include mergers, acquisitions, starting Internet businesses, restructuring, partnerships, reengineering, mass customization, supply chain enhancements, automating business processes, turning cost centers into profit centers, plus more.

In the midst of all my consulting and research, I also discovered the amazing qualities of absolutely fabulous leaders. You can use this information to model yourself after leaders who have track records that prove they are the best of the best.

Aim Breathtakingly High

In the long run, people hit only what they aim at.
Therefore, they had better aim at something high.

– HENRY DAVID THOREAU

Consulting I provide to many companies continually reinforces my observation that all incredibly successful companies spend 24 hours per day, 365 days per year progressing toward a big, exciting, compelling vision. Leaders at America's best-run companies always create a vision that focuses on becoming the *biggest* or *best* in their industry.

For example, The Ritz-Carlton Hotel Company's vision is the following: *Our key goal is to be the premier worldwide provider of luxury travel and hospitality products and services.*

Intuit's vision is this: *Our key goal is to revolutionize the way people do financial work.*

Robert Mondavi Corporation's vision is the following: *Our key goal is to be the world's preeminent fine wine producer.*

You probably noticed these visions are very big and ultra-exciting – "... premier worldwide provider ...," "... revolutionize ...," and "... world's preeminent ...." These are supremely compelling. Employees feel thrilled to work for a leader who aims breathtakingly high – and succeeds.

Cherish the Excitement

The greater the difficulty, the greater the glory.
– Cicero

As leaders make history, they cherish the *magic moments* they and their teams create. One reason for their success lies in the fact that they feel a tremendous thrill in making things happen on a grand scale. People who prefer calmer or smaller endeavors would fail in such big endeavors. But, absolutely fabulous leaders succeed mightily by simultaneously creating and feeding off the excitement of organizational change.

For example, Brooks Fisher, VP and General Manager of Intuit's Consumer Internet business, led the dynamic creation of Intuit's Internet business from scratch. While doing this, he reflected, *"This is a very special moment in time – and it won't last very long. Being part of this is tremendously exciting."*

Likewise, Mayor Stephen Goldsmith of Indianapolis led the charge to make improvements that governments seldom do: Cut taxes, reduce regulations, and improve government services. He and his staff thrilled in the excitement. Indeed, Goldsmith remarked, *"We have only so many days to change the world. So we need intensity and results."*

This sort of cherishing excitement is intensely craved – and enjoyed – by absolutely fabulous leaders. It creates a magnificent, self-perpetuating circle. The leader sets in motion organizational changes which, in turn, creates excitement which, in turn, is a sensation that absolutely fabulous leaders find delightful. William Blake summed up this feeling when he said, *"Energy is eternal delight."*

Speed Is Vital – & Always Keep Moving

In skating over thin ice, our safety is in our speed.
– Ralph Waldo Emerson

At Robert Mondavi Corporation, the famous wine company, senior vice president Alan Schnur led the planning of a major restructuring for six months – and then led implementation of much of the reorganization in only one week.

Onsale's president and COO Jeff Sheahan took under six months to implement three gigantic changes. These were adding e-tailing (online retailing) to Onsale's online auction business, acquired a business with a famous brand name – Egghead.com, and changing Onsale's name to the extremely recognizable Egghead.com brand name.

Brooks Fisher, an Intuit executive, launched the company's Consumer Internet business in only 90 days! In fact, Fisher colorfully described one key method to implement the change consisted of doing the following: *"Just run – and keep running."*

Indeed, Fisher also described the hyper-speed pace as *"like trying to sip water from a fire hose."*

Many other managers would have taken dramatically longer to accomplish similar feats. But, then again, most other managers have not climbed the leadership peaks of Schnur, Sheahan, and Fisher. After all, as Mae West wisely pointed out, *"He who hesitates is last."*

Optimism Fuels the Leader's Success

Pessimism never won any battle.
– DWIGHT D. EISENHOWER

My research revealed the fact that absolutely fabulous leaders are incredibly optimistic people. I had many absolutely fabulous leaders fill-out my my *Abilities & Behavior Forecaster*™ test. These leaders consistently scored high on the *Forecaster*™ test's Optimism scale.

This prompts the question: What is an optimist? In a book and audio-book I co-authored, *Spontaneous Optimism*™: *Proven Strategies for Health, Prosperity & Happiness*, my co-author and I defined an optimist as someone who focuses on solutions (not problems), possesses a vision of an exciting life, spends most of his or her time working on goals to achieve the vision, persists, and leads a prosperous life.

For example, Leonardo Inghilleri, senior vice president at The Ritz-Carlton Hotel Company, emphatically stated,

Optimism is absolutely significant. I'm an optimist in life – both my professional and personal life. You have to be positive. Nothing positive is created through negative thinking.

Starting when I was a teenager, I always have had a personal mission statement to help me in my life. It helps me know where I'm going even when I am challenged.

Or, as Ralph Waldo Emerson said, *"Nothing great was ever achieved without enthusiasm."*

Go Over, Under, Around or Through Your Critics & Doubters

Nothing will ever be attempted if all possible objections must first be overcome.
— SAMUEL JOHNSON

Every superb leader must manage doubters, rebels, and critics. Indeed, the second ingredient of my three-ingredient model of organizational change focuses leaders on handling employees who resist – or undermine – the change initiative. Actually, tackling negative people is a wise move in both your business life and personal life. Someone once pointed out that *no one ever erects statues of critics.* Only the doers get statues, status, recognition, and prestige.

At VF Corporation, the huge apparel manufacturer, vice president Tom Payne handled employees who resisted development of VF's sophisticated, highly successful supply chain management system in a number of ways. These superb methods included the CEO's continuous messages on the new system's importance and also consensus building. That is not all. At some points, a "war of attrition" was used in which, Payne explained, *"We wore everyone down until they accepted that we would make these changes."* This is wise leadership. At some point, a true leader just keeps plugging away until every person either participates or gets out of the way.

Along the same lines, I find this Chinese proverb delightfully sensible: *"Someone who says it cannot be done should not interrupt the person doing it."*

Persist – & Then Persist Even More

Nothing in the world can take the place of persistence. Talent will not; nothing is more common than unsuccessful people with talent. Genius will not; unrewarded genius is almost a proverb. Education will not; the world is full of educated derelicts. Persistence and determination alone are omnipotent.
— CALVIN COOLIDGE

Every organizational change takes time and intense work. Cutting short the endeavor would slash the height of the accomplishment. In fact, as a business psychologist who consults to companies, I continually observe that persistent people usually achieve more than less persistent people.

The Ritz-Carlton Hotel Company boosts its bottom line and outstanding reputation partly by holding a daily "Line-Up Meeting" for all employees at the start of each shift. This short meeting focuses every employee on how to better serve guests, as well as put into action the Ritz-Carlton's motto that employees live by: *"We are ladies and gentlemen serving ladies and gentlemen."*

What would happen if Ritz-Carlton stopped holding these daily meetings after a few months? What would happen to its magnificent service and superb reputation if Ritz-Carlton hotels stopped *persistently* holding *daily* "Line-Up Meetings?" If that happened, service might falter and its reputation could decline. As such, the persistence of Ritz-Carlton's leaders to hold daily meetings for thousands of employees is totally needed. Such persistence enables the company to fulfill its big, exciting vision *"to be the premier worldwide provider of luxury travel and hospitality products and services."*

Interestingly, in a way, the United States was physically founded on persistence. Columbus never wavered from his ultimate goal when he set off on his magnificent voyage. Despite horrible conditions, strife among his sailors, and continually having no land in sight, *every* day his diary repeated the exact *same* entry: "We proceeded south by southwest." That is persistence!

Benefit from Role Models

Some wisdom must thou learn from one who is wise.
– EURIPIDES

All the leaders I cite in my *Absolutely Fabulous Organizational Change*™ book found role models who taught them powerful life lessons. There is no reason to "reinvent the wheel" when someone can show you the way.

For example, Tim Gannon is the co-founder and senior vice president of astoundingly successful Outback Steakhouse, Inc. Gannon's top role model is Norman Brinker, the founder of two large restaurant chains, Steak & Ale and Chili's. Brinker also won the U.S. Open Championship in polo – just like Gannon later won. Importantly, Gannon admires that Brinker is a "self-made man." Gannon also is a self-made success. In all likelihood, Gannon's amazing achievements are partly due to Brinker being his top role model.

Thrill in the Realization: This is Your Life!
> *You can't build a reputation on what you are going to do.*
> – HENRY FORD

Absolutely fabulous leaders head up incredible organizational change. But, actually, being a magnificent leader carries deeper, profoundly personal significance. Indeed, I believe a key element in implementing major change is the leader's enthusiasm for living a big, fulfilling business and personal life. Leading change in a company is, in effect, a vibrantly large way to feel vital and intensely alive. It provides the vehicle for the leader to carry out Jonathan Swift's astute suggestion: *"May you live all the days of your life."*

Or, as George Bernard Shaw pointed out, *"The people who get on in this world are the people who get up and look for the circumstances they want and, if they can't find them, make them."*

Nourish Your Creativity
> *In order to be irreplaceable, one must always be different.*
> – COCO CHANEL

Results on my *Abilities & Behavior Forecaster*™ tests show that absolutely fabulous leaders are quite creative. On the *Forecaster*™ tests, the leaders' scores show a classic pattern for creative people: Specifically, they usually score both (A) low on the Following Rules scale and (B) high on the Creativity Motivation scale.

If you think about this, it makes perfect sense. After all, what is creativity? It is not always following all the rules, as shown in the leaders' low scores on the *Forecaster*™ test's Following Rules scale. But, that is not enough. On top of that, these leaders also feel strongly motivated to do creative work. When you combine creative thinking with motivation to do innovative work, you have classic hallmarks of creative people. Indeed, absolutely fabulous leaders certainly excel at conjuring up innovative, yet practical, solutions to propel a business.

In fact, a chief reason for success in business and in life is a person's ability continually to create opportunities. General Douglas MacArthur summed this up when he pointed out, *"There is no security in this life. There is only opportunity."*

Build Your Brainpower

> *To the dull mind, all of nature is leaden.*
> *To the illuminated mind, the whole world sparkles with light.*
>
> – RALPH WALDO EMERSON

Absolutely fabulous leaders usually are very smart people. This was verified in their scores on my *Abilities & Behavior Forecaster*™ tests. Specifically, these amazing leaders scored very high on the *Forecaster*™ test's Problem-Solving scale. This scale measures a person's general level of intelligence. The successful leaders also scored high on three other *Forecaster*™ test scales of mental abilities.

What does this mean for you? For starters, if you are a bright person, use your brains! If you have average intelligence, then do everything you can to boost your brainpower.

Take advantage of this old saying, "Use it or lose it." First, read books and articles to expand your mental horizons. Second, find absolutely fabulous leaders to be your role models. Carefully observe how they think through situations. Third, get the nutrition and rest you need to use your brain at its peak potential. Fourth, practice thinking through situations, and discuss your ideas with successful leaders who will help you sharpen your thinking. Overall, make sharp thinking into your habit.

Celebrate Your Victories

> *Happy are those who dream dreams and pay the price to make them come true.*
>
> – L.J. CARDINAL SUENENS

A little celebration goes a long way. And absolutely fabulous leaders use this fact to benefit everyone in their organization.

For example, IBM implemented magnificent changes in vendor processing that saved IBM $1-billion over three years. At key milestones along the way, Robert Hughes, manager of IBM National Accounts Payable, made sure *every major accomplishment was celebrated as a team.* For instance, when the team's monstrous accomplishments became the cover story on *Electronic Commerce* magazine, only Hughes' picture appeared on the cover. No one else's photo graced the magazine's cover.

So, at the picnic – complete with disk jockey, karaoke, and plenty of food – to celebrate being the *Electronic Commerce* cover story, two cartoon caricaturists drew each employee's face onto a mock-up cover of *Electronic Commerce* magazine. As such, each team member walked away from the celebration with his or her own 8-1/2-inch X 11-inch caricature drawing to proudly display on a wall.

A different type of celebration took place at Excell Global Services, an outstanding company that operates call centers in the U.S., Canada, Europe, and Asia Pacific. Lori Ulichnie, vice president of human resources, explained that when disasters strike – for example, when a hurricane affected Excell's call center in Florida – Excell offered all employees the opportunity to help handle calls at another call center. At the conclusion of this disaster-handling, Excell gave everyone who helped a tongue-in-cheek *Hurricane Survival Kit.* The kit contained "basic survival necessities," such as small bandages, crackers, and chocolate!

In fact, this demonstrates a key principle of social psychology: When people collaborate to effectively handle an extreme situation – such as a disaster – the result is people *emotionally bond* together. They tend to (A) like each other more, (B) enjoy working together more, plus (C) work more productively together. The extreme situation brings people together. Absolutely fabulous leaders celebrate teamwork that results in enjoyable work relationships and high productivity.

Grasp How Imperative It Is To Make Improvements

If we don't change our direction, we'll end up exactly where we are headed.
– CHINESE PROVERB

Recently, my aunt and I discussed changes she was making in her life. At one point in our conversation, she wisely observed, *"Everything's always different!"* How true!!

Similarly, in the business world, absolutely fabulous leaders anticipate needed improvements and head the organization in the needed direction. They see the world as it is, as it is becoming, and as it can be.

Now, It's Your Turn

The great goal in life is not knowledge but action.
— THOMAS HENRY HUXLEY

My book *Absolutely Fabulous Organizational Change*™ presented my three-ingredient model for highly effective change. It entails successfully (1) leading the change, (2) handling employee problems that pop up, and (3) serving as a fantastic role model for your employees.

My research on the amazing qualities of outstanding leaders gives you the groundwork to turn yourself into an absolutely fabulous leader. Importantly, most of the talents I discovered among highly successful leaders can be learned, practiced, and fine-tuned to perfection.

You can put your knowledge into action in an extremely exciting arena. In doing so, you take yourself and everyone around you on a magnificent – and tremendously rewarding – adventure.

Now, you can lead *absolutely fabulous organizational change*™.

Biography
of
Michael Mercer, Ph.D.

Dr. Mercer is a consultant, business psychologist, and speaker. He is founder and president of both The Mercer Group, Inc. and Mercer Systems, Inc. in Barrington, Illinois, U.S.A. He provides organizations with his expertise through his

- speeches
- workshops
- management retreats
- consulting
- pre-employment tests

He authored 5 important books:

- *Hire the Best – & Avoid the Rest*™
- *Absolutely Fabulous Organizational Change*™: *Strategies for Success from America's Best-Run Companies*
- *How Winners Do It: High Impact People Skills for Your Career Success*
- *Turning Your Human Resources Department into a Profit Center*™
- *Spontaneous Optimism*®: *Proven Strategies for Health, Prosperity & Happiness*

Dr. Mercer has *appeared on over 400 radio and TV talk shows –* including *Oprah, Leeza,* and *Today Show* – plus shows on ABC, CBS, FOX, NBC, CNBC, CNN, BRN, and NPR.

He delivers exciting *speeches, workshops* and *management retreats* at many companies, meetings, and conferences. Audience members describe his lively speaking style as "info-tainment."

Dr. Mercer developed 2 pre-employment *tests* that are used by companies across North America to help them select successful, productive employees:

- *Behavior Forecaster*™ test
- *Abilities Forecaster*™ test

He also has trained thousands of managers in how to conduct customized interviews of job candidates.

Articles quoting Dr. Mercer appear in major publications, including *The Wall Street Journal, Forbes, Fortune, Industry Week,* Gannett Newswire, Scripps-Howard Newswire, *Investor's Business Daily, Working Woman,* and *U.S. News & World Report.*

You can contact Dr. Mercer at
telephone = (847) 382-0690
or
e-mail = drmercer@mercersystems.com

Materials
You Can Order

Speeches, Workshops, & Management Retreats

Dr. Mercer can deliver customized speeches and workshops at your organization or conference. Also, he can conduct special sessions at your management retreat. Call Dr. Mercer and his staff to discuss your specific needs at (847) 382-0690.

Presentation topics include:

_____ *Absolutely Fabulous Organizational Change*™

_____ *Hire the Best – & Avoid the Rest*™

_____ *How Winners Do It: High Impact People Skills for Your Career Success*

_____ *Teambuilding: Improving Collaboration & Productivity*

_____ *Designing Your Organization's Future*

_____ *Turning Your Human Resources Department into a Profit Center*™

_____ *How To Negotiate, Influence & Persuade*

Tests

To discuss how Mercer Systems, Inc. can customize pre-employment testing for your company, call (847) 382-0690.

_____ *Abilities & Behavior Forecaster*™ tests
(Mercer Systems, Inc. can customize *Forecaster*™ tests for each job in your company.) *Forecaster*™ tests help you predict each job applicant's

- ◆ 3 interpersonal skills (friendliness, assertiveness, & teamwork)
- ◆ 5 personality traits (optimism, rules-following, reactions, calmness, & focus on feelings vs. facts)
- ◆ 5 motivations (money, helping people, creativity, power, & knowledge)
- ◆ 5 mental abilities (problem-solving, vocabulary, arithmetic, grammar, & small details)

_____ **P.A.S.S.-III® Character Survey**
Assesses job applicant's attitudes on work ethic, trustworthiness, and drugs/drinking.

Tool Kits
Call for information at (847) 382-0690.

_____ *Hire the Best Tool Kit™*
Customizable system to help your company hire successful employees:
- ◆ pre-employment tests (*Abilities & Behavior recaster™* tests)
- ◆ customizing of entire interview procedure for specific jobs in your company
- ◆ "Fast-Start" audio-tape & instructions to help you start quickly & easily
- ◆ over-the-phone consultations with Dr. Mercer and his staff to help you

_____ *Develop Winning Employees Tool Kit*
System to assess and develop key job skills and talents of your current employees:
- ◆ Assessment questionnaires for your employees to fill-out
- ◆ Action planning guides & audio-tapes on key job skills & talents
- ◆ "Fast-Start" audio-tape & instructions to help you start quickly & easily
- ◆ over-the-phone consultations with Dr. Mercer and his staff to help you

Consulting Services

For information, call (847) 382-0690.

_____ *Absolutely Fabulous Organizational Change*™ consulting

_____ *Teambuilding Sessions* – to improve collaboration and productivity

_____ *Ultra-Customized Evaluation of Job Candidates*

_____ *Intensive Coaching*® for individuals

_____ *Designing Your Organization's Future* consulting

_____ *Climate Survey* of your employees

Books

Print quantity you want on the line provided. Call (847) 382-0690 for discounts if you want to order two or more copies. Dr. Mercer will autograph books to you, unless you specify another person's name.

_____ *Hire the Best – & Avoid the Rest*™ by Dr. Michael Mercer Price: $25
☐ *Check here if you want Michael to autograph book to you.*

_____ *Spontaneous Optimism*®: *Proven Strategies for Health, Prosperity & Happiness* by Dr. Michael Mercer & Dr. Maryann Troiani, Price: $20
☐ *Check here if you want Michael and Maryann to autograph book to you.*

_____ *Turning Your Human Resources Department into a Profit Center*™ by Dr. Michael Mercer, Price: $65
☐ *Check here if you want Michael to autograph book to you.*

_____ *How Winners Do It: High Impact People Skills for Your Career Success*™ by Dr. Michael Mercer, Price: $25
☐ *Check here if you want Michael to autograph book to you.*

_____ *Absolutely Fabulous Organizational Change*™: *Strategies for Success from America's Best-Run Companies* by Dr. Michael Mercer, Price: $30
☐ *Check here if you want Michael to autograph book to you.*

Audio-books

Print quantity you want on line provided. Call (847) 382-0690 for discounts if you want to order two or more copies.

_____ *Spontaneous Optimism®: Proven Strategies for Health, Prosperity & Happiness* by Dr. Michael Mercer & Dr. Maryann Troiani, 2 audiocassette tapes, about 3 hours. Price: $20

_____ *How Winners Do It: High Impact People Skills for Your Career Success* by Dr. Michael Mercer, 6 audiocassette tapes, about 6 hours. Price: $60

_____ *Absolutely Fabulous Organizational Change™: Strategies for Success from America's Best-Run Companies* by Dr. Michael Mercer. For information on this, call (847) 382-0690.

All book and audio-book prices *include shipping & tax* in U.S.A.
Add U.S. $5 to ship to Canada.
Add U.S. $25 to ship outside U.S. & Canada.

Order materials from:

The Mercer Group, Inc.
25597 West Drake Road
Barrington, Illinois, U.S.A. 60010

Phone = (847) 382-0690
Fax = (847) 382-2250
E-Mail = drmercer@mercersystems.com